THE IMPERIAL REPUBLIC

Above all else, this book results from the love and support of my immediate family: Mimi Lord, Heather Wilson and Nathan Wilson

The Imperial Republic

A structural history of American constitutionalism from the colonial era to the beginning of the twentieth century

JAMES G. WILSON
Cleveland State University

Routledge
Taylor & Francis Group
LONDON AND NEW YORK

First published 2002 by Ashgate Publishing

Reissued 2018 by Routledge
2 Park Square, Milton Park, Abingdon, Oxon OX14 4RN
711 Third Avenue, New York, NY 10017, USA

Routledge is an imprint of the Taylor & Francis Group, an informa business

A Library of Congress record exists under LC control number: 2002100330

ISBN 13: 978-1-138-72786-1 (hbk)
ISBN 13: 978-1-138-72782-3 (pbk)
ISBN 13: 978-1-315-19020-4 (ebk)

Contents

Acknowledgments

Although the research and writing of this book required many hours of solitude stretching over several years, the process felt remarkably communal. There was the opportunity of learning from some of the greatest political thinkers, politicians, and historians of all time. Henry Adams was the guiding spirit behind this book, in terms of form and content. I like to imagine that he would have found my prose tolerable. It was also possible to sense what it might have been like for a wide range of people–ranging from pioneer settlers and exploited Native Americans to Southern slave owners–to live and die during this troubled era.

On a more immediate level, several readers representing a wide range of the existing ideological spectrum provided encouraging and thoughtful insights. Enduring thanks to Sheldon Gelman, Peter Fitzpatrick, Noam Chomsky, Paul Finkelman, Elizabeth Lord, David Snyder, Steve Lazarus, Peter Wilson, my colleagues who participated in two luncheon presentations at Cleveland State University, and the New York University Law School Legal History Symposium. There is also gratitude to Austin Sarat for including this book in his series on Law, Justice, and Power. Each reader must determine how much justice there is in this book, but there certainly is a great deal of law and power. I also wish to acknowledge Sandra Kerber, who imposed a Strunk and White aesthetic upon an all but final draft. Holli Goodman transformed the slightly chaotic manuscript into an elegant "camera ready" document. Finally, I want to thank the Cleveland-Marshall Fund for providing essential funds enabling me to work on this project over several summers.

Introduction

In his breathtaking autobiography, *The Education of Henry Adams*, Henry Adams recalled an insight he had during a dinner party with his close friend John Hay, who was directing American foreign policy after the victorious Spanish American War: "[A]s he sat at Hay's table, listening to any member of the British Cabinet, for all were alike now, discuss the Philippines as a question of balance of power in the East, he could see that the family work of a hundred and fifty years fell at once into the grand perspective of true empire-building, which Hay's work set off with artistic skill."[1] In other words, a "quest for empire" largely explained the words, motives, and actions of John Adams, John Quincy Adams, Henry's father Charles Adams, and Henry himself. The United States has always been simultaneously a republic and an empire, an imperial republic. And one of the immediate pleasures of empire was no longer knowing or caring who belonged to the British Cabinet. This perspective will probably jar some American readers' sensibilities; Americans tend to see themselves as virtuous republicans opposed to evil empires and arrogant imperialism. In popular culture, the *Star Wars* movies perpetuate this dichotomy by setting a corrupt empire, headed by an evil Emperor, against the beleaguered, disorganized revolutionary supporters of the Republic.

The imperial thesis has a corollary. While there has consistently been an overwhelming consensus on the need for empire, there have been sharp, even violent disagreements over the form and direction of that empire. The dichotomies have reverberated down to the present day; the wars between the French and English, the American Revolution, the debate over the ratification of the Constitution, the political conflict between the Republicans and Federalists, the sectional tensions between the North, South, and West which eventually led to the Civil War, and the debates over expanding American sovereignty beyond the North American continent to create permanent colonies.

---

[1] Henry Adams, *The Education of Henry Adams* (W.D. Brogan, intro., Boston, 1961), 363.

This book relies on two traditional historical standards to support its thesis that imperial ambition has continually[2] and profoundly influenced American constitutional history, politics, theory, and law – that Henry Adams was right. It first turns to the historical record for supporting and undermining evidence and then demonstrates how the claim generates interesting insights. Although this book relies on many words, actions, and beliefs for evidentiary support, it relentlessly emphasizes the leading politicians' frequent usage of the word "empire." On the crudest level, it is far easier to support the claim that a group of people is motivated by "empire" if they frequently employ that word.

To enable readers to make up their own minds about the definitions of the word "empire" and to better understand earlier Americans' beliefs about their country's emerging status in the world, this book presents numerous quotations containing the word "empire." No single instance proves the book's case, but the vast number constitutes a powerful body of evidence revealing an ambitious, expansionist constitutional ideology. This survey reveals that the word "empire" has long had multiple usages. On a very broad level, as a derivative of word "empirium,"[3] the word signifies any form of legal or political power. Thus, it could apply to virtually any legal right or authority. In the first volume of his Commentaries, William Blackstone equated "empire" with "sovereignty": "The meaning therefore of the legislature, when it uses these terms of *empire* and *imperial*, and applies them to the realm of England, is only to assert that our kin is equally sovereign and independent within these his dominions, as any emperor is in his empire; and owes no kind of subjection to any other potentate on earth."[4] One of the narrower applications of "empire" appeared in a Circuit Court opinion that Justice Story wrote in 1815 asserting a broad scope for admiralty jurisdiction: "[T]he soil, on which the tide ebbs and flows, may be parcel of a manor, and yet that the common law and the admiralty have there a divided empire, the former when the tide

---

2 This book rejects the frequently held belief that the United States had a brief bout of "imperialism" in the 1890s. It is not just romantic conservatives who deny or underemphasize pervasive imperial motivations, which can be traced back to the original English settlements' Royal Charters and cultural interactions with Native Americans. Michael Hardt and Antonio Negri, severe critics of the contemporary global "Empire," also fail to go far enough back in history: "In the first phase of the Constitution, between the presidencies of Thomas Jefferson and Andrew Jackson, the open space of the frontier became the conceptual terrain of republican democracy." Michael Hardt and Antonio Negri, *Empire* (Cambridge, 2000), 168.

3 James Harrington, *The Commonwealth of Oceana and a System of Politics* (J.G.A. Pocock, ed., Cambridge, 1992), 156 n.58.

4 William Blackstone, 1 *Commentaries on the Laws of England* (Chicago, 1979), 235 (italics in original).

ebbs, and the latter when it flows."[5] Consequently, admiralty's jurisdictional "empire" in a particular case might only extend to a few square feet. Of course, the federal courts' overall admiralty jurisdiction covered a large and important "empire" – the "empirium" the federal courts established to protect international and interstate trade. "Empire" was also a literary synonym/metaphor for dominion or control. Just moments before Jane Eyre met Mister Rochester's insane wife who lived in the attic, she described the silence following a sleep shattering scream: "No: stillness returned: each murmur and movement ceased gradually, and in about an hour Thornfield Hall was again as hushed as a desert. It seemed that sleep and night had resumed their empire."[6]

Such examples were uncommon among the political and legal materials studied in this book. Not surprisingly, America's leaders often used the word "empire" to describe such specific empires as Rome, Germany, China, or Britain. But more importantly, America's leaders frequently utilized the word to characterize their nation, even though "empire" had negative political connotations dating back to Aristotle, Caesar's Rome, Montesquieu, and the recently oppressive British Empire. At the Pennsylvania ratification debate, during his very influential speech on behalf of the proposed Constitution, James Wilson melodramatically explained why major constitutional change was necessary: "Ill fated America! thy crisis was approaching! Perhaps it was come! * * * Without a government! without energy! *** In such a situation, distressed but not despairing, thou desiredst to re-assume thy native vigour, and to lay the foundation of future empire!"[7] Perhaps some of these instances can be dismissed as bland synonyms for "sovereignty," "nation," or "country," but there is much additional evidence, in words and deeds, of the country's long-term commitment to glory, domineering growth, and power.[8] While some earlier Americans preferred a self-conception of innocence and virtue, others acknowledged that they, like the rest of the species, were motivated by the "lust for dominion" – a pleasure which included the satisfaction of no longer needing to learn powerful people's names, whether they be British Cabinet officials or Prime Ministers of Canada.

---

[5] *Delovio v. Boit*, 7 Cas. 418, 423 (1815).

[6] Charlotte Brontë, *Jane Eyre* (New York, 1973), 298.

[7] James Wilson, 'James Wilson's Summation and Final Rebuttal' (Dec, 11th, 1787), *1 The Debate on the Constitution* 834 (Bernard Bailyn, ed., 1993). In a speech that was more influential at the time than *The Federalist*, Wilson noted: "Let it be remembered then, that the business of the Federal Government was not local, but general; not limited to the views and establishments of a single state, but *co-extensive with the continent.*" 'James Wilson's Speech at a Public Meeting', ibid., at 65 (emphasis added).

[8] Richard W. Van Alstyne, *The Rising American Empire* (New York, 1960), 1-3. *See also*, Richard Koebner, *Empire* (Cambridge, 1961).

This historical perspective clashes with powerful strands in current American thought (including a great deal of American historiography). Many Americans across the political spectrum tend to see the country as being founded upon two original sins: racism and sexism. Such an approach is fundamentally reassuring because those two forces are appropriately under cultural and legal attack. Few upper middle class Americans look in the mirror and perceive a rampant bigot. But this book emphasizes a third original sin that remains a vibrant part of American political culture: the quest for power, wealth, and glory at the expense of others (citizens as well as noncitizens). From the moment contemporary Americans put on their clothes made by horrendously exploited Third World workers, they reenter the world of empire.

Early Americans often used the word "empire" normatively. Although America's leaders were well aware of Aristotle and Montesquieu's arguments that empires were inherently corrupt and anti-republican and were proud of their new nation's successful war against the entity known as the British Empire, they rarely used "empire" disparagingly. The historian Peter Onuf described Jefferson's imperial vision as "an empire without a metropolis, a regime of consent, not coercion."[9] Patrick Henry provided a

---

[9] Peter S. Onuf, *Jefferson's Empire: The Language of American Nationhood* (Charlottesville, 2000), 16. Onuf did not find disturbing connotations in the Americans' frequent usage of the word empire: "For provincial Britons 'empire' did not evoke, as it now does, centralized, despotic, and arbitrary rule." Rather, they felt they were part of a "transcendent, inclusive, imperial community" that secured law, liberty, and prosperity, Ibid., at 6. *See also* Anthony Pagden, *Lords of all the World: Ideologies of Empire in Spain, Britain, and France, C. 1500-C.1800* (New Haven, 1995).

It would border on the absurd to think that those early Americans employed the word "empire" to describe their country as fundamentally tainted by the word's worst possible connotations of corruption and arbitrary despotism. But it does not follow that they stripped the word of all potentially disturbing implications. There exist a wide range of meanings between an "evil empire" and an egalitarian American republican empire conceived as "a community of love," Onuf, op. cit., ibid., at 14. During this era, the word "empire" continued to suggest power, glory, dominion, and conquest. After all, the Framers were deeply aware of the histories of both the English and Roman Empires. Furthermore, we should not limit our review to Jefferson, who habitually glossed over his actions with sentimental abstractions. Other leaders, such as Alexander Hamilton, foresaw an American State very much in the traditional European image. Of course, the debate over "empire's" meanings merely reflects the underlying controversy over the early Americans' motivations, both conscious and unconscious. One of the reasons this book emphasizes the word "empire" by including so many contemporaneous usages of the word is to allow each reader to make his or her own assessments.

Although leading Americans have usually seen their nation as preordained to exert extraordinary power, few would have endorsed Hardt and Negri's contemporary definition of "empire" as a regime without boundaries, historically independent of conquest, and direct control of human nature. After all, they were still patriots. Their primary allegiance was to national power, not the global market, Hardt and Negri, op. cit., *supra* n.2, xiv.

rare exception during the Virginia debates over the ratification of the Constitution: "If we admit this consolidated government, it will be because we like a great, splendid one. Some way or other we must be a great and mighty empire; we must have an army, and a navy, and a number of things. When the American spirit was in its youth, the language of America was different: liberty, sir, was then the primary object."[10] For Henry, empire threatened liberty. But for the Federalists, empire protected liberty. Indeed, many Federalists believed the goal of empire was more important than equal liberty.

This book does not and should not stop with close historical and analytical consideration of the word "empire." To determine the effects of imperial ambition on America's republican constitution, it also explores the equally important words "republican" and "constitution." Relying on historical examples, the book sets forth some of various conceptions of the word "republican," combining them with the word "empire" to create a model of republican empires. This model asks a series of questions, some of which are relatively "objective" questions about structure (such as the amount and form of representation) while others are far more empirical or normative, to determine more systematically the particular nature of any republican empire.

The word "constitution" is also scrutinized.[11] In the United States, there is a strong tendency, particularly among lawyers, to equate the word "constitution" with the written Constitution and subsequent Supreme Court opinions. While that definition is central, it is incomplete. First of all, one should include the constitutional ideology lying behind the text. What were the Framers' purposes and beliefs, not all of which were overtly or fully expressed in the Constitutional text? Second, one cannot adequately understand how America's constitutional system operates by looking solely at text and judicial decisions. Somewhat like the British Constitution, the American constitution has numerous unwritten "constitutional conventions," defined and enforced by the polity, that combine with the judicial opinions to organize and regulate political action.[12] For instance, Congress retains the last word on determining what is an "impeachable offense." The 1999 Clinton-Lewinsky farce "held" that apparent

---

10 Patrick Henry (June 5, 1788), Jonathan Elliot, *1 Elliot's Debates* (Philadelphia, 1941), 53.

11 Hardt and Negri that the American constitutional order consists not just of the written document, but also of the "material, social constitution" that is made both by the judiciary and the citizenry, Hardt and Negri, op. cit., *supra*, n.2, at 168.

12 James G. Wilson, 'American Constitutional Conventions: The Judicially Unenforceable Rules that Combine With Judicial Doctrine and Public Opinion to Regulate Political Behavior', 40 *Buffalo Law Review*, 645 (1992).

Presidential perjury about consensual sex was not an impeachable offense, thereby creating another precedent defining and limiting the scope of that important Congressional power, a precedent that the Supreme Court would almost certainly find nonjusticiable under *Nixon v. United States*.[13] The relationship between law and convention is fluid. Much to the horror of Madison and Jefferson, Alexander Hamilton used his powers as President Washington's leading Cabinet Member to transform the system and culture from the Virginians' agrarian ideal into a fledgling modern nation state based upon public and private credit, commerce, and military force. Over subsequent decades, Chief Justice John Marshall consolidated many of Hamilton's conventions by turning them into constitutional legal doctrine. But it took a bloody civil war to resolve many of those disputes over the form and character of the American empire.

The ever-manipulative French diplomat Talleyrand provided another useful constitutional perspective. During the Jefferson administration, he never took American military threats seriously because he believed the United States had a defective "military constitution."[14] Part of American history is a gradual shift of the United States' "military constitution" from a relatively pacific system based upon Enlightenment aspirations to the brutal military machines that fought the Civil War.

We need Aristotle for a third crucial definition of the word "constitution." Aristotle defined a country's "constitution" as its distribution of wealth and power.[15] In our particular culture, that definition should emphasize the role of private power and its relationships with public power. Aristotle's definition also forces us to grapple with the racial and sexual implications of American empire building. Quite simply, American constitutional law and theory become far more intelligible and grounded when seen as part of a larger constitution, consisting of basic ideological norms and assumptions, political rules and powers that can be called "conventions," military structures, and private economic and social relationships.

The book seeks to avoid several traps created by its focus on the actual language of politicians and judges. First, the book does not exclusively base its thesis on contemporaneous usages of the word "empire." Even if nobody had ever used the term "empire" to describe the American system or even if everyone had used the word in the most innocuous way imaginable, it would still be easy to infer from the overall historical record

---

13 506 U.S. 681 (1997).

14 Quoted in Henry Adams, *History of the United States During the Jefferson Administrations* (New York, 1986), 661.

15 James G. Wilson, 'Commentary: Noam Chomsky and Judicial Review', 44 *Cleveland State Law Review*, 439 (1996).

that the majority of American leaders and average Americans consistently and strongly committed themselves to an exhilarating expansion of their nation, a goal that influenced their constitutional ideologies, politics, and legal doctrines. Second, the book avoids offering a preferred, much less an exclusive, definition of "empire" lest the entire inquiry be reduced to semantic squabbling. It is enough for now to recognize that the word has long had multiple meanings that serve multiple functions. Nor will the book attempt to define and categorize every usage of words like "republican," "empire," or "liberty." It would be tedious, distracting, and ultimately futile to attempt to "prove" what men like Franklin, Madison, Washington, Jefferson, and Calhoun exactly meant every time they used such words. Instead, this entire book – model, theories, definitions, and examples – is my best definition of America's "republican empire." Whatever particular meaning "republican" or "empire" may have had for any American speaker at any moment in time, one factor remained constant throughout the relevant period: a large majority of Americans consciously and effectively increased the power of their nation at the expense of other peoples and countries. At a very basic level, the growth of the American empire has not been all that different than any other nation's rise to prominence. All the classical tools of empire have been used: ideology, force, deceit, bribery, bluster, negotiation, propaganda, and persuasion. This book focuses on some of the "constitutional" dimensions of that history.

A few years before William Appleman Williams completed *The Contours of American History*, which explored the relationship between American imperial aspirations and economic ideology, he observed, "one of the central themes of American historiography is that there is no American Empire. Most historians will admit, if pressed, that the United States once had an empire. They then promptly insist that it was given away. But they also speak persistently of America as a World Power."[16] A few years later, Richard Van Alstyne said much the same thing: "[I]n the United States it is almost a heresy to describe the nation as an empire. [But] the founders so regarded it."[17] More recently, Michael Doyle began his inquiry of empires by quoting Lord Hailey: "Imperialism is not a word for scholars."[18] Although there has been an increasing amount of historical work on America's empire since Williams completed his provocative

---

[16] William Appleman Williams, 'The Frontier Thesis and American Foreign Policy', 24 *Pacific Historical Review*, 379-95 (1955).

[17] Van Alstyne, op. cit., *supra*, n.8, at 6.

[18] Michael W. Doyle, *Empires* (Ithaca, 1986), 11.

book,[19] the imperial theme has rarely appeared in discussions of legal history and legal constitutional theory. One has to reach back to George Bryan's *The Imperialism of John Marshall*,[20] written in 1924, to find a book focusing on the subject. Bryan's book is quite narrow, focusing excessively on the text of a single case, *Johnson v. McIntosh*. While such leading contemporary works as G. Edward White's biography of John Marshall[21] and Bruce Ackerman's two books on the relationships between constitutional history, law, and theory[22] have many virtues, they contain literally no discussion of empire as a major constitutional goal.[23] Although there are increasing signs of interest in the law review literature[24]

---

19 *See* Harry Magdoff, *The Age of Imperialism: The Economics of U.S. Foreign Policy* (New York, 1969); Reginald Horsman, *Race and Manifest Destiny: The Origins of American Racial Anglo-Saxonism* (Boston, 1981); William E. Weeks, *Building The Constitutional Empire* (Chicago, 1996); Bradford Perkins, *The Cambridge History of American Foreign Policy, Vol. 1, The Creation of a Republican Empire* (Cambridge, 1993); Andars Stephanson, *Manifest Destiny: American Expansion and the Empire of Right* (New York, 1995); Gregory H. Nobles, *American Frontiers: Cultural Encounters and Continental Conquest* (New York, 1997); Colin G. Calloway, *The American Revolution in Indian Country* (Cambridge, 1995); Noam Chomsky, *Year 501: The Conquest Continues* (Boston, 1993); and Francis Jennings, *The Creation of America: Through Revolution to Empire* (Cambridge, 2000).

20 George Bryan, *The Imperialism of John Marshall: A Study in Expediency* (1924, Boston). A recent foray is Christopher Tomlins' The Legal Cartography of Colonization, the Legal Polyphony of Settlement: English Intrusions on the American Mainland in the Seventeenth Century, 26 *Law and Social Inquiry* 315 (2001).

21 G. Edward White, *The Marshall Court and Cultural Change: 1815-1835* (New York, 1991).

22 Bruce Ackerman, *We the People: Foundations* (Cambridge, 1991) and Bruce Ackerman, *We the People: Transformations* (Cambridge, 1998).

23 Akhil Amar noted that contemporary lawyers ignore *The Federalist's* "geostrategic vision." He speculated that the vision is too imperialistic and genocidal, triggering "modern-day discomfort and guilt." Akhil Reed Amar, 'Some New World Lessons for the Old World', 58 *University Chicago Law Review*, 483, 492 (1991). I would add that inquiries into imperial motivations is disturbing not just for what it reveals about the past, but also for what it says but our existing political culture. Elsewhere, Amar emphasized how Marshall's *McCulloch v. Maryland* opinion facilitated the support of military forces throughout the continent, Akhil Reed Amar, 'Intratextualism', 112 *Harvard Law Review* 343, 753 (1999).

24 Sanford Levinson, 'Why the Canon Should Be Expanded to Include the Insular Cases and the Saga of American Expansionism', 17 *Constitutional Commentary*, 241 (2000); Ediberto Roman, 'The Alien-Citizen Paradox and Other Consequences of U.S. Colonialism', 26 *Florida State Law Review*, 1 (1998); Gerald Neuman, *Whose Immigration Law?: Citizens, Borders, and Fundamental Law* (Princeton, 1996); Earl M. Maltz, 'Citizenship and the Constitution: A History and Critique of the Supreme Court's Alienage Jurisprudence', 28 *Arizona State Law Journal*, 1135 (1996); Christine Klein, 'Treaties of Conquest: Property Rights, Indian Treaties, and the Treaty of Guadalupe', 26 *New Mexico Law Review*, 201 (1996); Efren Rivera Ramos, 'The Legal Construction of American Colonialism: The Insular Cases (1901-1922)', 65 *Review Jurisprudence University Peurto*

(particularly pertaining to the legal status of Puerto Rico),[25] the overall inattention makes it relatively easy to make numerous legal/political insights that are arguably "interesting."

Any originality in this book is probably more attributable to the lack of legal scholarly interest in the American empire than to the book's models or definitions. Nevertheless, model/hypothesis building and application helped construct this particular book, which contains numerous claims about America's constitutional development that I have not encountered elsewhere in the primary and secondary sources. It may be self-evident that Americans, like most other human beings, have been ambitious and aggressive. But models and historical abstractions help us organize and study the details – in this case, the United State's unique imperial constitutional ideology. To make the point by way of example, a model of republican empires makes it much easier to reach the conclusion that *The Insular Cases'* validation of America's racist empire after the Spanish-American War was in many ways worse than *Dred Scott v. Sandford's*[26] infamous defense of slavery. As most of us know, the Civil War and the Fourteenth Amendment repealed the worst aspects of *Dred Scott*. But very few of us are aware that *The Insular Cases* remain good law, the authority for the continuing subordination of the large colony of Puerto Rico.

Rico, 225 (1996); Gerald L. Neuman, 'Whose Constitution?' 100 *Yale Law Journal*, (1991); Gary Lawson, 'Territorial Governments and the Limits of Formalism', 78 *California Law Review*, 853 (1990); Gerald L. Neuman, 'Territorial Discrimination, Equal Protection, and Self-Determination', 135 *University Pennsylvania Law Review*, 261 (1987); Louis Henkin, 'The Constitution as Compact and as Conscience: Individual Rights Abroad and at Our Gates', 27 *William & Mary Law Re*view, 11 (1985); and Robert A. Katz, 'Note: The Jurisprudence of Legitimacy: Applying the Constitution to U.S. Territories', 59 *University of Chicago Law Review*, 779 (1992).

Just as this book was about to be published, Christina Duffy Burnett and Burke Marshall edited a series of essays on this issue. Unfortunately, I did not have the opportunity to incorporate their insights into this book. '*Foreign in a Domestic Sense: Puerto Rico, American Expansion, and the Constitution*' (Christina Duffy Burnett and Burke Marshall, eds., Durham, 2002).

[25] Gabriel A. Terrasa, 'The United States, Puerto Rico, and the Territorial Incorporation Doctrine: Reaching a Century of Constitutional Authoritarianism', 31 *John Marshall Law Review*, 55 (1997); Jose Trias Nonge, *Puerto Rico: The Trials of the Oldest Colony in the World* (New Haven, 1997); Alexander Aleinikoff, 'Puerto Rico and the Constitution: Conundrums and Prospects', 11 *Constitutional Commentary*, 15 (1994); Juan R. Torruella, *The Supreme Court and Puerto Rico: The Doctrine of Separate and Unequal* (San Juan, 1985).

[26] 60 U.S. (19 How.) 393 (1857).

1 Constructing a Model of Republican Empires

Empire building has consistently been a major force in the development of America's legal and political constitutions. This work verifies that claim by examining the historical record – the elite's and citizenry's words, plans, and actions – and by demonstrating the capacity of that thesis to improve our understanding of several major constitutional developments' causes, effects, and interrelationships. The work's primary contribution to the slight revival of interest in American imperial history consists of its description of how American territorial ambitions intermingled with Republicanism to create a succession of constitutional structures, different mixtures of judicial law and political "conventions." The survey covers a wide range of examples, including the texts of the original English colonial charters, Benjamin Franklin's 1854 Albany Plan, justifications for the American Revolution, differences between Montesquieu's Republican beliefs and those of Madison and Jefferson, and foreign policy effects of *Dred Scott* and the Fourteenth Amendment. The inquiry concludes in the early Twentieth Century, when the United States Supreme Court decided *The Insular Cases*, which constitutionalized the race-conscious empire established by the United States government after the victorious Spanish-American War in 1898.

There is no need to engage in conspiracy theorizing or even argue that imperial objectives must be inferred as "tacit understandings" from an ambiguous historical record. For example, early American leaders frequently used the word "empire" to express their desire to protect and enhance their country's political power, prestige, and size. A computerized search of a Library of Congress Internet website containing Elliott's Debates, Farad's, and early congressional records generated slightly more than two hundred different usages of "empire."[1] Both before and after the

[1] Thanks to modern technology, it is far easier to survey vast amounts of historical material to determine how often and in what context early Americans utilized various

American Revolution, American political beliefs, practices, and systems were consistently expansionist. Most notably, the Crown's original charters to the States of Massachusetts, Virginia, and Connecticut extended colonial jurisdiction to the Pacific Ocean.[2] During the French and Indian War, Benjamin Franklin[3] drafted and proposed The Albany Plan, which would have reallocated power among the State Assemblies, the State Governors, and the King of England. Its preamble bluntly stated its two objectives: "Plan of a proposed Union of the Several Colonies ... For their Mutual Defence and Security, and for *Extending the British Settlements in North America*."[4] This impetus did not come only from above. For decades, tens of thousands of unknown Americans participated in and even forced this relentless growth, often at the cost of their lives, families, and fortunes, by migrating to the Western frontier.[5]

Works like this book risk becoming entangled in semantics. It is impossible to determine how "republican" a particular "empire" is without attempting to define both "republican" and "empire." Compounding the difficulty is the inevitable uncertainty in determining what Eighteenth and Nineteenth Century Anglo-Americans had in mind when they used words like "empire." Were they only thinking of England's system? Perhaps they

---

important "political words" like empire. There are numerous search engines on the Internet that quickly review thousands of pages of important, relevant material, compiling examples of any important word or phrase. The very comprehensiveness of these search engines makes it less likely that the surveyor will miss or suppress examples that run contrary to that person's initial perspective. As of this date, one can easily scan *The Federalist*, Madison's *Notes on the Constitution*, *Elliott's Debates*, *Farrand's*, early *Congressional Broadsides*, early Congressional records, George Washington's manuscripts, Supreme Court opinions, lower Federal Court opinions, and Senator William Maclay's diary to determine how and when the word "empire" was put to use. These searches reveal that America's political leadership employed the word "empire" many hundreds of times. The number must reach into the thousands if one could look at everything. Thus, on one level, this book becomes slightly dated as soon as it is written. We can only hope that more primary sources will soon become accessible. Whether one is a historian trying to understand the past or a judge or lawyer attempting to construct a particular meaning out of a word or phrase, these searches guarantee a richer, deeper process. This approach admittedly does not achieve the same degree of context and understanding gained by reading all those texts in their entirety. But so long as one reads the entire document or section within which the particular chosen word is used, one can obtain a reasonable understanding of the meanings of that word and to a lesser degree, of the motives and values normally clustered around that word.

[2] Bernard DeVoto, *The Course of Empire* (Boston, 1952) 59.

[3] Lawrence H. Gipson asserted that Thomas Hutchinson wrote the Albany Plan, Esmond Wright, *Franklin of Philadelphia* (Cambridge, 1986), 92.

[4] Benjamin Franklin, 'The Albany Plan of Union', *Benjamin Franklin, Writings* (J.A. Leo Lemay, ed., 1987), 378.

[5] Eric Hinderaker, *Elusive Empires: Constructing Colonialism in the Ohio Valley, 1673-1800* (Cambridge, 1997) and Allan W. Eckert, *That Dark and Bloody River* (New York, 1995).

thought an "empire" was simply any large, powerful country. But they may also have included an aggressive, even an oppressive component. Conversely, their definition of empire sometimes could be quite general. One century earlier, the Republican thinker James Harrington frequently used the word "empire" as a synonym for "imperium," i.e., for political authority, a definition that applies to any type of government.[6] The inquiry into semantic history becomes even more indeterminate because a particular speaker may have had several overlapping definitions in mind when using any given word and/or may have used the word differently in different circumstances, even though the speaker's community had a generally favored definition. Even if there were no such barriers, we will remain tempted to impose our own conception(s) on empire on the country's formative thinking.

These insurmountable difficulties don't matter as much as one might first think. The great philosopher Ludwig Wittgenstein explained that a word gains its meaning or meanings within the context of the particular, purposeful game the speakers are playing.[7] In other words, the best way to understand the meaning of words like "republican" and "empire" during any era is to examine closely the speakers' particular situations, motives, plans, and actions. An overall semantic understanding can emerge, even if many instances are misleading, debatable, or uncertain. Ultimately, it is more important to try to ascertain what people wanted and how they acted than to obsess over precise definitions of their language or to expect uniform usage of particular words and phrases, to look at "things" more than "words." One can make a compelling case that a country has imperial ambitions even if nobody utters a word like "empire." Of course, the case is far stronger when the relevant actors have been as explicit as they have been throughout early American history about such hopes and expectations. The historical evidence will best determine whether this author has erroneously superimposed a contemporary conception of the word "empire" on early American constitutional history. After all, it can be just as anachronistic to deny that previous generations used a word in ways similar to contemporary practice as it is to superimpose changed meanings on past generations.

Immersed in a Marxist ideology of materialism and a consumerist culture of insatiable desires, progressives since Charles Beard have projected obsessions with wealth and greed on to the Framers, insightfully

---

6 Harrington, op. cit., *supra*, Intro, n.3, at 156 n.58.

7 Ludwig Wittgenstein, *Philosophical Investigations* (3rd ed., G.E.M. Anscombe, trans., Englewood Cliffs, N.J., 1958), 4. ("It disperses the fog to study the phenomena of language I primitive kinds of application I in which one can command a clear view of the aim and functioning of the words.")

concluding that the Constitution was partially designed to protect the rich.[8] But this approach is incomplete. Although wealth and greed seem to have been a constant part of the human condition, earlier Western cultures, particularly at the leadership level, were also strongly motivated by pride – the quest for honor, fame, and glory. During the late middle ages, Commines described Charles the Bold in almost Nietzchean terms: "He desired the great glory of fame, which more than anything else led him to undertake his wars; and longed to resemble those ancient princes who have been so much talked of after their death."[9] Douglass Adair concluded his famous paper, *Fame and the Founding Fathers*, with a similar depiction of the Founders' aristocratic quest for historical immortality: "These men drunk with the hope of fame looked to the classic past for models to emulate, as they made history in 1787, in order to win our applause – the praise that only we their posterity could grant."[10] A far darker motive lay underneath greed and the need for immortal glory: the pleasures of power. Bishop James Madison, a cousin of the Founder James Madison, called this impulse "the lust for domination."[11] Of course, the good Bishop was describing Europe's corrupt state of affairs, not the providentially blessed United States. He thought this new empire would be a unique, humane improvement that would eventually spread liberty and virtue throughout the world. But more sardonic thinkers, ranging from Alexander Hamilton to Henry Adams, would never immunize America from darker human motivations. Nor was it ever hard to find examples at every level of American society. In 1766, Benjamin Franklin lamented, "It grieves me to hear that our Frontier People are yet greater barbarians than the Indians, and continue to murder them in time of peace."[12] At the same time, wealthy speculators ranging from George Washington to William Johnson, the British official who oversaw England's imperial policy in the Ohio Valley, constantly engaged in new schemes to increase their wealth. One historian

---

8 Charles A. Beard, *An Economic Interpretation of the Constitution* (New York, 1935).

9 Quoted in Johan Huizinga, *The Autumn of the Middle Ages* (Rodney J. Payton and Ulrich Mammitzsch, trans., Chicago, 1996), at 76.

10 Douglass Adair, 'Fame and the Founding Fathers', Douglass Adair, *Fame and the Founding Fathers: Essays by Douglass Adair* (Trevor Colbourn, ed., Indianapolis, 1974), at 34.

11 Bishop James Madison, 'Manifestations of the Beneficence of Divine Providence Toward America', *Political Sermons of the American Founding Era: 1730-1805* (Ellis Sandoz, ed., 1990), 1311.

12 Letter from Benjamin Franklin to William Johnson (Sept. 12, 1766), quoted in Hinderaker, op. cit., *supra* ch. 1, n.5, at 162.

concluded: "Brash opportunism at the top was mirrored in the behavior of thousands of aspiring landowners below."[13]

Although it may be needless to say, any historical technique that employs a single theme to evaluate a broad range of topics runs the risks of reductionism and circularity. The emphasis on imperial motives should not be turned into the fallacious argument that imperial ambition was always the controlling variable, much less the exclusive factor.[14] We have already encountered the powerful argument that the Constitution was also created to protect the rich and powerful. It is not a fatal problem that "nearly every writer is an advocate of one out of many forces"[15] as long as both the writer and reader know that the temporary, focused examination of a particular theme is only a single step toward historical wisdom. Nor is this study presented as an expose. During the lengthy period studied, few Americans made any serious effort to hide their imperial aspirations. In addition, many Americans sincerely believed they were improving the world by enlarging their "city upon a hill."[16] Extending and protecting the humane political liberty created by republicanism was not a crude pretext for imperial, aggressive ambition. Republicanism was an inspiring goal that retains great moral validity. Just as the early European invaders thought they were saving souls, finding gold, conquering lands, and honoring themselves and their countries, so Americans combined several beliefs and motives, altruistic and selfish, to justify their existing power and continued geographical expansion.

Nor was there complete unanimity about the form and future of the Republic. As early as 1790, Southern Congressmen threatened secession during their furious assault against Quaker petitions to Congress raising the slavery issue.[17] Based upon a mixture of motives ranging from political partisanship, economic self-interest, and regional jealousy to humanitarianism, various individuals and groups sporadically and ineffectively opposed the inexorable imperial impulse.

Ultimately, each reader must determine how proud an American should feel about this history. This work will have accomplished one of its

---

13 Ibid., at 173.

14 Nor is this book implying that all Americans had the same beliefs about "empire." They disagreed over the form of their empire, its direction, its size, and sometimes its actions (particularly during the War of 1812 and the Mexican-American War). Another book could be written about the diverse, shifting ideologies and interests that have made up America's "anti-imperial" polity.

15 James Fitzjames Stephen, *Liberty, Equality, Fraternity* (Indianapolis, 1993), 118.

16 Quoted in Daniel J. Boorstin, *Americans: The Colonial Experience* (New York, 1958), 3.

17 Joseph J. Ellis, *Founding Fathers: The Revolutionary Generation* (New York, 2001), 81-119.

purposes if it helps undermine the continuing myth of "American innocence," replacing that myth with the proposition that the only defense of America's imperial history can be to compare it with other successful empires (an inquiry outside the scope of this piece). Indeed, the evolution of America's formal constitutional structure contains many of this country's most substantial contributions to humanity as well as some of its most venal moments. Both clusters of beliefs and deeds should be part of any comparison to other successful empires. Neither hagiography nor demonology can adequately explain America's exceptionalism, which includes an enthusiastic propensity, frequently immersed in an ocean of sentimentality, toward good and evil.

This book presents a four-stage model to refine the study of the range of definitions that invariably cluster around such important political concepts as "republican" and "empire," as well as such related words as "structure" and "citizen." It initially subdivides the words' different meanings into four categories: analytical/descriptive, empirical, "emotive," and normative. Next, it presents four historical examples to provide necessary context for its proffered definitions of each of those four words. It then utilizes these examples and definitions to create a model, presented as a series of questions, of "republican empires." Finally, the bulk of the book applies this model to American constitutional history from the colonial period through the *Insular Cases*.

The first step in creating the model of "republican empires" is to formulate one or more "descriptive/analytical" definitions of "republican" and "empire," supported by examples,[18] which individuals across the political spectrum can apply consistently. This technique is subject to a significant degree of verifiability since it requires that any proposed analytical definition must satisfy a diverse group of people who agree on little else. For instance, one might descriptively define "empire" as "the extension of formal geographical boundaries over time." This reasonable definition can be easily utilized by looking at a series of chronological maps. Under that definition, the United States was an empire during the Nineteenth Century, but not the late Twentieth Century. Political actors and theorists ranging from Hitler to Marx or Hume would reach the same

---

[18] Wittgenstein argued that a crucial part of any word definition is its accompanying example: "And this is just how one might explain to someone what a game is. One gives examples and intends them to be taken in a particular way." Wittgenstein, op. cit., *supra*, ch. 1, n.7, at 34. Consequently, words can only be understood through their application, ibid., at 27. In the Eighteenth Century, Benjamin Franklin quoted Dr. Turnbull: "But to teach Rules abstractly, or without Examples, and before the agreeable Effects the Observance of them tends to produce (which are in Reality their Reason or Foundation) have been felt, *is exceedingly preposterous.*" Doctor Turnbull, 'Liberal Education', quoted in Franklin, op. cit., *supra* ch. 1, n.4, at 336 (italics in original).

conclusion pursuant to that definition. The creation and application of such definitions resemble formal logic's syllogism: "If an empire is defined as a country that expands its geographical boundaries over time, and America increased its geographical boundaries throughout the Nineteenth Century, then America was an empire during that century." If someone persists in reaching contrary results, it will be very difficult, if not impossible, to have a viable political discussion (or perhaps any discussion at all). There may even be a "core" definition that most people would place at the top of any ranking of descriptive definitions; e.g., "empire" means "formal expansion," unless defined otherwise.

Such "descriptive"/"analytic" definitions cannot provide fully "right" answers. They only create a common vocabulary and methodology for subsequent political analysis, determining when political disputants can agree as well as disagree. They achieve their minimally "preferred" status by providing a starting point for political discussion, not by terminating it. "Analytical" definitions can, by themselves, generate partisan results, but only by making an excessively global and authoritative move. For instance, one could rely on the previously discussed definition of "empire" as "formal expansion" to deduce that the United States is no longer an "empire," a conclusion many would find reassuring. But, that approach converts one plausible, even useful analytical definition into the exclusive definition of empire. After all, there are other "objective" definitions of empire that we sometimes might want to utilize or which others have used in the past. One can also descriptively define "empire" as "large size," a definition covering the United States in the Eighteenth, Nineteenth, and Twentieth Centuries.[19] Although this book does not recommend any particular analytical definition of "empire" as the "best answer," many of its historical examples can be best interpreted as meaning, at least in part, "large size" and/or "expanding."

The second cluster of definitions associated with the word "empire" requires varying degrees of empirical study. The first subset consists of structural conceptions of empire that are less verifiable than the "geographical definitions" but still primarily descriptive. If one limits "empire" to those countries that have an "emperor," one must next define "emperor." That inquiry raises additional empirical issues. For example, if an "emperor" is defined as a "powerful, hereditary Chief-of-State," it is fairly easy to determine if a particular political system requires that a leader's power pass automatically to his or her progeny. But it will be

[19] The historian Frederick Jackson Turner wrote: "Indeed, the United States is, in size and natural resources, an empire, a collection of potential states, rather than a single nation." Frederick Jackson Turner, 'The Ohio Valley in American History', *Frederick Jackson Turner, The Frontier in American History* (New York, 1996), 158.

harder to ascertain how much power a "Chief-of-State" must have before designating that person an "emperor." No "emperor" can be "all-powerful," because every emperor needs advisers and an army.

In this book, James Madison's simple definition of "republicanism" as a "scheme of representation"[20] plays a major role in conceptualizing the structure of republican empires. Madison's definition – equating republicanism with electoral accountability – requires close analysis of any particular constitution, an inquiry that should produce results acceptable across the political spectrum. For example, both Hitler and Marx would probably agree that the United States House of Representatives is "republican" if one defines "republican" as any governmental branch whose members have been chosen through election. Controversy remains just below the surface; we will disagree over the form and nature of a "fair election." We will also disagree over whether electoral representation in a single part of a government makes a system sufficiently "republican."

A second subcategory of empirical definitions requires far more detailed work and is unlikely to generate any consensus, either in definition or application. Conceptualizing "empire" as a "powerful nation" requires a conception of the word "powerful." People will legitimately disagree over what factors should be used – military force, wealth, relative strength, popular morale, technology, and so on. They will then debate more fiercely how much weight should be given to those factors. They will be unable to achieve any consensus about the methods of measuring such variables, some of which are little more than predictions. For instance, only the savage test of war reveals certain aspects of a political culture's military strength, popular allegiance, and strength of will. But almost any empirical definition of "powerful" must include the United States at the end of the Twentieth Century. One simply contrasts other countries' strength to the United States' weaponry, gross national product, and capacity to impose its will on the rest of the world through persuasion, force, culture, and wealth. Yet one could have a more "spiritual" definition of "powerful" that would produce different results. Future historians may consider conquered Tibet to have been the most influential, important country in the late Twentieth Century: part of a country's power and glory consists of its capacity to inspire future generations.

In his study of "empire," Michael Doyle limited his initial broad definition of empires to those political systems that have unequal distributions of sovereignty: "Empire...is a system of interaction between two political entities, one of which, the dominant metropole, exerts political

---

[20] 'The Federalist No. 10' (James Madison) James Madison, Alexander Hamilton, and John Jay, *The Federalist* (Clinton Rossiter ed., 1961), 81.

control over the internal and external policy – the effective sovereignty – of the other, the subordinate periphery."[21] This definition can be read at least two ways. It requires a formal distinction between the core and the periphery, a distinction that arguably only minimally applies to the United States because almost all of its lands eventually became States with equal rights and powers. On the other hand, "effective sovereignty" is a far more empirical concept than formal inequality; some would insist that that New York City/Washington, D.C. area is the dominant metropole controlling internal and external policy not just in the United States, but also throughout the world, particularly South America. Eric Hinderaker extended the definition of "empire" beyond centrally organized states to "broadly shared economic, social, and cultural patterns – an empire, in other words, defined not by the dominance of a ruling elite but by patterns of activity and meaning that were common to the region at large…"[22]

Richard Van Alstyne's review of early American usage of the word emphasized its "emotive" connotations:[23] "Prior to the Seven Years War people had allowed to the term 'British Empire' only the limited meaning that the original Latin word 'imperium' conveyed, that is, a power or a sovereignty. But by 1760, under the influence of sweeping victories over France, the meaning of the term had been broadened so the emphasis was put upon territorial expanse and upon the people who inhabited it."[24] The word thereby intimated power, glory, unity, nascent nationalism, patriotism, domination, expansionism, and the conquest (or at least the defeat through purchase and absorption) of competing continental rivals. Most of this book's subsequent quotes that include the word "empire" fall primarily within this category.

The fourth cluster of definitions is purely normative. The word "empire" is a condemnation of "evil" nations that treat their neighbors unfairly. This definition easily degenerates into a conclusory propaganda technique employed to criticize rival countries. Hitler might argue that his Nazi Regime was not an "empire," because Germany was treating its neighbors as they deserved and was battling the world's truly evil empires, the Soviet Union and the British Empire. As long as there is political disagreement, there will be no consensus about the use of such a pejorative term. It may be needless to say, but American politicians did not employ the word that way to describe their own country and people. John Adams' pre-Revolutionary pamphlet captured the widespread, enduring belief that Americans are a chosen, blessed people: "If ever an infant country

21 Doyle, op. cit., *supra* Intro, n.18, at 12.
22 Hinderaker, op. cit., *supra* ch. 1, n.5, at 5.
23 Van Alystyne, op. cit., *supra* Intro., n.8, at 2n.1.
24 Ibid.

deserved to be cherished it is America. If any people deserved honor and happiness they are her inhabitants. They are a people whom no character can flatter or transmit in any expressions equal to their merit and virtue…"[25] Observe that these normative definitions rely far more heavily on exemplars than the more descriptive approaches (much less the analytical conceptions). Whenever the word "empire" is used as a synonym for "evil," it must contain a horrific instance as a "core" example. For most of us, Hitler's Germany more than satisfies that purpose. Once we have agreed upon an example as a baseline, we can then make analogies and distinctions based upon close study of beliefs, facts, institutions, and circumstances. It is not hard to develop more general principles from such a horrendous period. One defining characteristic of Nazi Germany was the government's elaborate organization of widespread, racist violence. Under that criteria, the United States acted far more like Hitler's Germany when it slaughtered Native Americans and enslaved African-Americans during the Nineteenth Century than when some of its citizens lynched African-Americans during the Twentieth Century. Although this normative approach immediately becomes complicated and controversial, it is still possible to create useful distinctions and categories. Political reasoning is similar to legal reasoning. In both situations, people subdivide venal acts into more manageable units. Political violence becomes "war," "terrorism," "genocide," "mass murder," or "totalitarianism," while private violence is divided into such elusive, often overlapping categories as "murder," "manslaughter," or "battery."

Although the four clusters of definitions influence each other, each grouping requires a different mode of reasoning. The "analytical" definitions mandate precise use of language and minimal use of facts (such as maps). Proper use of the "empirical definitions" consists of developing a simple, but useful definition of the relevant phrase and painstaking study of a particular political culture. "Emotive" definitions may be the hardest to determine because they require us to guess at what people felt and believed in when they used a particular word. Although it may be possible for some analysts to look dispassionately at "normative definitions," I believe one can best understand those terms by relying on one's own character as well as external, ethical constructs.[26]

---

[25] John Adams, 'The Earl of Clarendon to William Pym III', John Adams, *The Revolutionary Writings of John Adams* (Jan. 27, 1766) (C. Bradley Thompson, ed., Indianapolis, 2000), at 50.

[26] Finally, some definitions are hybrids. In his study of empires, Michael Doyle proposed "the behavioral definition of empire as effective control, whether formal or informal, of a subordinated society by an imperial society," Doyle, op. cit., *supra* Intro., n.18, at 45. Britain's domination of India easily satisfies the formal component of that definition, because Indians had far less rights than their British rulers. But it is far harder to determine when there is "informal subordination." One could argue that the contemporary

The semantic problems become even more complex because Western political thought from the time of the ancient Greeks has consistently commingled most of its crucial political words into something resembling a simultaneous equation. For example, Benjamin Franklin believed that "liberty" and the Republican conception of "consent" were essential components of "property," all of which were part of the English "constitution": "[I]t is essential to English liberty, that the subject should not be taxed but by his own consent or by the consent of his elected representatives."[27] A person did not have any "property" if that property could be taken away without his or her "consent." Such consent could only be given either through individual concurrence or through a majority of one's elected representatives. All men had a fundamental "liberty" interest in these rights and in representative government. Consequently, Franklin concluded that Parliament's direct taxation schemes of the Colonies "unconstitutionally" violated the colonialists' liberty by taking their property without their concurrence: "I say … [the American colonists] will not tamely give up what they call their natural, their constitutional rights. Force must therefore be made use of."[28] We cannot understand what Franklin meant when he used words like "liberty," "property," or "empire" without being aware of how they fit into his overall political philosophy that was partially composed of many such words. Only then can we better grasp the well-developed ideology that lay beneath his Revolutionary rhetoric.

A. Defining "Republic" and "Republicanism"

Thomas Jefferson all but used this four-pronged approach to understand the meanings of the word "republic." After acknowledging "that the term republic is of very vague application in every language,"[29] he proposed a

---

American "society of the affluent" run an empire that informally subordinates many of their fellow citizens as well as billions more throughout the world. The word "subordination" has normative connotations, particularly in a culture that prides itself on equality, that will render many of its applications (such as the one above) controversial.

[27] Benjamin Franklin, 'Reasons and Motives for the Albany Plan of Union', Franklin, op. cit., *supra* ch. 1, n.4, at 387.

[28] Benjamin Franklin, 'Pax Quaeritur Bello', ibid., at 579.

[29] Letter from Thomas Jefferson to John Taylor (May 28, 1816), *Thomas Jefferson: Writings* (Merrill D. Peterson, ed., 1984), at 1392. While President, John Adams expressed similar sentiments: "The words 'Republican Government' have imposed on many very imperfect ideas under them – as there are none in our language more indeterminate, they may be interpreted to mean anything." John Adams, 'Address of John Adams to the Inhabitants of Rutland, Vermont', *quoted from* Richard N. Rosenfeld, *American Aurora* (New York, 1997), at 177.

core descriptive definition, which he conceded could not be practicable beyond the example of a New England township:

> [I] would say, purely and simply, [republic] means a government by its citizens in mass, acting directly and personally, according to rules established by the majority; and that every other government is more or less republican, in proportion as it has in its composition more or less of this ingredient of direct action of the citizens.[30]

It is easy to apply Jefferson's equation of "republic" with "pure democracy." One simply determines when the "citizens in mass" engage in "direct action." Under that definition, who could argue that any aspect of the current American constitutional system has the features of a "republic?" Criminal and civil juries come closest in terms of "direct action" by the citizenry, but they are not acting "in mass."

For larger, more complex societies, Jefferson twice diluted this definition of pure republicanism by including more "indirect" republican forms and political constitutions that combine republican and nonrepublican institutions:

> Other shades of republicanism may be found in other forms of government, where the executive, judiciary and legislative functions, and the different branches of the latter, are chosen by the people more or less directly, for longer terms of years or for life, or made hereditary; or where there are mixtures of authorities, some dependent on, and others independent of the people.[31]

This approach commingles two analytical conceptions. First, one needs to determine how and when government officials are "chosen by the people more or less directly." In addition to elections, several other republican techniques create responsibility and accountability: juries, direct participation by the citizenry at town meetings, specific instructions to elected representatives, referendums, recalls, and delegated influence – electors choose officials who in turn select other important constitutional actors.[32] Second, one must determine if a particular constitution contains a

---

30 Jefferson, op. cit., at 1392.

31 Ibid., at 1393.

32 Jefferson explained: "Hence, with us, the people (by which I mean the mass of individuals composing the society) being competent to judge of the facts occurring in ordinary life, they have retained the functions of judges of facts, under the name of jurors...." Letter from Thomas Jefferson to P.S. Dupont de Nemours (April 24, 1816), ibid., at 1385. I would include the jury, a "palladium of liberty," as another republican institution; a group of citizens represented the people in major lawsuits. Indeed, the jury, particularly in criminal cases, is the last remnant of direct democracy, acting at the point when community participation is most needed. We do not want to cede our liberties to the complete discretion

"mixture of authority," a combination of republican and non-republican institutions. In other words, one needs to distinguish "mixed" governments from those that are purely republican. For example, England in Jefferson's time only permitted a limited portion of the populace, generally those with substantial wealth, to elect members of the House of Commons. The English Crown and the House of Lords were completely hereditary. Thus, only one third of the English Constitution satisfied, to a very limited degree, Jefferson's broader definition of "republican." Nevertheless, the people's capacity to participate in this "mixed constitution" by electing members of the House of Commons inspired many Seventeenth and Eighteenth-Century republicans, most notably Montesquieu.

Jefferson included another important, easily verifiable republican structural component: the length of time in office. Like many other republicans, he believed governmental officials subject to frequent elections would be more responsive than those who receive lengthy or lifetime appointments. Many American citizens from that era believed all important, non-judicial officials must be elected annually to a single legislative branch for a truly republican government to exist.[33] When Chief Justice John Marshall's decisions infuriated Jefferson, Jefferson qualified his earlier definition of republicanism: "The Judiciary [is] seriously anti-republican, because for life..."[34] In other words, the Judiciary may have formally satisfied his basic republican definition because it was selected by the President and the Senate, both of whom are ultimately accountable to the electorate, but lifetime tenure effectively transformed the judicial branch into a bastion of anti-republicanism.

At least while writing his portion of *The Federalist*, James Madison would not have agreed with his close friend about the Federal Judiciary. Madison argued that all three branches of the Federal government were ultimately accountable to the People, making the proposed political Constitution "unmixed," wholly republican. The People directly elected all the members of the House of Representatives. By directly electing their State legislators, who then chose two of their members to be United States Senators, the voters indirectly selected the Senate. The electorate had a more focused form of indirect selection by selecting each States'

---

of government officials known as judges. Although he did not label juries as "republican," Jefferson believed that even civil juries helped maintain a republican society, because juries tend to be wary of the rich, who generally benefit from the technicalities of law.

33 "Never was any measure so thoroughly discussed as our proposed new Constitution... As to the new chambers [of Congress], I am of your opinion that one alone would be better..." Letter from Benjamin Franklin to M. Le Veillard (Oct. 28, 1788), quoted in Rosenfeld, op. cit., *supra* ch. 1, n.29, at 731.

34 Letter from Thomas Jefferson to John Taylor of Caroline (May 28, 1816), Jefferson, op. cit., *supra* ch. 1, n.29, at 1393.

Presidential electors. Finally, the President, indirectly accountable via these Republican techniques, nominated Supreme Court Justices, whom the Senate could reject. Admittedly, the President and Senate chose the Justices for life, neither of which the People directly selected. But that two-step process did not make the judicial system "nonrepublican" or the Federal judiciary inherently "anti-republican." As Madison pointed out in *The Federalist*, all major government officials could trace their appointments back to the electorate. He summarized his defense of this completely indirect system with a simple analytical definition in Federalist Number Ten: "A Republic [is] a Government in which the scheme of representation takes place…"[35]

Madison did not see any republican defects in the creation of the Constitution. State Legislators, whom the populace elected, had chosen the Framers. Even though the Framers exceeded their original mandate to alter the Articles of Confederation to facilitate commerce, their proposed Constitution had no legal authority until ratified by nine out of thirteen State Conventions. Admittedly, the People never directly endorsed the Constitution, but they participated in a "scheme of representation" by electing State representatives to Special State Constitutional Conventions. More than once, State Conventions rejected the voters' electoral preferences, ratifying the Constitution even though Anti-Federalists started the meetings with a majority of the delegates.[36] Madison observed that the People, acting through their representatives, removed any alleged improprieties by participating in the Constitutional ratification process.

People across the political spectrum should reach similar results when they apply to other constitutions Madison's analytical definition of "Republic," a definition that includes as a "core example" his discussion of the proposed Constitution. The United Kingdom's Constitution remains "mixed" because the Crown and many members of the House of Lords are hereditary positions (although the Labor Government is currently transforming the House of Lords). Madison's definition is quite "analytical" because it can be easily understood, applied, and even "refuted." One need only bring forth a group of thinkers who can explain how they can reach different conclusions while using Madison's definition. But it will be hard to find such thinkers because this mode of reasoning closely resembles formal logic. If "republican government" means "representation," and "representation" means an electoral constitutional ratification process that initially places all authority in elected officials who

---

35 'The Federalist Number 10' (James Madison), op. cit, *supra* ch. 1, n.20, at 81.

36 Only defiant Rhode Island had a belated referendum after all the other States had complied with the Framers' requests to hold ratification conventions that accepted the new Constitution.

then select additional constitutional actors, then the United States Constitution, in formation and organization, is purely "republican."

Before turning to more complicated, value-laden definitions of "republic," it is important to concede that anyone can assert that the Jefferson/Madisonian emphasis on representation focuses on the wrong core. One might believe that the expressly normative value of "civic virtue" is the heart of any true Republic. Nevertheless, we should retain Madison's analytical definition. Republics differ structurally from their alternatives by giving some power to the populace to influence government through elections. In addition, the degree of electoral participation is far easier to define and agree upon than such overtly normative standards as "civic virtue." Not that these alternative conceptions should be completely rejected; they are aspects of a more morally acceptable conception of a "republic." For instance, I believe a true "republic" must include not only elections, but also a rich, humane conception of "civic virtue" and a commitment to the "rule of law." However, almost any norm or institution can be characterized as "republican" under these more extensive, amorphous definitions. The American slave owners' argument that the peculiar institution of race slavery was "republican"[37] demonstrates that there is no "objective" or "logical" boundary once we proceed beyond the more analytical, structural definitions.

Both Madison and Jefferson had a vision of "republicanism" that reached far beyond the electoral process, touching virtually every aspect of American society. For them, the ultimate purpose of republicanism was not the creation of an electoral process but the establishment of an enlightened, humane society that would facilitate every man's "pursuit of Happiness." They believed republics needed additional institutions, such as the jury and free press; wealth redistribution mechanisms like the elimination of primogeniture and entail; and the inalienable right of freedom of conscience. Conversely, institutions like national banks, a standing army, political parties, and a national debt threatened their republicanism. The two Virginians' vision of republicanism included America's political economy and culture. Only industrious, independent farmers can maintain a republican culture, because cities inevitably spawn a large number of dependent poor, corruption and luxury. Unpretentious manners and dress manifested the republican spirit, not militarism, war, conquest, and ceremonial glory. Above all, the republic would be animated and protected by the "civic virtue" of its leaders and citizens. No matter what its design,

---

[37] Larry E. Tise, *Proslavery: A History of the Defense of Slavery in America, 1701-1840* (Athens, 1987), 347-63.

a constitutional republic would collapse once its citizenry and magistrates became hopelessly corrupt.

This far-reaching Republican ideology, a clear reflection of Madison and Jefferson's preferences and backgrounds, is bound to be debatable in theory and practice. Although it is simple to verify whether such institutions as juries and national banks exist, there will never be a permanent consensus that they ought to exist. Rights of conscience and press remain uncertain in definition and application. The two Virginians' cultural norms are bound to be even more controversial. Most of us who live in cities would oppose the notion that we are inherently dangerous, corrupt threats to any humane and enlightened republic. In other words, we might agree with Madison and Jeffersons' ultimate purposes, but reject some of their preferred means. Nor should republicanism of any form be the ultimate standard. A Hobbesian would test each institution's legitimacy by its capacity to protect a commonwealth from civil war and invasion. Thus a standing army of some sort would usually be necessary. A Burkean would determine how effectively a particular institution has prevented tyranny.[38] The Constitution's protection of slavery constituted its most egregious effort to protect private tyranny instead of preventing tyranny. In addition, many of these subsequent criteria are harder to define. What do "corruption" and "luxury" mean? By themselves, the rival notions of "corruption" and "civic virtue" are little more than normative conclusions. So there will be many disagreements, first about the definitions of these words and then about the subsequent application of agreed-upon definitions.

Of course, many people will not accept the basic norms and institutions. After all, why should a society want electoral representation? Others will find some norms and institutions to be insufficient. Is accountability through elections the ultimate end (and thus the terminus of our inquiry into the meanings of "republic"), or is it a means to other more important goals? Any answer to such questions will be purposeful, a collection of normative political preferences.

B. Defining "Empire" and "Republican Empire"

During the Constitutional Ratification debate, Federalists frequently and unapologetically used the word "empire." Although we never can be confident what any speaker completely meant in any particular situation,

---

[38] James G. Wilson, 'Justice Diffused: A Comparison of Edmund Burke's Conservatism with the Views of Five Conservative, Academic Judges', 40 *University Miami Law Review*, 913 (1986).

we should remember that the country had recently revolted from a powerful entity known as the "British Empire." Apparently, any analogy between the "British Empire" and America's nascent "empire" did not trouble the Federalist advocates. In private writings,[39] at the Constitutional Convention,[40] and in *The Federalist*, James Madison periodically, even casually, described America as an "empire." After all, the word "empire" powerfully reinforced his underlying insight that the United States' republic would be stabilized by its vast size.[41] For instance, in *The Federalist* he dismissed the argument that Americans were too culturally diverse to unify:

> Hearken not to the unnatural voice which tells you that the people of America, knit together as they are by so many cords of affection, can no longer live together as members of the same family; can no longer continue the mutual guardians of their mutual happiness; can no longer be fellow citizens of one great, respectable, and flourishing empire.[42]

During the Constitutional Convention, Gouverneur Morris lamented: "Among the many provisions which had been urged, [he] had seen none for supporting the dignity and splendor of the American Empire."[43] Alexander Hamilton's second sentence in *The Federalist No. 1* assumes the existence of an American empire: "The subject (of the proposed Constitution) speaks its own importance; comprehending in its consequences nothing less than the existence of the UNION, the safety and welfare of the parts of which it is composed, the fate on an empire in many respects the most interesting in the world."[44] Later in *The Federalist*, Hamilton converted the Anti-Federalists' fears of a large republic into an additional reason for a powerful, central government: "[T]he very difficulty itself drawn from the

---

39 "1. If the minority happen to include all such as possess the skill and habits of military life, & such as possess the great pecuniary resources, one-third only may conquer the remaining two-thirds." James Madison, 'Vices of the Political System of the United States', *The Mind of the Founder: Sources of the Political Thought of James Madison* (Marvin Meyers, ed., Hanover, 1971), 59.

40 "... would the small States be more secure against the ambition & power of their larger neighbours, than they would be under a general Government pervading with equal energy every part of the Empire, and having an equal interest in protecting every part against every other part?" James Madison, *Notes of the Debates in the Federal Convention of 1787* (Adrienne Koch, intro., Athens, Ohio 1984), 146.

41 "The laws are so far from being uniform, that they vary in every state; whilst the public affairs of the union are spread throughout a very extensive region, and are extremely diversified by the local affairs connected with them, and can with difficulty be correctly learned in any other place, than in the central councils, to which a knowledge of them will be brought by the representatives of every part of the empire." 'The Federalist Number 53' (James Madison), op. cit., *supra* ch. 1, n.20, at 333.

42 'The Federalist Number 14' (James Madison), ibid., at 104.

43 Madison, *Notes*, op. cit., *supra* ch. 1, n.40, at 255.

44 'The Federalist Number 1' (Alexander Hamilton), op. cit., *supra* ch. 1, n.20, at 33.

extent of the country, is the strongest argument in favor of an energetic government; for any other can certainly never preserve the Union of so large an empire."[45] John Dickinson asserted that the proposed Constitution was "necessary to the good government of an extensive republican empire."[46] Quite simply, the Constitutional Federalists wanted a republic *and* an empire. The broad based support for empire included many Anti-Federalists. Although Madison fought Anti-Federalists like Patrick Henry over the possibility and desirability of a large republican empire, many other Anti-Federalists had different concerns (and even Henry was profoundly inconsistent given his obsession over protecting Western rights to the Mississippi). The most effective criticism of the Constitution was its failure to provide a Bill of Rights. Many Anti-Federalists eventually reached a compromise on this issue by supporting those State Conventions that would ratify the existing Constitution while also recommending prompt Amendments. Those who sought a Bill of Rights were mainly concerned about Federal oppression of individuals or States. Once that issue was resolved to their satisfaction, they could and would easily support the new republican empire.

One could plausibly argue that the Constitution's advocates defined "empire" as "large size," a definition that obviously included the existing thirteen colonies. After all, Hamilton wrote of "preserving" the empire. But we shall see that these same men also had expansion in mind. It is hard to conceive of Hamilton as ever being uninterested in further power and glory for himself and his country; he gave a lengthy speech at the Constitutional Convention recommending the British Constitution as the best model for an "energetic" government.

Aristotle, Thomas Hobbes, and David Hume had already laid the foundation for much of Madison's thinking about the virtues of large size. Aristotle observed: "[L]arge states are less liable to faction than small ones, because in them the middle class is large; whereas in small states it is easy to divide all the citizens into two classes who are either rich or poor, and to leave nothing in the middle."[47] Thomas Hobbes praised the equilibrium gained by maintaining a balance of power among domestic

---

45 'The Federalist Number 23' (Alexander Hamilton), ibid., at 157.

46 "Fabius" [John Dickinson], 'Observations on the Constitution Proposed by the Federal Convention VIII', 2 Bailyn, op. cit., *supra* Intro., n.7, at 424. Several years before the Constitution was created, George Washington sent a circular to the State Governors, in which he observed: "The foundation of our Empire was not laid in the gloomy age of Ignorance and Superstition; but at an Epocha when the rights of mankind were better understood and more clearly defined, then at any other period." 'Circular to State Governments', *George Washington, Writings* (John Rhodehamel ed., 1997), 517.

47 Aristotle, Politics, 2 *The Complete Works of Aristotle* (J. Barnes, ed., Princeton, 1984), 2057.

factions: "[N]o great Popular Common-wealth was ever kept up; but either by a forraign Enemy that united them; or the reputation of some one eminent Man amongst them; or by the secret Counsell of a few; *or by the mutuall fear of equall factions*; and not by the open Consultations of the Assembly."[48] David Hume emphasized the virtues of size:

> Though it is more difficult to form a republican government in an extensive country than in a city; there is more facility, when once it is formed, of preserving it stead and uniform without tumult and faction... In a large government, which is modeled with masterly skill, there is compass and room enough to refine the democracy, from the lower people, who may be admitted into the first elections or first concoction of the commonwealth, to the higher magistrates, who direct all the movements. At the same time, the parts are so distant and remote, that it is very difficult, either by intrigue, prejudice, or passion, to hurry them into any measures against the public interest.[49]

Many anti-Federalists relied on Montesquieu's double-edged proposition[50] that pure republics can only endure by remaining small, while monarchs or despots are necessary to rule large empires. Montesquieu's concerns presented two problems for Madison, who wanted both a republic and a large empire: Madison had to demonstrate that republics could be large and empires not necessarily become despotic. As many scholars have observed, Madison answered the question of size in *Federalist Number Ten* and elsewhere by arguing large republics were preferable to small

---

48 Thomas Hobbes, *Leviathan* (C.B. MacPherson, ed. New York, 1968), 311.

49 David Hume, 'Idea of a Perfect Commonwealth', *David Hume, Essays: Moral, Political, and Literary* (Eugene F. Miller, ed., Indianapolis, 1985), 527-28. Gibbon's famous history undermined Montesquieu's dichotomies between peace-loving republics and aggressive empires: "The principal conquests of the Romans were achieved under the republic; and the emperors, for the most part, were satisfying with preserving those dominions..." Edward Gibbon, 1 *The History of the Decline and Fall of the Roman Empire* (David Womersley, ed., 1994), 31.

50 "[T]he natural property of small states is to be governed as republics, that of medium-sized ones, to be subject to a monarch, and that of large empires to be dominated by a despot..." Montesquieu, *The Spirit of the Laws* (Anne M. Cohler, et al., trans. & ed., 1989), 126. Montesquieu's distinction was not as helpful as many anti-Federalists believed. After all, he admired the British system, a "republic which disguises itself under the form of a monarchy," in part because it relied upon commerce more than civic virtue to expand its authority over a vast area, Paul A. Rahe, *3 Republics Ancient and Modern, Inventions of Prudence: Constituting the American Regime* (Chapel Hill, 1992), 46. Hamilton also pointed out in The Federalist that even if the Americans subdivided their existing country into at least six separate republics, those areas would still exceed Montesquieu's "dimensions" for small republics. Moreover, Montesquieu offered the same solution as the Federalists: a confederation of republics that would combine the freedom and virtue of small government with the energy and power of monarchies, 'Federalist Number Nine' (Hamilton), op. cit., *supra* ch. 1, n.20, at 74.

republics, much less pure democracies, because there would be so many groups and interests that the majority could never coalesce into a tyrannical faction, capable of oppressing minorities for economic, religious, or other improper motives.[51]

Montesquieu's aversion to large empires and conquest was part of an alternative intellectual tradition. Aristotle wrote elsewhere in *The Politics* that "[E]xperience shows that a very populous city can rarely, if ever, be well governed; since all cities which have a reputation for good government have a limit of population."[52] He also equated "empire" with dominion and conquest:

> Many modern writers have taken a similar view; they commend the Lacedaemonian constitution, and praise the legislator for making conquest and war his sole aim, a doctrine which may be refuted by argument and has long been refuted by facts. For most men desire empire in the hope of accumulating the goods of fortune; and on this ground Thibron and all those who have written about the Lacedaemonian constitution have praised their legislator, because the Lacedaemonian, by being trained to meet dangers, gained great power. But surely they are not a happy people now that their empire has passed away, nor was their legislator right. How ridiculous is the result, if, while they are continuing in the observance of his laws and no one interferes with them, they have lost the better part of life! * * * Neither is a city to be deemed happy or a legislator to be praised because he trains his citizens to conquer and obtain dominion over their neighbors, for there is great evil in this.[53]

In 1784, Immanuel Kant stated that expansionism undermines the quest for moral maturity:

> But as long as states apply all their resources to their vain and violent schemes of expansion, thus incessantly obstructing the slow and laborious efforts of their citizens to cultivate their minds, and even deprive them of all support in these efforts, no progress in this direction can be expected.[54]

One of the greatest threats to any empire, republican or otherwise, is excessive conflict between the "party of privilege"[55] and the less well off. The fruits of empire do not rest exclusively in external conquest; they also consist of the labor and capital obtained from the weaker members of the citizenry. Such local class-based conflicts as Bacon's Rebellion, the 1771

---

51 'Federalist Number Ten' (Madison), ibid., at 83-84.

52 Aristotle, op. cit., *supra* ch. 1, n.47, at 2104-05.

53 Ibid., at 2116.

54 Immanuel Kant, 'Idea for a Universal History with a Cosmopolitan Purpose', *Kant, Political Writings* (Hans Reiss, ed., Cambridge, 1970), 49.

55 Turner, *The Old West*, op. cit., *supra* ch. 1, n.19, at 111.

Battle of the Alamace,[56] the Shays Rebellion, the Fries Rebellion, and the Whiskey Rebellion reconfirmed the need for an energetic central government capable of subduing the poor. The problem for the wealthy Framers of the Constitution was to provide enough democracy to satisfy the people while creating a system that would protect their class's interests over the long run. For many decades preceding and following the Constitution's ratification, large segments of America's leadership were eager to minimize the rights of the fellow white male citizens through property qualifications for voting and office and through legislative malapportionment. Perhaps the bluntest statement occurred half a century later, during the debates over a new Virginia State Constitution:

> The principle is that the owners of the slave property must be possessed of all the powers of government, however small their own numbers may be, to secure their property from the rapacity of an overgrown majority of white men. This principle admits of no relaxation, because the weaker the minority becomes, the greater will their need for power be according to their own doctrines.[57]

The Constitutional convention left the scope of franchise to each of the states. But whatever system any State chose, American voters would select their representatives from a large base that would provide more honorable citizens as candidates. A larger electorate thus could "filter" out less worthy representatives.[58] Once a written Constitution precludes rule by a King or an aristocracy, large countries become less vulnerable to corruption and cabal. The national legislature would only pass laws that truly advance the public good. Consequently, the large republican empire would neither collapse from internal bickering nor degenerate into corruption and despotism.[59] To use the hackneyed phrase once again, Madison "stood Montesquieu on his head." Madison had relied upon his core analytical conception of republicanism as electoral representation to design a republic that avoided the problems of pure participatory democracy, which was clearly unworkable on such a large scale and dangerously prone to

---

[56] Ibid., at 119.

[57] Ibid., at 115.

[58] Gordon S. Wood, *The Creation of the American Republic* (Williamsburg, 1969), 506-18. *See also* 'The Federalist Number 10' (Madison), op. cit., *supra* ch. 1, n.20, at 82-83.

[59] "[T]he fewer the distinct parties and interests, the more frequently will a majority be found of the same party; and the smaller the number of individuals composing a majority, and the smaller the compass within which they are placed, the more easily will they concert and execute their plans of oppression," Ibid., at 83.

tumultuous factionalization.[60] Indeed, many Federalists asserted that direct democracy was a poor form of government, irrespective of size and feasibility.[61] Madison thereby rejected Jefferson's core example of New England Meetings as pure "republics." Under Madison's terminology, such communities were unstable "pure democracies," allowing the populace to participate directly in government.

Such an interpretation of Madison, which relies heavily upon *Federalist Number Ten*, is illuminating, but incomplete.[62] In *Federalist Number Sixty-three*, Madison revisited the question of size. He first analyzed the ancient Greek republics to determine if they had ever used "a scheme of representation." He pointed out that Athens had elected nine Archons to govern them; Carthage elected a Senate; and Sparta was partially ruled by the Ephori, "elected by the whole of the people."[63] With these facts as background, Madison wrote a paragraph worth considering line-by-line. In the first sentence he rejected the commonly held opinion that the Greek City States were pure democracies and that modern Europe had invented the concept of representation:[64] "From these facts, to which many others may be added, it is clear that the principle of representation was neither unknown to the ancients, nor wholly overlooked in their political constitutions."[65] He then explained in a completely italicized sentence that the crucial difference between the American and Greek systems is that the American people "in their collective capacity" take no

---

[60] For example, Noah Webster wrote that "the moderns have invented the doctrine of *representation*, which seems to be the perfection of human government." Quoted in Rahe, op. cit., *supra* n.76, at 42 (italics in original).

[61] Fisher Ames was predictably blunt: "The representation of the people is something more than the people. I know, sir, but one purpose which the people can effect without delegation, and that is, to destroy a government. That they cannot erect a government is evinced by our being thus assembled, on their behalf. * * * [Pure participatory democracy] would be government not by laws, but by men. Such were the paltry democracies of Greece and Asia Minor, so much extolled, and so often proposed as a model for our imitation." Fisher Ames, 'Fisher Ames on Biennial Elections and on the Volcano of Democracy' (January 15, 1788), Bailyn, *1 Debate*, op. cit., *supra* Intro., n.7, at 892. *See also* 'The Federalist Number 10' (Madison), op. cit., *supra* ch. 1, n.20, at 81.

[62] Lance Banning characterized the choice between small and large republics as a question of degree and probability: "[P]rivate liberties and public good *might both be safer* in a large than in a small republic." Lance Banning, *The Sacred Fire of Liberty: James Madison and the Founding of the Federal Republic* (Ithaca, 1995), 207-208 (Emphasis added).

The Federalists also argued that their proposed Constitution was consistent with Montesquieu, who had recommended that republics form federations to prevent external conquest, Montesquieu, op. cit., *supra* n.76, at 131.

[63] 'The Federalist Number 63' (Madison), op. cit., *supra* ch. 1, n.20, at 387.

[64] Ibid.

[65] Ibid.

direct part in the political constitution. In other words, the Greeks erred by allowing any direct, majoritarian democracy. Every part of the political constitution must be representative; the "mass" must never have a direct voice in government. But purging a constitution of pure democracy did not[66] provide sufficient protection from factionalization. For Madison, context remained as important as theory or text: "[T]o ensure to this advantage [of pure representation] its full effect, we must be careful not to separate it from *the other advantage, of an extensive territory*." Madison then annihilated Montesquieu's belief in small republics: "For it cannot be believed that any form of representative government, could have succeeded within the narrow limits occupied by the democracies of Greece."[67]

Madison did not just "stand Montesquieu on his head" in that paragraph by arguing that a very big republic is better than a small one; he asserted that republican governments had no alternative to being of great size.[68] There are no qualifications like those in the conclusion of *Federalist Number Ten*: "Does [large size] consist in the *greater security* afforded by a greater variety of parties, against the event of one party being able to outnumber and oppress the rest?"[69] In *Federalist Number Sixty-Three*, the foreseeable effects of size do not raise questions of degree or even probability, but of kind! Republicans have no choice but to pursue and protect empire. Applying another cliché, Madison "cut Montesquieu off at the knees" in this later *Federalist*. The imperial republic would be safer for two basic reasons: It would be less likely to dissolve into factional conflict, and it would be less vulnerable to foreign threats.

Federalists like Hamilton frequently warned of foreign machinations should the Constitution not be ratified: "Foreign powers, also, will not be idle spectators. They will interpose; the confusion will increase; and a dissolution of the Union will ensue."[70] Hamilton sounded like Thomas Hobbes in explaining the need for central domestic strength. Because "men love power," they will gravitate toward the most powerful public

---

66 This paragraph demonstrates how brilliantly Madison formulated and used precise definitions. "Republicanism" is separated from "pure democracy" by a verifiable form of decision-making: elections versus direct participation by the collective citizenry. Thus, on one level at least, all Americans who support the Constitution are republicans.

67 Ibid., at 387.

68 This analysis conflicts with Paul Rahe's conclusion that the debate over size was exaggerated. According to Rahe, Madison primarily sought to combat polarization of factions by creating a multiplicity of interests: "[Madison's] argument is essentially an economic argument and only tangentially a geographical argument." Rahe, op. cit., *supra* n.76, at 54.

69 'The Federalist Number Ten', (Madison), op. cit., *supra* n.46, at 84 (emphasis added).

70 Alexander Hamilton, (June 18, 1788), *1 Elliot*, op. cit., *supra* Intro., n.10, at 200.

institutions, which tend to be at the state level in any confederacy: "All the passions, then, we see, of avarice, ambition, interest, which govern most individuals, and all public bodies, fall into the current of the states; and do not flow into the stream of the general government. The former, therefore, will generally be an overmatch for the general government, and render any confederacy in its very nature precarious."[71] Overall, the leading Federalists offered a tragic, Hobbesian choice. If citizens want a stable republic, they also need an extensive empire, which makes factions less powerful through the ancient doctrine "divide and conquer": "Divide et imperia, the reprobated axiom of tyranny, is under certain qualifications, the only policy, by which a republic can be administered on just principles."[72] Imperial success advances the ideal of republicanism as much as republican structures protect large empires. Quite simply, Madison imbedded an imperial mandate into the American Constitutional system, just as he used size to protect private power's wealth and religious minorities from "majority tyranny." The Framers' two major goals of wealth protection and empire building cannot be fully found within the Constitution's text.[73] Because of its foreseeable effects, external reality – particularly size – was a basic part of the Madisonian system. In other words, some of the Constitution's most fundamental purposes and structures can only be understood by looking beyond the text. Madison proudly concluded in *Federalist Number Fourteen*: "Americans can claim the merit of making the discovery of the basis of unmixed and extensive republics."[74] Knowing that all political choices involve tradeoffs, he offered a new constitution that would simultaneously enhance the empire, guarantee republicanism, and protect minorities (particularly the wealthy and religious sects) from majority tyranny.

Only hindsight would reveal how much darker Hamilton's views were than Madison's theory. While Madison hoped and believed that the basic structure and size of the new republic would facilitate the selection of virtuous republican leaders at the expense of fractious demagogues, Hamilton concluded that the new central government would need to rely heavily upon "ambition, avarice, and interest." The two co-authors of *The Federalist* would split almost immediately over this difference; Hamilton preferred to manipulate public credit and debt to create a group of wealthy merchants committed to the central government, while Madison fulminated

---

71 Ibid.

72 Letter of James Madison to Thomas Jefferson (Oct. 24, 1787), 1 Bailyn, op. cit., *supra* Intro., n.7, at 201.

73 A small country could adopt this Constitution without changing a word.

74 'The Federalist Number 14' (Madison), op. cit., *supra* n.46, at 101.

over the destruction of such local, community norms as the protection of the interests of those who actually fought in the Revolutionary War.

James Wilson's opening address to the Pennsylvania ratifying convention probably had more influence on the ratification debate than *The Federalist*. Instead of distinguishing Montesquieu, Wilson recruited him. Because the new nation would be a "federal republic," it would combine the virtuous spirits of both monarchy and republicanism, the benefits of internal liberty and external empire:

> In this dilemma, a Federal Republic naturally presented itself to our observation, as a species of government that secured all the internal advantages of a republic, at the same time that it maintained the external dignity and force of a monarchy. The definition of this form of government may be found in Montesquieu, who says, I believe, that it consists in assembling distinct societies, which are consolidated into a new body, capable of being increased by the addition of new members; an expanding quality peculiarly fitted to the circumstances of America.[75]

One could attempt to infer from these arguments that Federalists like Wilson and Madison defined "empire" only as a country of large size, a variant of Edmund Burke's definition: "An empire is the aggregate of many states under one common head, whether this head be a monarch or a presiding republic."[76] The Founders certainly knew they were planning to regulate an extraordinarily large expanse of land and population currently under the jurisdiction of may State governments. Jefferson wrote in his *Notes on the State of Virginia* that Virginia alone was "one third larger than the islands of Great Britain and Ireland."[77] Limiting the meaning of "empire" to big countries has the conceptual advantage of being as "analytic" and "descriptive" as defining "republics" purely in terms of indirect accountability to the people. Such a static definition of empire is particularly reassuring to those who want to see Madisonian republicanism as a pervasively humane ideology. Under this narrow definition, Madison already lived in an empire; he was merely trying to preserve and improve that large country. Consequently, no reason exists to attribute any of the more disturbing connotations of the word "empire" – much less its cognate "imperialism," or, even worse, "imperious" – to Madison's goals. The Madisonian dilemma is reduced to a technical problem in political science,

---

[75] James Wilson, 'James Wilson's Opening Address', Bailyn, *1 Debate* (Nov. 24, 1787), op. cit., *supra* Intro., n.7, at 793.

[76] Quoted in Walter Lafeber, *The New Empire: An Interpretation of American Expansion 1860-1898* (Ithaca, 1963), 1.

[77] Thomas Jefferson, 'Notes on the State of Virginia', Jefferson, op. cit., *supra* ch. 1, n.29, at 127.

having few moral connotations or costs. As the historian Jack Rakove put it, Madison's capacity to analyze and solve the problem of size was a triumph of "pragmatism" over Montesquieu's "clichés about small republics."[78]

But we have already encountered a more unsettling "analytic" definition of "empire" that is now worth employing. One can also reasonably define an "empire" as a geographically growing country. In this sense, most Americans (including Madison) were not satisfied with their existing empire. In a very influential speech that helped establish the grounds for subsequent debate about the proposed Constitution throughout the nation, James Wilson explained to the Pennsylvania ratifying convention:

> To frame a Government for a single city or State, is a business both in its importance and facility, widely different from the task entrusted to the Federal Convention, whose prospects extended not only to thirteen independent and Sovereign States, some of which in territorial jurisdiction, population, and resource, equal the most respectable nations of Europe, but likewise to innumerable States yet unformed, and to myriads of citizens who in future ages shall inhabit the vast uncultivated regions of the continent.[79]

This imperial urge to grow long predated the Revolution, much less the formation and ratification of the Constitution. In his history of the lengthy struggle between European and American empires over the fate of North America, the historian Bernard DeVoto concluded that the United States, having national boundaries of continental size resulted from

> [A] feeling which, historically, the American people have always had, a feeling that properly they must become what they have become, a single society occupying a continental unit. That feeling was a powerful force in the creation of the American nation and the American empire.[80]

One of the primary objectives of Franklin's Albany Plan was to "extend the British settlements in North America."[81] As early as 1751, Franklin explained why England must support its Colonies. The Indians had to be displaced because their hunting-based economy took up too much land,

---

[78] Jack N. Rakove, *Original Meanings: Politics and Ideas in the Making of the Constitution* 55 (New York, 1996). These objective definitions of "empire" and "republic" are also consistent with the erroneous historical argument that Rome changed from a "republic" to an "empire" when Julius Caesar took over. So long as Rome retained its electoral process, it remained a republic.

[79] James Wilson, 'James Wilson's Opening Address, Pennsylvania Ratifying Convention' (Nov. 24, 1787), Bailyn, *1 Debate*, op. cit., *supra* n.7, at 791.

[80] DeVoto, op. cit., *supra* n.28, at xxxi.

[81] Franklin, 'Reasons and Motives', in Franklin, op. cit., *supra* n.30, at 383.

land that could be more efficiently used for farming to support a huge Anglo-American population.[82] Indeed, every European power would soon be contending for more American lands to increase national power through larger populations.[83] This racially inspired vision led Franklin to oppose race slavery (even while retaining domestic Africans until he later turned against slavery late in his life):[84]

> And while we are, as I may call it, *Scouring* our Planet, by clearing *America* of Woods, and so making this Side of our Globe reflect a brighter Light to the Eyes of Inhabitants in *Mars* or *Venus*, why should we in the Sight of Superior Beings, darken its People? Why increase the Sons of *Africa*, by Planting them in *America*, where be so fair an Opportunity, by excluding all Blacks and Tawneys, of increasing the lovely White and Red? But perhaps I am partial to the Complexion of my Country, for such Kind of Partiality is natural to Mankind.[85]

The Colonists rarely thought small. In 1764, the colonist Stephen Hopkins explained why Parliament had acted ungratefully toward its loyal colonists by imposing the Stamp Act after the victorious French and Indian War:

> These colonies having thus planed and defended themselves and removed all enemies from their borders, were in hopes to enjoy peace and recruit their state, much exhausted by these long struggles; but they were soon called upon to raise men and send out to the defense of other colonies, and to make conquests for the crown. They dutifully obeyed the requisition, and with ardor entered into those services and continued in them until all encroachments were removed, and all Canada, and even the Havana, conquered. They most cheerfully complied with every call of the crown; they rejoiced, even exulted, in the prosperity and exaltation of the British Empire.[86]

Exalting the British Empire primarily meant furthering British conquest and glory, not extending republicanism. Thus, the more troubling notions of "glory" and "conquest" were also associated with "empire."

Holmes had been provoked by Parliament's Proclamation of 1763, which barred American colonists from moving beyond the Allegheny Mountains to settle in the Ohio River valley. The Proclamation stated

---

[82] Franklin, 'Observations Concerning the Increase of Mankind, Peopling of Countries, &c.', ibid., at 368.

[83] Ibid., at 372-73.

[84] Jennings, op. cit., *supra* Intro., n.19, at 193.

[85] Ibid., at 374.

[86] Stephen Hopkins, 'The Rights of Colonies Examined', *1 American Political Writing During the Founding Era 1760-1805* (Charles S. Hyneman and Donald S. Lutz, eds., Indianapolis, 1983), 58-59.

Americans could not survey, own, or settle that land. Those who already lived there had to leave.[87] Bernard DeVoto concluded that the English wanted the Ohio River valley undeveloped to protect their valuable fur trade and the Indians who made it possible. England was also worried about continuing clashes between two groups of its subjects: the Indians and the Colonists.[88] One official warned: "Were [the Indians] driven from their forests, the peltry trade would decrease and it is not impossible that worse savages would take refuge in them."[89] Those "worse savages" were migrating American colonists.

Once the Revolution began, colonists looked far beyond their existing borders. One doesn't have to rely on words like "empire" and "continent"[90] for evidence. During the debate in the First Continental Congress over whether to seek formal independence, one delegate stated: "That France & Spain had reason to be jealous of that rising power which would one day certainly strip them of all their American possessions."[91] The Colonists had more than long-term aspirations. In September 1775, the First Continental Congress authorized General Schuyler to invade Canada. Those politicians knew that such an aggressive military action would reduce the likelihood of reconciliation with England and would shift the American role from purely defensive to aggressive.[92] Soon after he began the invasion, General Schuyler used purely moral abstractions for justification:

> [T]he only views of Congress were to restore to them those rights which every subject of the British empire, of whatever religious sentiment he may be, is entitled to; and that in the execution of these truths he had received the most positive orders to cherish every Canadian, and every friend to the cause of liberty, and sacredly guard their property.[93]

---

87 DeVoto, op. cit., *supra* n.28, at 235.

88 I thank Paul Finkelman for pointing this out to me.

89 Ibid., at 264.

90 In 1776, an anonymous writer observed: "The happiness of individuals is secured to them by the community, and happiness of the separate Colonies can only be secured by the Continent..." [Anonymous], 'Letter II in Four Letters on Interesting Subjects', 1 *Political Writing*, op. cit., *supra* n.112, at 374. The word "continent" rarely should be interpreted as a synonym for North America. It usually alluded to the Colonies. After all, they called their army the Continental Army, their Congress the Continental Congress, and their currency "Continentals." Nevertheless, the colonists' choice of the word may well indicate conscious and unconscious aspirations toward future growth.

91 Thomas Jefferson, 'Autobiography 1743-1790' (January 6, 1821), Jefferson, op. cit., *supra* ch. 1, n.29, at 14.

92 David Ramsay, *1 The History of the American Revolution* (Lester H. Cohen, ed., 1990), 213.

93 Ibid., at 215.

The invasion was a disaster, largely because the Americans had erroneously hoped Canadians, particularly the French in Quebec, would rally to their side. The rumblings of sedition, which ranged from Quebec and Nova Scotia to Bermuda and the Bahamas, never congealed into revolution.[94] Judging from their actions and inactions, most Canadians did not perceive the Americans as liberators.

That failure did not deter either Congress or the American citizenry. Many pamphleteers and preachers demanded using more force against Canada; both God and Republicanism were on America's side.[95] In early 1776, Congress authorized another attempt to annex Canada. Delays prompted outrage. One anonymous writer castigated Congress: "[T]hey have thrown cold water on the necessary military proceedings of this province and continent, and have been abettors...in procrastinating the expedition to Canada, which, by that *delay only*, may probably not now succeed."[96] Once again, the Americans did not expect to win solely through violence. Congress informed the Canadians that they would enter Congress as political equals; they would not reduce Canada to a subordinate group of colonies.[97] Persuasion played a part in Congress' foreign policy; a printer, printing press, and a clergyman accompanied the invading army.[98] The Americans again failed to convince Canadians of their good intentions. American soldiers plundered local citizens,[99] while General Benedict Arnold seized enough goods in Montreal to set up a profitable business for his nephew back in America.[100] Defeat and retreat soon followed.

The two invasions reveal how far apart England and America were long before the Second Continental Congress formally declared independence on July 4, 1776. At least three allegations in the Declaration of Independence appear to have been references to British resistance to colonial expansion.[101] First, the Declaration criticized the King for "prevent[ing] the population of the states; for that purpose obstructing the laws for naturalization of foreigners, refusing to pass others to encourage their migrations hither." That same sentence also attacked the King for "raising the conditions of new Appropriations of Land." Although the revolutionaries were certainly

---

94 Kevin Phillips, *The Cousins' Wars: Religion, Politics, & the Triumph of Anglo-America* (New York, 1999), 271.

95 Ramsay, op. cit., *supra* n.118, at 250.

96 Anonymous, 'The Alarm: or, an Address to the People of Pennsylvania on the Late Resolve of Congress', 1 *Political Writings*, op. cit., *supra* ch. 1, n.86, at 327.

97 Ramsay, op. cit., at 215.

98 Ibid., at 250.

99 Ibid., at 252.

100 Ibid., at 259.

101 Pauline Maier, *American Scripture: Making the Declaration of Independence* (New York, 1997), 114.

thinking of the British occupation of Boston when they condemned "standing Armies without the Consent of our legislators," they may also have been complaining about the forts the English built in the West to protect the fur trade and the Native-Americans from western migration.[102] They had never forgiven England for the Proclamation of 1763, which prohibited American westward migration.[103] The Quebec Act of 1774 was even worse, protecting Roman Catholics while extending Quebec's boundary to the Ohio River.[104] It was particularly galling to the colonists that Parliament was taxing the colonies to pay for that military force. The Colonists felt they were being taxed to support their jailers. Thus it was hardly surprising that once the Revolution began, the Americans would turn aggressively to the West as well as North to Canada. The Continental Congress ordered Lachlan McIntosh to "invade the Indian territory and destroy their towns," a goal he was able to accomplish, unlike his initial mission to conquer Detroit.[105] Later, General John Sullivan would destroy "forty [Iroquois] villages, numerous isolated houses, at least one hundred sixty thousand bushels of corn, and an uncounted quantity of other vegetables..." throughout the Finger Lakes region of New York.[106]

All the Virginians who would later become President – Washington, Jefferson, Madison, and Monroe – sought to expand the country, particularly westward. A major investor in Western lands, Washington triggered the French and Indian War by killing a French ensign and nine of his troops who had been lurking around Washington's camp during a period of relentlessly increasing military tensions.[107] In early 1787, John Jay's willingness to cede to Spain navigation rights on the Mississippi in exchange for increased New England fishing rights convinced Madison that the country had to quickly replace the Articles of Confederation with a more consolidated form of government that would better represent and protect the West. Madison believed that Jay's proposal might well force the South and West to withdraw from the Union.[108] President Jefferson and Secretary of State Madison endorsed Monroe's Louisiana Purchase, which included far more land than Monroe had been authorized to seek. The

---

[102] Ibid., at 236.

[103] John C. Miller, *Origins of the American Revolution* (Stanford, 1943), 74-78.

[104] Ibid., at 373-75.

[105] Jennings, op. cit., *supra* Intro., n.19, at 244, 254.

[106] Barbara Graymount, *The Iroquois in the American Revolution* (Syracuse, N.Y., 1972), 218.

[107] The French claimed that Washington ordered his troops to open fire while the French were trying to talk to him; Washington claimed that the secretive French "snatched their guns the moment they saw the English." Francis Parkman, *2 France and England in North America* (New York, 1983), 945.

[108] Banning, op. cit., *supra* n.88, at 105.

Monroe Doctrine laid the groundwork for subsequent United States military, political, and economic supervision of all of Latin America.[109]

Of the four Virginian Presidents, Jefferson expressed the most global ambitions. Soon after the Revolution, he speculated that North and South America could "nourish 1200 millions of inhabitants..."[110] While President, Jefferson described to James Monroe, who was governor of Virginia at the time, the beneficiaries of this growth:

> However our present interests may restrain us within our own limits, it is impossible not to look forward to distant times, when our rapid multiplication will expand itself beyond those limits, & cover the whole northern, if not the southern continent, with a people speaking the same language, governed in similar forms, & by similar laws; nor can we contemplate with satisfaction either blot or mixture on that surface.[111]

For Jefferson, the republican form of government was not only good for its own sake. It was the best way for this "rising nation"[112] to rule its vast expanses: "...a government by representation is capable of extension over a greater surface of country than one of any other form."[113] In other words, Jeffersonian-Madisonian republicanism easily coexisted with Jeffersonian imperial aspirations.[114] It is also worth noting Jefferson's intolerance, containing intimations of force and racism, of any "blots or mixtures" that would disfigure his hemispheric empire. The United States' longevity has verified Madison's belief that the American people could create and maintain an enduring empire that satisfied the basic republican principle of ultimate electoral control of all parts of the Federal government. Using the Aristotelian criteria of "self-sufficiency," it might seem easy to agree with

---

109 The relationship between the Monroe Doctrine and America's nineteenth century empire is discussed in Van Alystyne, op. cit., *supra* n.8. *See also* Dexter Perkins, *A History of the Monroe Doctrine* (Boston, 1941).

110 Thomas Jefferson, 'Answers and Observations for Demeunier's Article on the United States in the Encyclopedie Methodique, 1786' (January 24, 1786), Jefferson, op. cit., *supra* ch. 1, n.29, at 589.

111 Letter from Thomas Jefferson to the Governor of Virginia [James Monroe] (Nov. 24, 1801), ibid., at 1097.

112 Thomas Jefferson, 'First Innaugural Address' (March 4, 1801), ibid., at 492.

113 Letter from Thomas Jefferson P.S. Dupont de Nemours (April 24, 1816), ibid., at 1387.

114 Jefferson did not consistently require the future empire to be under a single government; the people were to live under "similar forms" of government. He even foresaw the existing Union might be better off divided into parts: "Whether we remain one confederacy, or form into Atlantic and Mississippi confederacies, I believe not very important to the happiness of either part." Letter from Thomas Jefferson to Dr. Joseph Priestley (Jan. 29, 1804), ibid., at 1142. But just a year earlier, he had proposed to "finally consolidate our whole country into one nation only," Letter from Thomas Jefferson to Gov. William H. Harrison (Feb. 27, 1803), ibid., at 1120.

Jefferson that Montesquieu's arguments were "brilliant fallacies"[115] and with Professor Rakove that Montesquieu created "hoary maxims."[116]

Unfortunately, experience has also validated some of Montesquieu's apprehensions about republican empires, fears that reflected his competing, normative definition of "republicanism." Many of Montesquieu's arguments against republican empires were not so much repudiated as ignored by Madison, particularly in public writings like *The Federalist*. Montesquieu's republicanism, like Jefferson and Madison's, extended throughout a political culture; all three men sought an agrarian society of independent yeoman, untainted by corruption and luxury. Montesquieu, however, believed that the "spirit" of empire is conquest, while the two Virginians foresaw nonviolent growth. Whether justifiable or not, the United States' numerous military actions, wars, and conquests – ranging from race slavery, battling with Native-Americans, Jefferson's defeat of the Barbary pirates, the Mexican War, the Civil War, the World Wars, continuing "gunboat diplomacy," and the defeat of Iraq in the Oil War – confirm Montesquieu's prediction that a large republican empire would frequently rely on violence and aggression. Montesquieu differed from Madison and Jefferson (and even more from many other Americans) by including pacific and static norms as a crucial part of his ideal republic: "The spirit of monarchy is war and expansion; the spirit of republics is peace and moderation."[117] According to Montesquieu, republics never start wars: "One takes up arms, in the republic, only to defend the laws and the homeland; it is because one is a citizen that one becomes, for a time, a soldier."[118] Charles Pinckney expressed similar views during the Constitutional Convention: "Conquest or superiority among other powers is not or ought not ever to be the object of republican systems."[119] This primarily static, peaceful vision had little in common with the continental ambitions of the vast majority of America's leaders and populace, many of whom were more than willing to pick up weapons, particularly against Native-Americans, to extend their homeland. Many of them would reject Montesquieu's definition of the "right of conquest" as "a necessary, legitimate, and unfortunate right, which always leaves an immense debt to be discharged (to those who have been conquered)."[120]

---

[115] Letter from Thomas Jefferson to Francois D'Ivernois (Feb. 6, 1795), ibid., at 1024.

[116] Rakove, op. cit., *supra* n.104, at 133. Rakove also described Montesquieu's thoughts as "cliches about small republics," ibid., at 55.

[117] Montesquieu, op. cit., *supra* n.75, at 132.

[118] Ibid., at 69.

[119] Madison, *Notes*, op. cit., *supra* ch. 1, n.40, at 185.

[120] Montesquieu, op. cit., *supra* n.75, at 142.

Empire building also conflicted with other classical Republican criteria. Continued growth would cause additional conflict with Native-Americans; some sort of a standing army would be necessary to protect settlers and guarantee continued expansion. Providing for military expenses would increase the need for a national bank. When Jefferson ended his eight years in office, he complained about Hamilton's Bank but concluded that it had become such a basic part of the system that he could not remove it.[121] Furthermore, if the new country fulfilled Montesquieu's prediction of aggressive expansion, it would eventually face European powers that still controlled much of North and South America. The Constitution anticipated this problem by giving Congress the right to declare War for whatever reason, including conquest.

Once Hamilton became the equivalent of a Prime Minister within Washington's first Cabinet, he did everything he could to guarantee that the Presidency, which he conceptualized as a unitary executive, would have the "energy" to facilitate the growth of empire. More than any other Founder, Hamilton was determined to build a modern, aggressive nation-state built upon the English model of economic power, military force, public credit, national debt, a national bank, unethical but legal "corruption" that bound the wealthy to the national government, and a powerful executive. For Hamilton, unified national power[122] was far more important than republicanism, which he saw as a dubious, albeit noble experiment that the Constitutional Convention had to accept due to popular opinion.[123] Even for those who were less ambitious, centralization of power and force was a Hobbesian necessity. The Federalist historian David Ramsay, who opposed conquest, explained why all republics need a single person in charge of military operations:

> The result of the experiment was, that however favorable republics may be to the liberty and happiness of the people in the time of peace, they will be greatly deficient in that vigor and dispatch, which military operations require, unless they imitate the policy of monarchies, by committing the executive departments of government to the direction of a single will.[124]

Madison and Jefferson straddled the issue, by hoping that the new Republic would not become tainted by overt conquest and militarism while

---

121 Letter from Thomas Jefferson to P.S. DuPont de Nemours (Jan. 18, 1802), Jefferson, op. cit., *supra* ch. 1, n.29, at 1101.

122 Hamilton and Burr's duel can be traced back to Hamilton's belief that Burr was negotiating with Federalists who wanted to separate New England and New York from the Union. Ellis, op. cit., *supra* ch. 1, n.17, at 44-45.

123 Madison, *Notes*, op. cit, *supra* ch. 1, n.40, at 134.

124 Ramsay, *2 Revolution*, op. cit., *supra* ch. 1, n.92, at 514.

continuing to increase in size and power. They hoped America would become the world's first peaceful empire. Jefferson apparently did not foresee much resistance from Native-Americans or remaining European powers. His influential Republican colleague Joel Barlow explained how and why America should expand its "empire" to the North and West without turning to conquest (or a standing army): "I hope none will infer from the observations in this article (about expansion), that I am an advocate of *conquest*, in any case whatever; and still less that I would extend the limits of a dominion by colonies and foreign possessions."[125] After leaving the Presidency, Jefferson concluded that the recent history of the ever-expanding American regime refuted Montesquieu. Large republics can thrive and expand without using force:

> I have much confidence that we shall proceed successfully for ages to come, and that, contrary to the principle of Montesquieu, it will be seen that the larger the extent of the country, the more firm its republican structure, if founded, not on conquest, but in principles of compact and equality.[126]

Jefferson must have been alluding to his most important presidential act, the Louisiana Purchase, to prove how the American Republic could grow by "compact and equality."

Like the country he helped found, Jefferson vacillated between sentimentality and ruthlessness. Nauseated by his fellow citizens' continual use of racist violence against the Native-Americans, a race that he admired, Jefferson wanted the United States to buy their lands, not seize them. His Rousseauian admiration for those "noble savages" had its limits. Elements of sharp practice, duress, and even coercion lurked behind his republican commitment to purchase. In a letter, he explained how the United States could purchase the Indian lands for very little money. Hemmed in by white settlements based upon previous purchases, the Indians would no longer be able to roam and hunt. Forced to farm smaller plots of land, they would have to purchase manufactured necessities (such as plows). These expenses would drive them into debt, which in turn would force them to sell much of their remaining lands.[127] Should such non-violent means fail, Jefferson noted "we have only to shut our hand to

---

[125] Joel Barlow, 'To His Fellow Citizens of the United States. Letter II: On Certain Political Measures Proposed to Their Consideration', *2 Political Writings*, op. cit., *supra* ch. 1, n.86, at 1124.

[126] Letter from Thomas Jefferson to Francois de Marbois (June 14, 1817), Jefferson, op. cit., *supra* ch. 1, n.29, at 1410.

[127] Letter from Thomas Jefferson to Governor William H. Harrison (Feb. 27, 1803), op. cit., ibid., at 1118.

crush them."[128] Nor was Jefferson squeamish once war began. In another letter, he described the best way to conduct the War of 1812: "I hope we shall confine ourselves to the conquest of their possessions, and defense of our harbours, leaving the war on the ocean to our privateers."[129]

By dwelling on Jefferson and Madison, two of the more pacific statesmen of that era, this book has sought to prove its case at a most difficult point. First of all, there were many other leaders, such as Hamilton, who did not care much about republicanism. They sought money, power, and personal glory (military and political). Second, a large segment of the American public acted on a more brutal definition of "republicanism"; they used whatever force and fraud needed to drive the Native Americans further West. Every treaty violation was a form of conquest. A large part of the expanding American empire was gained in the traditional imperial fashion: massacres, skirmishes, and battles. This grisly history[130] demonstrates that at least for the constitutional concept of "republican empire," we know all too well what the average American had in mind. We do not encounter the interpretive and evidentiary problems that usually bedevil constitutional analysis. Jack Rakove observed that it is hard for us to determine what the average voter thought phrases like "liberty" or "necessary and proper" meant in the Constitution, particularly when that voter had to either accept or reject the Constitution in its entirety.[131] Nor is it much easier to determine what any collective group believed, be it the Framers or the Ratifiers at State Conventions. But when it comes to "republican empire," Thomas Pynchon's fictional characters Mr. Slough and Oily Leon in *Mason & Dixon*, typified widespread American sentiments as much as Jefferson's hand-wringing when they explained to Mason and Dixon why they massacred several pacific families of Moravian Indians:

> "You can't just come minuetting in from London and expect to understand what's going on here," advises Mr. Slough.
>
> "This is about Family, sure as the History of England. Inside any one Tribe of Indians, they're all related, see? Kill you one Delaware, you affront the Family at large. Out here, if it's Blood of mine, of course I must go out and seek redress * * *

---

128 Ibid.

129 Letter from Thomas Jefferson to General Thaddeus Kosciusko (June 28, 1812), ibid., at 1265.

130 Eckert, op. cit. *supra* n.31.

131 Jack N. Rakove, 'Fidelity Through History (Or To It)', 64 *Fordham Law Review* 1587, 1604 (1997).

"These were said to be harmless, helpless people," Dixon points out in some miraculous way that does not draw challenge or insult in return * * *

"They were blood relations of men who slew blood relations of ours," Jabez explains.

"Then if You know who did it, for the Lord's sake why did You not after them?"

"This hurt them more," smiles a certain Oily Leon * * *

"What's the complaint?" demands Oily Leon. "We're out here as a Picket for Philadelphia, – we've cleared them a fine safe patch, from Delaware to Susquehanna. Now may they prance about foolish as they may."

"Aye, Penns, handing us and our children about like Chattel."

"Damme, – like Field Slaves!"[132]

In a very influential and controversial pamphlet, the Philadelphia Quaker Benjamin Franklin condemned this slaughter: "The barbarous Men who committed the atrocious Fact, in Defiance of Government, of all Laws human and divine, and to the eternal disgrace of their Country and Colour, then mounted their Horses, and huzza'd in Triumph, as if they had gained a Victory, and rode off – *unmolested*!"[133] But observe that Franklin was only criticizing their particularly savage means, not their goal of making the land accessible to white settlers.

Montesquieu's pacific republicanism was not the only available republican model. J.G.A. Pocock described a more militant republican tradition in *The Machiavellian Moment*. According to Pocock, Renaissance republicans systematically substituted secular metaphors for religious beliefs to compensate for their loss of faith in an afterlife: "The republic, being a mode of temporal authority, is viewed in the context of empire, and empire in the context of universal salvation, apocalyptically conceived."[134] In other words, one can't have a republic without some notion of empire. Machiavelli believed that most republics could only endure by creating a body of armed citizens who would be willing to defend and expand the

[132] Thomas Pynchon, *Mason & Dixon* 343-44 (New York, 1997).

[133] Benjamin Franklin, 'A Narrative of the Late Massacres, in Lancaster County, of a Number of Indians, Friends of this Province, by Persons Unknown with Some Observations on the Same,' Franklin, op. cit., *supra* n.30, at 544 (1764).

[134] Machiavelli, *Discourses on Livy* (Harvey C. Mansfield & Nathan Tarcov, trans. Niccolo, Chicago, 1996), 50.

republic.[135] Although republics should and would act democratically and justly within their boundaries, they needed a ruthless foreign policy.[136] Imperial motivation and militarism were imbedded in republicanism. In the course of bringing Machiavelli's thoughts to England, James Harrington described the ideal state of Oceana as a "commonwealth for increase."[137] Although he opposed conquest as "a great robbery,"[138] Harrington did not rely on sentimentalism to justify his republicanism. Because they could generate powerful citizen armies, republics would prove to be most effective forms of government.[139] Nor were republican motives purely benign; Pocock concluded that the pursuit of glory, honor, and fame had replaced the quest for salvation.[140] Even this interpretation may be somewhat romantic; many republicans, like so many other humans, pursued empire for immediate wealth and pleasure.

Machiavelli provides many insights that help explain some enduring traits of America's republican empire. His description of the life of those who lived under the "zone of influence" of a republic will be familiar to many Latin Americans:

> And of all hard servitudes, that is hardest that submits you to a republic. First, because it is more lasting and there can be less hope of escape from it; second, because the end of the republic is to enervate and to weaken all other bodies so as to increase its own body.[141]

This grim view of republics' double standard explains some seemingly "paradoxical" aspects of the United States' political culture. The United States can be the freest country in the world in terms of protecting its own citizens' rights while still ruthlessly violating its near neighbors' human rights. The United States, however, has not adopted all of Machiavelli's preferred means. He praised the Roman Republic for:

> [I]ncreasing the inhabitants of one's city, getting partners and not subjects, sending colonies to guard countries that have been acquired, making capital out of booty, subduing the enemy with raids and battles and not with sieges,

---

135 Ibid., at 269.

136 Ibid., at 213.

137 Harrington, op. cit., *supra* n.3, at 7.

138 Ibid., at 249.

139 Ibid.

140 J.G.A. Pocock, *The Machiavellian Moment: Florentine Political Thought and the Atlantic Republican Tradition* (Princeton, 1975), 133. *See also* Douglass Adair, op. cit., *supra* n.36. Fisher Ames was more direct: "that love of distinction, which is one of the most powerful agents in the transactions of mankind." Fisher Ames, 'Hints and Conjectures Concerning the Institutions of Lycurgus', Fisher Ames, *1 Works of Fisher Ames* (W.B. Allen, ed., Indianapolis, 1983), 100.

141 Machiavelli, op. cit., *supra* n.160, at 133.

> keeping the public rich and the private poor, and maintaining military exercises with the highest seriousness is the true way to make a republic great and to acquire empire.[142]

Nor were Machiavelli and Harrington the only respected authority to visualize militarily powerful republics. Plutarch described the Roman Republic as an "empire."[143] From Plutarch's perspective, Caesar did not change Rome from a Republic to an Empire, but from a Republican Empire to a Tyrannical Empire.

For both Montesquieu and Machiavelli, "corruption" posed the greatest threat to republics. While Machiavelli worried about sloth, stagnation, and decadence, Montesquieu predicted that imperial republics would deteriorate into selfish, violent non-republican societies. In a large country, some people would eventually gain a great deal of wealth. Their selfish pursuit of luxury would undermine the republican virtue of frugality.[144] They would consider their self-interest to be far more important than their republic's well being.[145] It would be difficult for the majority to express its will at all, even on issues that clearly benefit the public good: "In a large republic, the common good is sacrificed to a thousand considerations."[146] Corruption and courtiers, symptoms of despotism and monarchy, would flourish. A quick review of the daily news is enough to convince many of us that Montesquieu's concerns were not "hoary maxims," but legitimate fears that cannot be easily dismissed. The District of Columbia is filled with courtiers – now known as lawyers, lobbyists, public relations experts, and Congressmen – who are primarily interested in advancing their own interests and those of their wealthy, powerful masters. Even Presidents believe they must engage in the tawdriest types of fund-raising to win the next election.

Madison's private anxieties were not completely different from Montesquieu's predictions. Even while arguing in *The Federalist* that the new Constitutional system would sort out those proposals that truly advance the common good from those reflecting majority tyranny, thereby eliminating the threat of the "many," he wrote a letter expressing fears that a powerful minority faction of the "few" might seize control of the

---

142 Machiavelli, op. cit., ibid., at 172-73.

143 Plutarch quotes Romulus, who founded Rome and created the Senate, as saying he built "a city to be the greatest in the world in empire and glory." Plutarch, *The Lives of the Noble Grecians and Romans* (John Dryden, trans., rev's by Arthur Hugh Clough, Modern Library ed.), 44.

144 Montesquieu, op. cit., *supra* n.75, at 124.

145 Ibid.

146 Ibid.

system.[147] Soon after the Constitution was ratified, Madison must have questioned the rosier public propositions he had made during the Ratification Debates to persuade the electorate that an aristocracy would not control the new Constitution. He believed the Washington administration, led by his co-author of *The Federalist*, Alexander Hamilton, passed numerous oppressive laws that benefited a minority of the population at the expense of the "common good." He and Jefferson opposed Alexander Hamilton's plan to pay the face value of all governmental debts to the holders of the paper while offering nothing to those original recipients who fought in the Revolutionary War.[148] The officers had already received a five-year pension, and now those who purchased the paper, often without telling the original holders that it was about to appreciate in value, were main beneficiaries. Indeed, most of Hamilton's financial schemes handsomely rewarded friendly participants. For example, William Duer relied upon inside information to profit on federal securities after he left the Treasury Department.[149] Many Congressional members voted on laws that immediately increased the value of their own securities. The Federalists chose to reward themselves and their class, not the citizen soldiers who risked everything to win the Revolution. To achieve his vision of empire, Hamilton needed capital to be concentrated in the hands of the "merchant class, who were committed to the growth of national government and national power."[150] The Federalists responded to this dissent with repression by passing the Alien and Sedition Act.[151] By 1796, Madison considered his old allies' Federalist government to be "Despotic."[152]

Another normative definition of empire emphasizes the selfish pursuit of power and glory, what eighteenth century preachers and politicians like Benjamin Franklin called "the lust for dominion."[153] At all levels of power, many people receive great pleasure in watching other people react with fear and deference. Politicians, generals, and political theorists knew

---

[147] In a letter to Jefferson about the need for a Bill of Rights, Madison conceded that "the danger of oppression" could come from "a succession of artful and ambitious rulers" as well as from a majority of the people, letter from James Madison to Thomas Jefferson (Oct. 17, 1788), in Madison, *Mind*, op. cit., *supra* ch. 1, n.39, at 158.

[148] Stanley Elkins and Eric McKitrick, *The Age of Federalism* (New York, 1993) 143-45.

[149] Ibid., at 274.

[150] Ibid., at 115-23.

[151] *See, e.g.*, Rosenfeld, op. cit., *supra* ch. 1, n.29.

[152] Letter from James Madison to Thomas Jefferson (Feb. 8, 1799), James Madison, 17 *Papers Of Madison* 229.

[153] Letter from Benjamin Franklin to Lord Howe (July 20, 1776), Franklin, op. cit., *supra* n.30, at 991.

that those who lead countries to conquest and victory achieve enduring fame, which many of them coveted now that they doubted that they would achieve true immortality after death. Might did not just mean right, it also meant historical immortality. It would be absurd to think that these men were uniquely immune to self-aggrandizement. Indeed, Madison had shown why they should not separate their republican ideals from their glorious, imperial ambitions and their dreams of historical importance. At one moment during the Revolutionary War, John Adams groused: "I don't wish to be under obligations to [France]... and I am very unwilling they should rob Us of the Glory of vindicating our own Liberties."[154] An anonymous pamphleteer explained: "The union of the Colonies is not only our glory, but our protection."[155] In his popular history of the American Revolution, published in 1789, David Ramsay concluded: "The love of power and of property, on the one side of the Atlantic, were opposed by the same powerful passions on the other."[156]

C. Defining "Citizen"

One of the crucial decisions in any republican system is determining which inhabitants are citizens authorized to participate in and benefit from that system. Just as each republican government will have its own mixture of representative institutions, it will also formulate its own "shape," which will be determined by the answers to four interrelated questions which revolve around the political/legal concept of "citizens": (1) Who are full "citizens" within a republic; (2) How do they become citizens; (3) How is the citizenry distributed throughout the empire; and (4) What relationships do those citizens have with the rest of humanity, at home and abroad? Each of the following four subsections addresses these questions, primarily through historical examples.

This book will not attempt to answer any of those questions completely. As Aristotle pointed out over two thousand years ago, the word "citizen" is a crucial legal/political word containing multiple

---

[154] Letter from John Adams to James Warren (April 27, 1977), quoted in Rosenfeld, op. cit., *supra* ch. 1, n.29, at 322. John Adams also was envious of Benjamin Franklin for being called the "Founder of the American Empire," Letter from John Adams to Arthur Lee (April 10, 1783), ibid., at 237-38.

[155] Anonymous, 'The Alarm', *1 Political Writing*, op. cit., *supra* ch. 1, n.86, at 323. That same writer also lambasted Congress for failing to conquer Canada, ibid., at 327.

[156] Ramsay, *1 History*, op. cit, *supra* ch. 1, n.92, at 51. Over two centuries later, Theodore Draper reached the same conclusion, Theodore Draper, *A Struggle for Power: The American Revolution* (New York, 1996) 517-18.

definitions.[157] Aristotle's preferred definition of "citizen" predictably included some of his other important political norms: only "citizens" could create a just, moral society.[158] Close factual analysis of ancient republics is difficult because both Republican Athens and Republican Rome had different degrees of citizenship. In addition, a person may be a "citizen" for certain purposes but not others. Contemporary American women have many equal constitutional rights but presently do not have the constitutional right/obligation to participate in armed combat, which many earlier cultures considered the "essence" of citizenship. In every modern society, most children are considered to be citizens even though they cannot yet vote, participate in government, or join the military. Rogers Smith's meticulous historical survey of changes in the changing citizenship rights of American women, children, slaves, aliens, immigrants, colonists, and conquered peoples demonstrates that the word "citizen" cannot be reduced to a single definition.[159] Nor does the Fourteenth Amendment's protection of state and national citizenship completely resolve the problem because its Framers distinguished between the "political" right to vote and such "rights of citizens" as "the right to acquire property, the right to go and come at pleasure, the right to enforce rights in the courts, to make contracts, and to inherit and dispose of property."[160]

An analytical definition of "full citizen" somewhat ameliorates these problems by only including those people who have the opportunity to elect those representatives that constitute part or all of a legal/political sovereign, the legal right to run for those offices, and full property rights. Under such a definition, American women were not full "citizens" until the passage of the Nineteenth Amendment[161] even though the Antebellum Supreme Court had recognized that a white American woman had certain political rights of citizenship that she could lose by choosing to live under British protection.[162] Class distinctions also permeated early constitutional conceptions of citizenship. The franchise was initially limited to those with

---

157 Aristotle, op. cit., *supra* n.73, at 2023.

158 Philip Brook Manville, *The Origins of Citizenship in Ancient Athens* (Princeton, 1997), 211.

159 Rogers M. Smith, *Civic Ideals: Conflicting Visions of Citizenship in U.S. History* (New Haven, 1997).

160 Quoted in Brest, Levinson, Balkin, and Amar, *Processes of Constitutional Decisionmaking: Cases and Materials* (New York, 2000), 242.

161 Justice Ward Hunt, sitting on circuit, denied Susan Anthony any right to vote under the Fourteenth Amendment, 24 F. Cas. 829 (N.D. N.Y. 1873). Hunt relied upon a Supreme Court decision upholding a state law prohibiting female attorneys, *Bradwell v. Illinois*, 83 (16 Wall.) 130 (1873). Two years later, the Supreme Court held that States could withhold the vote from women even though they were American citizens, *Minor v. Happersett*, 88 U.S. (21 Wall.) 162 (1875).

162 *Shanks v. DuPont*, 28 U.S. (3 Peters) 242, (1830).

some resources. As late as 1842, Supreme Court Justice Story upheld the States' rights to arrest, restrain, and remove from their borders any "idlers, vagabonds, and paupers."[163] Reducing citizenship to these fundamentals of political and economic power somewhat simplifies our inquiry. A country's laws tell us who can vote and be in office. Such an analytical definition makes this part of the model resemble real science, because it is hard to dispute who is a legal citizen under these relatively straightforward criteria. Of course, such simplifications are contestable, begging important questions. For instance, the Fourteenth and Fifteenth Amendments gave the freed male slaves the right to vote, but in reality they lost this right within a decade with the end of Reconstruction. Nevertheless, if we are primarily interested in exploring the meanings of "republican empire," converting most of the related concepts into single, easily verifiable definitions makes it less likely we will create a hopelessly muddled model. This approach is "quasi-scientific": we try to hold steady all the variables but those we are most interested in studying.

1. Athens' Limited Citizenship and Overtly Exploitive Foreign Policy

There are good reasons to emulate Madison's method of studying the histories of ancient Greece and Rome. These two eras provided the prototypes for republic systems, complete with some of the greatest political analysis of all time as well as numerous compelling historical examples of those system's strengths and weaknesses. Athens' imperial republic consisted of approximately fifteen thousand Athenians, who participated directly and indirectly in running their empire. They elected officials, sat on large juries, and formulated domestic and foreign policy. The most dramatic and tragic example was their catastrophic decision to invade Sicily.[164] On the other hand, Athenians delegated some of their power to elected representatives. Through this combination of republican and purely democratic forms, they ruled approximately two hundred thousand people who lived in Athens. Athenian women, slaves, farmers, and artisans were not citizens. According to Aristotle, citizens needed sufficient underlings to have the needed "leisure" to develop the moral,

---

163 *Prigg v. Pennsylvania*, 41 U.S. (16 Peters) 536 (1842). *See also* The Passenger Cases, 48 U.S. (7 How.) 283 (1849). For an in depth analysis, *see* Gerald Neuman, *Strangers to the Constitution: Immigrants, Borders, and Fundamental Law* (Princeton, 1996), 23. In 1952, Congress finally stated that "[t]he right of a person to become a naturalized citizen of the United States shall not be denied or abridged because of race or sex." Immigration and Nationality Act of 1952, c. 477, Title III, ch. 2, s 311, 66 Stat. 239.

164 Thucydides, *The Peloponnesian War* (T. Hobbes, trans., Chicago, 1989), 378-93.

intellectual, and experiential capacities necessary to create and maintain a just society.

The Athenians also demanded tribute and military support from the many city-states they conquered. To insure compliance, they gave significant rights to those residents who assisted them. Called *pronexos*, these local leaders had privileges that "might include legal safeguards for the *pronexos* and his family, the right to seek redress in Athens at the court of the polemarch, and even an invitation to have dinner in the Athenian *prytaneion*."[165] Indeed, some colonists received full citizenship rights.[166] Although one of the most democratic societies in early history, the Athenian empire was rife with inequality – both within Athens and throughout its domain.

This brief summary generates two structural questions. First, who is a "citizen" within the formal boundaries of the dominant country? Second, how do that country's "citizens" treat those who live in subordinate parts of the empire – colonies, territories, and conquered lands? In other words, how much equality exists between the Athenian rulers and other Athenian adults and between Athens's citizens and the inhabitants of its subordinate lands? The Athenian system demonstrates that a "republican empire" need not be fully egalitarian at home and can be ruthlessly aggressive and unequal abroad. The Athenian model also raises difficult empirical questions, particularly the careful study of other mechanisms of control that are part of any empire. Such institutions include tribute, slavery, trade regulations, taxes, military force, ideology, and propaganda.

Athens remains a disturbing reminder that a republic can be an empire, a continual refutation of the frequently made argument that democracies are never aggressive and warlike. Athens laid the foundation for the Peloponnesian Wars through harsh treatment of subordinate regions and an expansionist ideology based upon the virtues of Athenian culture and democracy. This self-gratifying approach threatened its more authoritarian neighbors both by direct force and appeals to the internal populace to revolt, thereby providing the Spartans the opportunity to foment a counter-rebellion. In addition, the Athenians did not use these norms to create euphemisms to obscure their own ambition. Angry at the opposition to execute all rebellious Mytilanaeans, the Athens leader Cleon began his speech by raising the question that is the theme of this book: "I have often on other occasions thought a democracy incapable of dominion over others, but most of all now for this your repentance concerning the Mytilanaeans."[167] He warned: "[Y]ou ought not to alter your former decree

---

[165] Manville, op. cit., *supra* n.184, at 207.

[166] Ibid.

[167] Thucydides, op. cit., *supra* n.190, at 175.

(of execution) nor to offend in any of these three most disadvantageous things to empire, pity, delight in plausible speeches, and lenity."[168] Diodotus's plea for clemency also appealed to the victors' self-interest. The death penalty will not be sufficiently coercive because men from all classes have often been willing to risk their lives for necessity, pride, passion, liberty, and dominion over others.[169] Because it is foreseeable that other colonies will revolt in the future, it is better not to kill all the rebels because future rebels might stop fighting if they had some hope of a pardon. The Athenian people proved the ruthlessness of democracies by agreeing with Cleon, just as they would later support Alcibiades' disastrous proposal to conquer Sicily for "both glory and profit."[170] Thucydides' analysis of their motives raises recurring, disturbing questions about republican imperial motivation: "[T]he Athenians longed very much to send an army against it, out of a desire to bring it all under the subjection, which was the true motive, but as having withal this fair pretext of aiding their kindred and new confederates."[171]

The Madisonian solution to the cruel and ill-conceived foreign policy judgments made by the Athenian citizenry was to eliminate the average citizen from any direct participation in foreign policy decision-making. Under his system, the average American citizen would have the important rights to vote and sit on juries, but could only influence major foreign and domestic policy through the electoral process. Quite simply, the Athenian citizen had had too much constitutional power. This basic decision has never been revisited; most constitutional disputes in America would be over which inhabitants had these important, but limited citizenship rights, not over the actual structural limits themselves.

2. *The British Empire in the Eighteenth Century and the American Revolutionary Response – From Virtual Constitutionalism Based Upon Mercantilism to Equality Throughout the Empire*

The English system in the eighteenth century varied in many ways from Athens' empire. Aside from the jury, the English populace did not directly participate in any governmental deliberations. The House of Commons was elected, while the King and the House of Lords were hereditary. Furthermore, by the time of the American Revolution, the ruling class had narrowed the franchise to only five percent of English males (probably a

---

[168] Ibid., at 178-79.
[169] Ibid., at 182-83.
[170] Ibid., at 385.
[171] Ibid., at 378-79.

lower percentage than in Athens). Thus, the English system was far less democratic (defined as direct participation by the citizenry) and far less republican (defined as the capacity to elect or indirectly select all major governmental officials) than the Athenian political constitution. Although its wealth requirements did not permanently ban most Englishmen to second-class citizenship, they were not "full citizens" because they could neither vote nor hold major office.

The British Constitution's defenders devised the doctrine of "virtual representation" to smooth over glaring disparities caused by the significant property qualifications and the grotesque distribution of seats in the Commons created by the "rotten borough" system. This doctrine maintained that votes were sufficiently scattered throughout the country among a large variety of groups and interests, creating an existing electorate that would be sufficiently informed and concerned about England's well being. This group would choose the sort of representatives that the others would also have selected had they been properly informed and had the vote. Thus Parliament would adequately and fairly represent all (propertied) Englishmen, not just an Aristotelian elite. This argument overlooks the fact that limiting the franchise to relatively the well off and giving many seats to nobility through "rotten boroughs" necessitated that the rich and powerful control the system. But the British Constitution's supporters would find that outcome desirable for another reason. Those who held enough property to be permitted to vote would naturally do the best job of protecting the English Empire and the rights of property, the two appropriate interests of the disenfranchised. According to Locke, the underlying purpose of government is the protection of life, liberty, and property. The wealthy and powerful have more capacity, leisure, and understanding to increase the power and wealth of the entire country. Overall, the poor would benefit from the wisdom of their economic and social betters.

There were at least two more constitutional safeguards. All statutes applied to all Englishmen (except the King). The limited group of electors would be unlikely to pass burdensome taxes or oppressive laws that would harm them as much as those who had no vote. Furthermore, all Englishmen were protected by the Common Law, a reflection of the more ghostly notion of "the rights of Englishmen." Nor were any Englishmen permanently barred from voting. They could move to a district that had a representative and/or they could make enough money to satisfy the property requirements. Women and people of color were placed in an inferior legal status. However, in 1772, the English judiciary improved the constitution by outlawing slavery within England.[172] That reform reeked with hypocrisy. English blacks could in theory become full citizens if they gained enough wealth, while English merchants and the British government continued to profit from the sale of slaves to the American colonies.

England's relationship with the American colonies was more sophisticated and enlightened than Athens's relentless demands for tribute and military assistance. Like Athens, the English did not give their colonists any citizenship rights to elect Members of Parliament. Like so many Englishmen, the Americans had to be satisfied with "virtual representation." But in all but two colonies, the colonists entered into charters with the King authorizing them to create their own representative assemblies. The colonists also felt protected by the "rights of Englishmen" and the English Common Law. Most importantly, for many decades, the English government let them run their internal affairs. England, like Athens, ran its empire for profit and glory. However, England's mercantile system relied on the exchange of goods and services, not direct confiscation via tribute. Using such monopolies as the East India Company and the Hudson Bay Company, England exploited her colonies by forcing them to participate in a monopolized market. This technique is less oppressive than tribute; at least the Companies paid something to the Colonists in return for goods and services rendered. There was some reciprocity and mutual benefit via this closed market system. That system also encouraged the colonials to work hard because they could make handsome profits despite the constraints. Nevertheless, the price was high. Benjamin Franklin claimed that forcing Americans to use English ships sometimes increased the cost of American imports by as much as thirty percent.[173]

England's policies also differed from the Athenian approach by not impressing its colonial subjects into battle. As Stephen Holmes pointed out, many colonists willingly and proudly fought on behalf of the British Empire during the French and Indian War. Overall, the English Constitution was slightly more egalitarian than the Athenian system. At least in theory, internal representation was diffused through England, not limited to a geographically small, largely predefined group of people and families. Abroad, the colonies were treated more as equals, instead of as complete subordinates. The colonials' right to property prevented direct confiscation.

For many decades, this constitutional structure worked reasonably well, but it ultimately proved as fatally unstable as Athen's domain. The

---

172 Sommersett's Case, 20 Howell's State Trials 1 (K.B. 1772).

173 Franklin, 'Causes of the American Discontents Before 1768', Franklin, op. cit, *supra* n.30, at 613. Franklin had this letter reprinted in 1774 to demonstrate to the English that Colonial complaints and arguments predated the Stamp Act, ibid., at 607-12.

colonists were generally allowed to run their governments through their elected representatives and the King's governors. England provided them with military defense, while they supplied troops to help defeat England's rivals. They also indirectly gave a great deal of wealth to England through the mercantile system, which required them to trade exclusively with Englishmen, use English ports and ships, and not develop local rival manufactures.

One country's republican victories can come at the expense of another. After the Glorious Revolution in 1688, England developed the doctrine of parliamentary sovereignty: The King-in-Parliament has the last word on all legal/political questions. Once a law had been passed by the House of Commons, the House of Lords, and accepted by the King, it became completely valid. English courts, much less American colonists, could not reverse any such law. This doctrine echoed the Athenian system of local predominance; only Englishmen had all the "rights of Englishmen." For many years, this doctrine remained an irrelevant abstraction because the English did not use it against their brethren in America. But the continuing economic burdens of English mercantilism and taxation and the formal inequality of constitutional rights became ever more galling as the Colonies increased in population and power. In addition, Americans felt far more secure militarily after they had helped England win the French and Indian War in 1763. The English perceived the victory differently; the colonists had an obligation to help reduce the huge debt caused by the War. Parliament proposed direct taxes like the Stamp Act, thereby forcing the colonists to reconceptualize the appropriate structure of republican empires. Of course, much of the colonial opposition to direct taxation was not based upon constitutional theory. They became far more sensitive about their legal subordination once they had to pay more taxes to England. They believed Parliament was acting in bad faith, forcing them to pay more than their share for defense. They also concluded that much of new money would go to corrupt English officials, not to legitimate imperial objectives. As noted earlier, it was particularly infuriating that some of the new tax revenues would subsidize such continuing expenses of the Empire as the maintenance of the British forts and Armies that had been posted West of the Alleghenies to prevent further colonial immigration.

To justify colonial taxation, the English leadership again invoked the doctrine of "virtual representation." Those Englishmen who could vote would adequately represent the colonists because both groups had the same goals of expanding and protecting the entire British Empire. Ultimately, Parliament and the King must decide what was best for everyone. Not only did they have the power and authority under the doctrine of parliamentary sovereignty, but also they had a better perspective of the complete Empire's needs. Many Englishmen saw the American colonists as ungrateful, hypocritical swindlers, unwilling to pay their fair share for the recent war, which benefited them, and complaining about unequal rights, all while using slaves. They also perceived the American settlers to be threats to another profitable group of subjects, Native-Americans.

Benjamin Franklin was a reluctant revolutionary.[174] For many years, he attempted to preserve the empire. For instance, he rejected John Dickinson's distinction in the widely read *Letters From a Farmer in Pennsylvania* between legitimate "regulatory" and unconstitutional "revenue" taxes. For Franklin, there could be no such "middle doctrine."[175] But in 1772, a personal political defeat cost him any chance of gaining a royal grant to vast western lands as part of his scheme to transform Pennsylvania into a royal colony.[176] The discovery of Massachusetts's Governor Thomas Hutchinson's letters advocating harsh treatment of the fractious colonies completed the process of alienation.[177] Franklin would lead the Colonies' intellectual and political responses to England's various legislative and executive actions premised upon the theory of parliamentary sovereignty. James Madison later praised him as the primary theorist of the revolution.[178] According to Franklin, the colonies were established under a prior English Constitution that had a different imperial structure. When the King granted the colonial charters in the early 1600s, he had complete dominion over their jurisdiction: "Our former Kings Governed their Colonies, as they Governed their Dominions in France, without the Participation of British Parliaments."[179] Thus, Parliament's victory over the King in 1688, which generated the doctrine of Parliamentary Sovereignty, could not repeal or alter those original contracts between King and the Colonies. Consequently, only the King remained sovereign over all his subjects; the colonists owed allegiance exclusively to him. Amongst themselves, all English subjects are equal.[180]

Franklin supplemented this historical argument with the more abstract principle of equality of citizenship throughout the empire. Parliament represented English subjects, who had no constitutional authority to reduce the Colonial subjects to their subjugation. The doctrine of Parliamentary

---

[174] Jennings, op. cit., *supra* Intro., n.19, at 127-39.

[175] Ibid., at 130.

[176] Ibid., at 137.

[177] Ibid., at 132.

[178] James Madison, 'Preface To Debates In The Convention Of 1787' Max Farrand, *3 The Records of the Federal convention of 1787* (New Haven, 1911), 540 n.1.

[179] Letter from Benjamin Franklin to William Strahan (Nov. 26, 1769), Franklin, op. cit., *supra* n.30, at 849-50.

[180] Ibid., at 850.

Sovereignty turned Americans into "subjects of subjects."[181] This argument carried particular weight in terms of direct taxation. Because Parliament only represented England, it had no authority to raise taxes, because the taxation power would enable England to take the colonists' property without their consent via their own representatives. Parliament was merely another representative body equal to the locally elected colonial Assemblies. Parliament had no more authority to tax the colonies than the colonial assemblies had to tax Englishmen. The Colonists thus rejected the Athenian model of one region's maintaining imperial superiority over others, preferring instead an empire without geographical discriminations. Of course, the colonists retained many egregious internal distinctions (notably the lack of rights for women, slaves, Native Americans, and the poor). They preferred James Harrington's egalitarian, expansionist vision in *Oceana* "that whatever falleth into her empire must fall equally, and if the whole earth fall into your scales it must fall equally."[182]

In 1774, Jefferson first gained national attention when he drafted *A Summary View of the Rights of British America*.[183] The powerful prose in this work helped lead to his appointment to be the leading member of the committee that drafted the Declaration of Independence. In the *Summary View*, he clearly articulated the Americans' new conception of republican empires premised upon equal citizenship and equal representation throughout the empire:

> [England should] no longer persevere in sacrificing the rights of one part of the empire to the inordinate desires of another; but deal out to all equal and impartial right. Let no act be passed by any one legislature that may infringe on the rights and liberties of another. This is the important post in which fortune has placed you, holding the balance of a great, if a well poised empire.[184]

The English leadership rejected this last effort at reconciliation. Revolution soon followed.

3. *The Constitutional Settlement of "Compact and Equality"*

In 1787, the Constitutional Convention revisited the questions of equal statehood and subjecthood. The Ratification process reflected the

---

181 Franklin, 'Subjects of Subjects', op. cit., ibid., at 616.

182 Harrington, op. cit., *supra* n.3, at 220.

183 Ellis, op. cit., *supra* ch. 1, n.17, at 29.

184 Thomas Jefferson, 'A Summary View of the Rights of British America', Jefferson, op. cit., *supra* ch. 1, n.29, at 121.

assumption that the existing thirteen States were equal sovereignties; each State had an equal right to decide to enter the new compact. The new Constitution would become effective upon nine States' ratification but would not include those States that chose not to join. Nor would the new United States force recalcitrant States into joining the Union. Although the Constitution represented "We, the People," it also acknowledged residual, equal sovereignty among the entering States through such important devices as the State legislatures' election of United States Senators, minimal constraints on State power over individuals, the enumeration of Congressional powers, and the complete inability to use the Constitutional amendment process to change the number of Senators a State receives without first obtaining that State's consent. And as John Calhoun would point out a few decades later, the constitutional text actually began with the phrase "We, the People of the United States," which Calhoun construed to mean that the "People of each State" as States were the original contracting parties, not "We, the People" as a whole.[185]

On the other hand, republican egalitarianism expanded the Federal Government's power over the States; the national government was obligated to guarantee that every State maintain a republican form of government. In other words, each State must have the same ("equal") basic form of government: republicanism. Finally, the Framers reversed the preexisting structures of republican empires, which centered in cities like Rome and London, by not providing any national representation to the newly formed seat of the Federal Government, the District of Columbia. People living within the new Capitol would have less constitutional rights than their fellow citizens. This structure may have been designed to reduce the likelihood that Montesquieu's fears of consolidation and corruption at one central location would inevitably accompany empire. To this day, the District's citizens remain under a system of "virtual representation," a classic example of recurring gaps between American constitutional principles and practices.

The Convention did not agree so easily about the Territories' constitutional rights. Everyone agreed that citizens who moved into the new Territories in sufficient numbers could create States that would eventually become parts of the Union, not perpetual colonies. But many delegates did not want to treat the new entrants equally. Gouverneur Morris proposed an American version of "rotten boroughs"; the Atlantic States would retain power in the House of Representative by keeping a majority of the Seats

---

[185] John C. Calhoun, 'A Discourse on the Constitution and Government of the United States', John C. Calhoun, *Union and Liberty: The Political Philosophy of John C. Calhoun* (Ross M. Lence, ed., Indianapolis, 1993), 93.

even after the majority of American citizens had moved South and West.[186] Toward the end of the Convention, several Framers proposed an admissions system that was formally equal and unequal: "If the admission be consented to, the new States shall be admitted on the same terms with the original States. But the Legislature may make conditions with the New States concerning the public debt."[187] The new States should pay off more than their equal share of the national debt incurred by the Revolutionary War for the privilege of joining the Union. Such conditions were not as "unequal" as Morris' abortive plan that would have perpetuated constitutional inequality. New States, like new members of a club, would merely have to pay for the privilege of becoming equal members.

James Madison successfully opposed this double-standard: "[T]he Western States neither would nor ought to submit to a union which degraded them from an equal rank with other States."[188] He had several practical reasons for his position. Like the rest of his Southern colleagues, he sought to empower the West to counterbalance the existing Northeastern majority. In addition, Virginia's western citizens, who would soon form the State of Kentucky, had reacted to Jay's treaty proposal to give Spain control of the Mississippi by contemplating leaving the Union to join Spain. Any effort to diminish their representative power would alienate them not only from the new Constitution, but also from the underlying Union.

Madison's position also had its moral component. The Revolution had been premised on the constitutional theory that all parts of a republican empire should be equal. To create a double standard discriminating against Territories would violate that principle. It would "degrade" those people who lived there, destabilizing the new republic: "[Western settlers] will have the same pride & other passions which we have and will either not unite with or will speedily revolt from the Union, if they are not in all respects placed on an equal footing with their brethren."[189] Madison's foresight was justified. In Virginia's contentious Ratifying Convention, western delegates constituted the swing vote.[190] Despite Patrick Henry's flamboyant, eloquent speeches, enough western Virginians joined Madison to form a majority in favor of the Constitution, an action they probably

---

186 Farrand, op. cit., *supra* ch. 1, n.178, at 571.

187 Madison, Notes, op. cit., *supra* ch. 1, n.40, at 552. For a general discussion, *see* Rakove, op. cit., *supra* n.104, at 70-79.

188 Madison, ibid., at 552.

189 Farrand, *1 Records*, op. cit., *supra* ch. 1, n.178, at 578-79. *See also* Madison, *Notes*, op. cit., *supra* ch. 1, n.40, at 552.

190 Rakove, op. cit., *supra* n.104, at 275.

would not have taken if the Convention had facially discriminated against them.

The Constitution guaranteed perpetual equal representation, based upon population among the States, by requiring a Census of the entire population (free and slave) every ten years. In other words, Constitution clearly guaranteed proportional representation among the States, although not within the States.[191] The country's egalitarian republicanism could never be distorted by existing States' refusal to reallocate representatives to new States that had more rapid population growth. Overall, the new Constitution was sufficiently formed in "compact and equality" that it could adapt to the society's subsequent movement toward more democratic norms, particularly universal suffrage for white men,[192] and the empire's westward expansion. After all, one of the foreseeable, desirable effects of the new "empire for liberty" would be the power (the "liberty") it gave to individual settlers to move westward at the expense of Native Americans. The Constitution thereby ratified a process that helped cause and sustain the American Revolution: "The Revolution invented a powerful new engine of imperial expansion: the liberty of its people, freed to act outside of older constraints of public authority* * * The Revolution established a dynamic national empire in the Ohio Valley, and left an indelible legacy of violence and conquest that shaped the development of the region and the nation for generations to come."[193]

Republican egalitarianism also influenced the constitutional definition of "citizen." Until late in the Convention, the delegates wanted two classes of citizens whose rights would differ based upon wealth. One set of monetary standards would screen out undesirable voters and a second set would limit access to office. Gouverneur Morris moved that the federal franchise be limited to freeholders.[194] George Mason proposed that "qualified" elected officials must have land and no outstanding accounts or

---

[191] For a defense of continuing unequal representation within a State, see Americanus [Timothy Ford], 'The Constitutionalist: Or, An Inquiry How Far It is Expedient and Proper to Alter the Constitution of South Carolina', *2 Political Writings*, op. cit. *supra* ch. 1, n.86, at 900-935. This is one of the many shocking arguments to contemplate: "The constant example of slavery stimulates a free man to avoid being confounded with the blacks * * * If then domestic slavery, so far from being inconsistent, has in fact, a tendency to stimulate and perpetuate the spirit of liberty in the low country [which had more than a proportional share of the votes], it is to be fairly inferred, that under their management the personal rights would receive as effectual and as permanent protection, as under any other people." Ibid., at 934.

[192] Alexis De Tocqueville, *1 Democracy in America* (Phillips Bradley, ed., New York, 1945), 206-14.

[193] Hinderaker, op. cit. *supra* n.31, at xiv.

[194] Madison, *Notes*, op. cit., *supra* n.66, at 401.

debts with the United States government.[195] Elbridge Gerry concurred, because "we might have a Legislator composed of public debtors, pensioners, placemen & contractors."[196] For some reason, there was never a similar motion to exclude federal creditors because of their potential conflict of interest. A draft of the Constitution in July made it more difficult for the average man to serve as a Senator than as a Member of the House; Senators would only receive "a fixed compensation"[197] while Representatives would be paid "an adequate compensation."[198] The Framers ultimately avoided making any precise definition of full citizenship by delegating to the States the power to determine who could have the franchise and run for office.[199] Congress still retained an important role in defining citizenship by having plenary power over Naturalization issues. Thus, despite continued effort by many delegates, the Framers did not entrench England's class discrimination into the written Constitution. They were aware that their proposal would have to be accepted by a more egalitarian electorate,[200] which at that time consisted of over half of all American white males, many of whom were not even freeholders.[201]

With the notable exceptions of Benjamin Franklin and James Wilson, the Framers did not support universal suffrage. Overall, American citizens would have "virtually" the same set of constitutional rights wherever they lived. Those citizens who could not vote in a particular State because of restrictive property requirements could move to a more progressive State. Even if an Englishman could not vote because he did not have much money, he had other constitutional rights, such as the right to a jury in criminal cases. After much dispute,[202] the Framers also guaranteed that subsequent naturalized citizens would, with the exception of becoming President, have the same rights as native-born citizens.[203]

Overall, the new republic made major steps toward a Republic truly formed by the principles of "compact and equality." The Americans

---

195 Ibid., at 372.

196 Madison, ibid., at 377.

197 Ibid., at 383.

198 Ibid., at 380.

199 The convention allocated representation within the House "in proportion to the whole number of white and other free citizens of every age, sex, and condition...and three fifths of all other persons (slaves)." Rakove, op. cit., *supra* n.104, at 70.

200 Joyce Appleby, *Liberalism and Republicanism in the Historical Imagination* (Cambridge, 1992), 217.

201 Madison, *Notes*, op. cit., ibid. at 401. By delegating the issue to the States, the Framers did not imbed prevailing sexist norms into the Constitution. States could have given women the right to suffrage but refused.

202 Elbridge Gerry wanted future eligibility limited to natives, Madison, op. cit., ibid. at 437.

203 Ibid., at 439.

rejected the Athenian and British models subordinating newly settled lands to serve a central metropolis. But many problems of citizenship remained to be resolved, ultimately by war and protracted political conflict. The Framers had retained Athen's policy of internal slavery and England's limitation of citizenship to men.

4. *The American Republic After the Fifteenth and Nineteenth Amendments*

The Constitution's allocation of the scope of the franchise to the States and Naturalization issues to Congress made it all but inevitable that the Supreme Court would eventually need to resolve the legal status of free African-Americans and slaves. When Chief Justice Taney faced this issue in *Dred Scott v. Sandford*, he argued that the Framers precluded not only all slaves from national citizenship but also all other African-Americans, including those who had become free before the Revolution.[204] It took a Civil War and the Fourteenth Amendment to repeal this part of *Dred Scott*.

In *United States v. Anthony*,[205] a Federal Circuit Court claimed that the Constitution gave the States the exclusive power to determine if women could be full citizens with the right to vote. The Nineteenth Amendment reversed this decision, finally creating a desirable, albeit minimal conception of republican citizenship that included everyone born in the United States and those who achieved citizenship through naturalization. Many years later, in *Trop v. Dulles*, the Supreme Court reinforced the importance of American citizenship when it held that Congress violated the Eighth Amendment's ban against cruel and unusual punishment by passing a law authorizing, as a penalty for a crime, the termination of citizenship.[206] No political branch could alter this basic component of individual sovereignty. At long last, the republic was officially grounded in "compact and equality" for all natural born and naturalized people living within the States. At least on a formal level, almost all American adult inhabitants would have equal rights to all constitutionally protected benefits of citizenship. For some, this resolution of the American constitution's shape has become the appropriate stopping place. But for others, "equal citizenship" and "republicanism" require much more than the fundamental rights to vote, participate in juries, and own transferable property.

---

[204] 60 U.S. (19 How.) 393 (1857).

[205] 24 Fed. Cas. 829 (C.C.N.D.N.Y.) (1873).

[206] 356 U.S. 86 (1958).

D. A Model of Republican Empires

It is time to blend those four historical examples into a structural model of republican empires, a model framed as questions. The model makes "empire" the most contested, dynamic concept by "freezing" such related notions as "democratic," "republican," and "citizen" into more descriptive definitions. Furthermore, it begins descriptively, asking a series of questions that are quite easy to verify. But as it develops, it presents more difficult problems that only can be explored by a close study of the evidence.

> How much of the political constitution is "democratically" under the direct control of the populace?
>
> How much of the political constitution is "republican," accountable to the people directly or indirectly through the electoral process? Are there parts of the government that are hereditary or otherwise completely immune from the electorate?
>
> Who are "full citizens," defined as those who can participate in all the republican components of the constitution and have access to all elected positions? Are there barriers based upon such factors as sex, race, or class? Or does the constitution extend full, equal citizenship to all native-born and properly naturalized persons? Do these citizens have rights to "property" that cannot be taken away with "due process of law?"
>
> Does the republican empire's constitution control subordinate lands, which can later become full members of the empire? In the meantime, do residents in those lands have all other constitutional rights? Or are residents in some geographical areas perpetually deprived of equal constitutional rights?
>
> What other means and institutions does the empire use to extend its influence, internally and externally? Does it provide an equal trade zone within the empire? Does it demand tribute and force colonialists into combat? Does it turn conquered people into slaves? How is wealth and power distributed within the nation? What is the role of concentrated private power?
>
> How does the republic influence, even control, nations beyond its formal boundaries, through persuasion, example, trade, force, money, and power?
>
> What are the legal and political relationships between the central government and any local governments?

> What are the legal and political relationships between the different branches of the central government: the Executive, the Legislature, the Judiciary, and the Military? Does the empire have such supporting institutions as standing armies, national banks, public credit, and influence over the media?
>
> What clusters of motives, intentions, purposes, and ideologies influence the empires' leadership and citizenry? Protecting and enlarging a republican empire? Saving souls? Protecting one's family? Creating a particular political economy and culture? Exercising religious freedom? Greed? Glory? The lust for dominion?

This analytical, empirical model omits the most contentious issue: the two competing normative conceptions of "republic" and "empire." Montesquieu believed a "republican empire" was a doomed oxymoron, while Machiavelli, Harrington, and Alexander Hamilton admired aggressive republics. Much of early United States' political history can be seen as both a struggle between these competing visions and an effort to reconcile them into a newer, better form of republican power.

2 Early Constitutional Structures

From their moment of inception, the English colonies' constitutional designs contained explicit imperial directives. The Seventeenth Century Charters of Massachusetts (1628 and 1691), Virginia (second charter in 1609), Connecticut (1662), and both Carolinas extended the Crown's colonial jurisdiction from the Atlantic to the Pacific Ocean. Although these grants were based upon the "geographic fantasy" thát the Pacific was nearby, they helped provide the legal/political foundation for the United States to claim title to all land east of the Mississippi when they ratified the Articles of Confederation in 1781.[1]

Although the Royal Charters vaguely guaranteed the colonists the rights of Englishmen, their initial authorization of colonial self-government did not mandate any particular constitutional system. With written, legal charters as the basis of their political authority and title to land, the colonists drafted written constitutions to regulate their internal affairs. Most importantly, the colonists consistently founded their constitutions on electoral representation even though they came from different regions and classes in England and had very different social/political cultures.[2] The middle-class Puritans fled religious persecution in the 1620s, while their rivals, the aristocratic Cavaliers, migrated during Cromwell's ascendancy two decades later. Both groups despised the gentle Quakers who lay between them in Pennsylvania and New Jersey. Powerful family "cousinages" controlled Puritan New England and the Cavalier South, while Pennsylvania was a creature of William Penn and his family. Although many colonists were committed republicans, the British government also prodded the colonists to adopt some form of representative government. As early as 1618, the London council ordered

---

1 DeVoto, op. cit., *supra* n.28, at 59-60.

2 David Hackett Fischer, *Albion's Seed: Four British Folkways in America* (Oxford, 1989).

Virginia's governor to implement a representative form of government.[3] Thus American constitutional history begins in irony. The American colonies would have had far more difficulty unifying against England if any of them had not developed long traditions of representative government, traditions that the English government helped create.

These republican governments varied dramatically in the extent of suffrage. In 1631, Massachusetts extended the vote to all "freemen," not just to those "freeholders" who held a significant amount of acreage, so long as those "freemen" were members of an appropriate church.[4] The *Massachusetts Body of Liberties* included all freemen who would take an oath of fealty: "It is the libertie of the freemen to choose such deputies for the General Court out of themselves, either in their owne Townes or elsewhere as they judge fittest."[5] South Carolina limited the franchise to all free white men who had resided in the State for a year and either had a freehold of at least fifty acres or had paid at least twenty shillings in taxes.[6] Needless to say, Native Americans were never included. In 1630, the Massachusetts Bay Colony proscribed the shooting "off a gun on any unnecessary occasion, or at any game except an Indian or a wolf."[7]

Even though such republican forms of government were pervasive, the early settlers defined themselves primarily in terms of their religious and ethnic heritages, not political structures and rights. The 1658 *[Puritan] Laws and Liberties* set forth the purposes of the Mayflower Compact: "[T]o erect a plantation and Collonie of English; Intending the Glory of God *the enlargement of his (Majesty's) dominions* and the speciall good of the English Nation."[8] There was not as much consensus over the appropriate use of force. The Massachusetts Body of Liberties prohibited the Commonwealth from requiring its citizens from joining in an "offensive war," while authorizing the draft for "vindictive and defensive warres in our owne behalfe, or behalfe of our freinds, and confederats..."[9] This opposition to offensive war should not be confused with pacifism. Three years later, Massachusetts included in its codification of laws and liberties the power to banish Ana-Baptists, "some whereof as others before them

---

3 *Colonial Origins of the American Constitution: A Documentary History* (Donald S. Lutz, ed., 1998), 327.

4 [Massachusetts Election Agreement] (May 18, 1631), ibid., at 40.

5 The Massachusetts Body of Liberties, paragraph 68, ibid., at 79.

6 Act to Ascertain the Manner and Form of Electing Members to Represent the Province, ibid., at 351-52 (1721).

7 Quoted in David E. Stannard, *American Holocaust: The Conquest of the New World* 241 (New York, 1992).

8 '[Puritan] Laws and Liberties', Lutz, op. cit. *supra* n.235, 145-46 (emphasis added).

9 Ibid., at 72.

have denied... the lawfulness of making warre."[10] The Rhode Island Constitution provided a musket, one pound of powder, twenty bullets, and other basic weaponry to help resist "ye many incursions that we are subjected vnto."[11]

The colonies did not see themselves as isolated political entities. In 1643, four New England colonies conducted the first New World experiment in confederation. This early attempt contained two themes that have reverberated through American constitutional history: a military need for widespread unity and a federal structure of representatives "chosen by" each of the colonies. These colonies entered "into a present consociation among ourselves, for mutual help and strength in all our future concernments," to be called "the United Colonies of New England."[12] Although they did not have such authority under the texts of their Royal Charters, they asserted that they needed to form such an alliance because they were surrounded by "people of several nations and strange languages" and combinations of hostile "natives." These rivals had become particularly dangerous because England was unable to provide "advice" and "protection" due to the "sad distractions" of its own vicious Civil War. Although the military justifications for the alliance may have been temporary, the colonies created "a firm and perpetual league of friendship and amity for offense and defense." Almost the entire agreement involved mutual obligations during war. For example, Massachusetts was required to immediately send 100 armed troops and the other colonies "45 or so" armed men to aid any colony that had been invaded. Two commissioners from each Colony would "determine all affairs of our war or peace leagues, aids, charges, and numbers of men for war, division of spoils and whatsoever is gotten by conquest."[13] All this constitutional militarism served a higher purpose, the colonists' religious culture: "Whereas we all came to these parts of America with one and the same end and aim, namely, to advance the kingdom of our Lord Jesus Christ and to enjoy the liberties of the Gospel in purity with peace."[14] The Confederation stopped operating in 1664, soon after the termination of the English Civil War, and formally disbanded in 1684.[15]

The Confederation's demise did not end merger proposals; there were at least fourteen other major schemes considered prior to the Revolution.[16]

---

10 'The Laws and Liberties of Massachusetts', ibid., at 100-01 (1647).
11 'Acts and Orders of 1647, sections 29-30', ibid., at 184 (1647).
12 'The New England Confederation', ibid., at 399 (1643).
13 Ibid., at 368.
14 Ibid., at 365-66.
15 Notes of Donald S. Lutz, ibid., at 365.
16 Ibid., at 387.

In 1688, a Royal Commission recommended unifying New England, New York, and the Jerseys.[17] Nine years later, William Penn proposed a Plan of Union that recommended unity to solve commercial as well as political differences. Two Deputies would "be appointed by each Province" as members of a federal "Congresse" that would "hear and Adjust all matters of Complaint or difference Between Province and Province."[18] In particular, they would pursue all fleeing debtors and prisoners and would support the colonies against any "Publick Enemies." The omission of any religious overtones or references indicates the pragmatic, economically focused nature of Penn's "briefe and plaine scheam."

Benjamin Franklin adopted Penn's secular constitutionalism when he wrote the Albany Plan of Union in 1754. He modified Penn's rule of two representatives for each colony by first mandating a minimum of two representatives per colony in the General Council and then apportioning representatives (up to seven) based upon the amount of money each colony paid into the general treasury. More importantly, he explicitly required that all the representatives be "chosen by the representatives of the people of the several colonies," eliminating ambiguities caused by Penn's use of the passive voice, which failed to clarify who in each of the Provinces would appoint the representatives. Franklin thereby combined degrees of republican equality among the States and between the citizens of the States with some inequality based upon a mixture of population and wealth, since those colonies that paid the most taxes would usually be the most populated. Franklin's immediate concern was the Colonies' relationship with the Iroquois, not internal commercial disputes. Appointed by the King, the President-General, "with the advice of the General Council," would enter into treaties with Indians and "make peace or declare war with Indian nations," and to "make such Laws as they Judge Necessary for regulating all Indian Trade." Franklin had excised more than religion from the New England Confederation; the Plan endorsed "Mutual Defence and Security," not "conquest." The Native-Americans were to be treated as equal human beings having fully vested property rights. In the future, only the central government could purchase lands from the Indians for future settlement to fulfill the Plan's goal of "Extending the British Settlements in North America."[19] This constitutional system did not preclude conquest; the colonies might benefit from any British victories over rival European empires.

In a desperate attempt to keep the British Empire intact when colonial relationships radically deteriorated in 1774, the Tory Joseph Galloway

17 Ibid.

18 William Penn, 'William Penn's Plan of Union', ibid., at 390.

19 Franklin, 'The Albany Plan of Union', op. cit., *supra* n.30, at 380.

submitted a Plan of Union. This futile effort, which might have prevented the Revolution, had some enduring value through its subsequent influence on the Articles of Confederation. Because this proposal was designed to avert revolution, it had a broader scope than any of its precursors. After affirming that the colonies would preserve their present constitutions and the "powers of regulating and governing [their] own internal police," the new Constitution would create a Grand-Council, elected every three years by the colonies' "respective assemblies," that would "hold and exercise all the rights, liberties, and privileges, as are held and exercised by and in the House of Commons of Great-Britain." To insure harmony among the colonies, their neighbors, and England, the King would appoint a President-General, whose authority was constrained by the "advice and consent of the Grand-Council." The President General would hold and exercise all the legislative rights, powers, and authorities, necessary for regulating and administering all the general police and affairs of the colonies, in which Great-Britain and the colonies, or any of them, the colonies in general, or more than one colony, are in any manner concerned, as well civil and criminal as commercial."[20]

In 1775, after the Revolutionary War began, Benjamin Franklin submitted a set of "Proposed Articles of Confederation" to the First Continental Congress. As had been the case with Franklin's earlier Albany Plan, the recommended Articles sought to strengthen the "United Colonies of North America" through "perpetual Union."[21] With the colonies already at war with England, it is hardly surprising that the Articles' initial objective was to provide for "their Common Defence against their Enemies." The goal of "common defence" did not limit Congress to defensive wars. Article X prohibited the Colonies from pursuing an offensive war without first receiving Congressional authorization, more than implying that Congress could engage in offensive war whenever it wanted. After all, Congress had already launched an offensive war by ordering an army to invade Canada. Article XI explicitly authorized Congress to enter into a "perpetual Alliance, offensive and defensive," with the Six Nations [The Iroquois Confederation]. Article V envisioned future growth of by giving Congress the power of "Planting …new Colonies when proper." Furthermore, every English colony in North America was invited to join the Union. Franklin's definition of "North America" was amazingly broad: "[Ireland], the West Indies Islands, Quebec, St. Johns, Nova Scotia, Bermudas, and the East and West Floridas." Franklin concluded the Proposal by restating that the union shall be "perpetual" if the Colonies

---

[20] Joseph Galloway, 'A Plan of a proposed Union between Great Britain and the Colonies', Lutz, op. cit., *supra* n.235, at 392-93.

[21] Franklin, 'Proposed Articles of Confederation', op. cit., *supra* n.30, at 730.

cannot reconcile their differences with the King. Like the Albany Plan,[22] the new Articles would treat Native-Americans as human beings, endowed with legitimate property rights that could only be relinquished by sale to the central government: "[T]heir land not to be encroach'd on, nor any private or Colony purchases to be made of them hereafter to be held good; nor any Contract for Lands to be made but between the Great Council of the Indians at Onondaga and the General Congress."[23] The recommended constitution also turned inward, providing "for the Security of [the Colonies'] Liberties and Propertys, the Safety of their Persons and Families, and their mutual and general welfare." Although not accepted at the time, this draft and Galloway's proposal provided the foundation for the Articles of Confederation of 1787.

Compared to its predecessors, The Articles of Confederation[24] created a detailed, complex system of representative government designed to serve multiple purposes.[25] The State legislators had "two schemes of representation" to control Congressional members. They selected the Congressmen and retained the power to recall any of them during the year. Congress would be responsible for the post office, federal public credit, foreign policy, interstate disputes, the raising of an army and navy, and questions of war and peace. Aside from permitting Congress to charge postage to cover post office expenses, the Articles did not give the federal government one of the most basic aspects of sovereignty: taxation. Congress could only raise its money indirectly through the States which exclusively retained the power to tax. Because all thirteen States had to agree to any amendment of the Articles to create Congress taxation power, Congress never raised sufficient revenues during either war or peace. The most notorious example was Rhode Island's rejection of a five percent impost tax. This single-state veto power guaranteed that the States remained constitutionally equal among themselves, retaining effective

---

22 The Albany Plan stated that the President General, with the advice of the Grand Council, "make such Laws as they Judge Necessary for regulating all Indian trade. That they make all Purchases from Indians for the Crown, of Lands not within the Bounds of Particular Colonies." Franklin, 'Albany Plan', ibid., at 380.

23 Franklin, 'Proposed Articles', ibid., at 732.

24 *See, e.g.*, Arthur R. Landever, 'The Indispensable Articles of Confederation – Stage in Constitutionalism, Passage for the Framers, and Clue to the Nature of the Constitution', 31 *Arizona Law Review* 79 (1989). Although George Washington disliked the Articles of Confederation's failure to provide adequate federal power, he wrote a circular in 1783 to the State Governors which demonstrated that the American Empire was already in existence: "The foundation of our Empire was not laid in the gloomy age of Ignorance and Superstition; but at an Epocha when the rights of mankind were better understood and more clearly defined, than at any other period. George Washington, 'Circular to State Governments' (June 8, 1783), Washington, op. cit., *supra* ch. 1, n.46, at 517.

25 Landever, op. cit., *supra* n.256, at 79.

sovereignty over Congress with the notable exception of foreign policy. Finally, the Framers constitutionalized their continued expectations of territorial expansion in Article XI:

> Canada acceding to this confederation, and joining the measures of the united states, shall be admitted into, and entitled to all the advantages of this union; but no other colony shall be admitted into the same, unless such admission be agreed to by nine states.[26]

The Articles gave Congress control over the Western lands. Although States and speculators were reluctant to cede any rights to Congress, the economics of war pressured every State, most notably Virginia, into making concessions. In *Common Sense*, Thomas Paine explained the essential role the new territories would play: "It is by the sale of those lands that the debt may be sunk, without burthen to any, and the quit-rent reserved thereon, will always lessen, and in time, will support the yearly expence of government."[27]

Despite the constitutional limitations, the Confederation Congress helped reorganize and defend the Union. It gained power when New York and Virginia ceded to Congress their claims to Western lands. Thomas Jefferson initiated the Ordinance of 1784, which stated that these lands should eventually be admitted into the Union as equals,[28] reaffirming the principle of "equality throughout the empire" that he had so eloquently articulated in his pre-Revolutionary plea to England. When Congress passed the Northwest Ordinance in July 1787, it created another desirable precedent for the regulation of its colonies.[29] The statute referred to the vast extent of land as a "territory," not a "colony" or "plantation." Congress would initially treat the lands like traditional colonies, appointing a territorial governor, a secretary, and three judges. Once the Territory reached a population of 5,000 [white male, free] adults, it could select its own legislature to work with a council appointed by the governor and Congress. When the future state grew to 60,000 white adults, it could apply for Statehood to become an equal member of the Union. Jefferson's revolutionary ideology of equality throughout a Republican Empire had become fully developed law.[30] Furthermore, Article VI prohibited slavery,

---

26 'The Articles of Confederation, Article XI', Lutz, op. cit., *supra* n.235, at 383.

27 Thomas Paine, 'Common Sense, Appendix', Paine, *Collected Writings* 50 (New York, 1995).

28 Dumas Malone and Basil Rauch, *Empire for Liberty: The Genesis and Growth of the United States* (New York, 1960), at 211.

29 Peter S. Onuf, *Statehood and Nation: A History of the Northwest Ordinance* (Bloomington, 1987).

30 Malone and Rauch, op. cit., *supra* ch. 2, n.28, at 214-16.

thereby providing some degree of equal citizenship to all males: "There shall be neither slavery nor involuntary servitude in the said territory otherwise than in the punishment of crimes." Subsequent historical developments in the Territories show that analysis of republican empires cannot end at the textual level. Article VI probably helped prevent the rampant growth of slavery, but both the institution of slavery and widespread support for slavery continued for decades in the area covered by the Ordinance. In 1828, only sixty percent of the population of Illinois supported a referendum to eliminate slavery in that State after another twenty years.[31]

None of these constitutional documents and developments fully captures the colonists' expansionist impulse. While the lower classes ventured west to battle the Native Americans, the upper classes speculated in Western lands and dreamed of a vast empire. In 1753, Benjamin Franklin procured a subscription to outfit a ship to search for the proverbial Northwest Passage.[32] Fourteen years later, he explained to his son why Americans needed to settle in Illinois: "[A] settlement should be made in the Illinois country... raising a strength there which on occasions of a future war might easily be poured down the Mississippi upon the lower country and into the Bay of Mexico to be used against Cuba, the French Islands, or Mexico itself."[33] We have already encountered Jefferson's musings of a republican culture covering both continents. Before he became President of the United States, George Washington was president of the Potomac River project, which planned to link the Potomac with the Ohio River and Great Lakes.[34] He thought the plan would help bind the Western settlers to the Union: "I need not remark to you Sir, that the flanks & rear of the United States are possessed by other powers – & formidable ones, too; nor, how necessary it is to apply the cement of interest, to bind all parts of the Union together by indissoluble bonds – especially that part of it, which lies immediately west of us, with the middle states."[35]

Madison's 1780 draft of a Continental Congress letter directing John Jay's diplomatic negotiations with Spain and France summarized the Revolutionary generation's imperial ideology, a mixture of economics,

---

[31] Paul Finkelman, *Slavery and the Founders: Race and Liberty in the Age of Jefferson* (Armonk, 1996) 79.

[32] 'Letter from Benjamin Franklin to Cadwallander Colden' (Feb. 28, 1753) Franklin, op. cit., *supra* n.30, at 468.

[33] Quoted in Turner, 'The Significance of the Mississippi Valley in American History', op. cit., *supra* ch. 1, n.19, at 182.

[34] In 1770, Washington had considered a proposal to improve the Potomac. But he was not willing to commit any funds to the plan, 'Letter from George Washington to Thomas Johnson' (July 20, 1770) Washington, op. cit., *supra* ch. 1, n.46, at 137-40.

[35] Letter of George Washington to Benjamin Harrison (Oct. 10, 1784) ibid., at 562.

military threats, legal doctrine, and dramatic human rights rhetoric.[36] Ever the westward looking Virginian, Madison ordered Jay not to just to protect United States boundaries, but also to demand equal navigation rights on the Mississippi River and to have access to at least one "free port" in West Florida. He dismissed all Spanish legalisms: "It is unnecessary to take notice of any pretensions founded on a priority of discovery, of occupancy, or on conquest." The Americans now claimed title to all land England had gained during the French and American War. Military victory established sovereignty: "That if a right to the said territory depended upon the conquests of the British posts within it, the United States have already a more extensive claim to it than Spain can acquire, having by the success of their arms obtained possession of all the important posts and settlements on the Illinois and Wabash, rescued the inhabitants from British domination, and established civil government in its proper form over them."[37] Nor was the United States limited to its original jurisdiction. It had the right to seize Canada and even the "remote and unimportant island of Bermuda" from its English rival.[38]

Geography supplemented force as a justification. The Americans' claim to all lands east of the Mississippi is "a more natural, more distinguishable, and more precise boundary than any other that can be drawn eastward of it; and consequently will be less liable to become a source of those disputes which too often proceed from uncertain boundaries between nations."[39] Madison then played America's trump card; American settlers were bound to move into the area irrespective of treaties, interrupting the "perpetual" "harmony" between the two nations. Already those Americans who had settled in the region have their allegiance with the United States, not Spain. On a more pragmatic level, the land was of "less value" to Spain than to the United States because the new nation needed to keep the land out of the hands of its military opponent, Great Britain.[40] The original, ambitious state charters (which frequently gave land rights all the way to the Pacific) were an additional source of legal authority. Furthermore, the United States had all the rights to territory that Spain and France had ceded to England in 1763 after the French and Indian War.

Madison next turned to the question of the right to equal navigation on the Mississippi, a right that did not deductively follow from any of the above principles. His first argument was pragmatic economics. Because

---

36 *Journals of the Continental Congress, 1774-1789* 935 (Oct. 17, 1780).
37 Ibid., at 937-38.
38 Ibid., at 943.
39 Ibid., at 939.
40 Ibid., at 940.

"the navigation of that river will essentially tend to the prosperity and advantage of the citizens of the United States that may reside on the Mississippi," Spain's control over the mouth of river at New Orleans "cannot be deemed a natural or equitable bar to the free use of the river." He immediately upped the rhetorical ante: "Such a principle would authorize a nation disposed to contravene the clear indications of nature and Providence, and the general good of mankind." Madison quoted the international lawyer Vatel for legal authority for this "innocent passage." Once again, Madison reminded any readers that local Americans would not settle for anything less. The migrating population will relentlessly swell, generating agricultural surpluses that must be sent abroad while simultaneously increasing the demand for "foreign manufactures." At the least, Spanish resistance would force Americans to go North and trade with the British. Finally, geography dictated the need for a free port: "From the rapid current of this river, it is well known that it must be navigated by vessels of a peculiar construction, and which will be unfit to go to sea."[41]

[41] Ibid., at 944.

3 Creating the Imperial Constitution

A. The Federalist Empire

We have already seen in *Federalist No. Sixty-Three* how Madison brilliantly combined his republicanism with the maintenance and growth of empire. This book seeks to avoid the error of equating nascent constitutional thought with Madison, a tempting proposition given Madison's intellect, contributions, and character. To an unknown degree, Madison echoed contemporary thinking in the course of creating and justifying new constitutional structures. For example, the issue of size had frequently been considered. As early as 1778, Theophilus Parsons observed that the rich in England use bribery to easily control small electoral districts, while larger districts produce "the most upright and able statesmen in parliament" simply because it is impossible to bribe a large electorate.[1] After mapping out legislative and executive powers, Parsons concluded that it would be difficult, but not impossible to "balance a large society on republican or general laws."[2]

Other Federalists made many of *The Federalist's* most important arguments before the publication of *The Federalist* during the crucial New York Constitutional Convention. At the Pennsylvania Convention, which was first considered the Constitution, James Wilson confronted the Anti-Federalists' reliance on Montesquieu's proposition that republics must remain small or degenerate into despotism. Wilson first observed that the argument created a seemingly insoluble problem; America was a vast country but its people would always oppose despotism. Wilson then spun Montesquieu around, quoting him to solve the dilemma: A "confederate republic" has "all the internal advantages of a republican together with the

---

1 Theophilus Parsons, 'The Essex Result', *1 Political Writing*, op. cit., *supra* ch. 1, n.86, at 498-99.

2 Ibid., at 520.

external force of a monarchial government."[3] Wilson also cited Montesquieu's observation that such an "assemblage of societies" would grow easily, a particularly important feature for the new republic: "The expanding quality of such government is peculiarly fitted for the United States, the greatest part of whose territory is yet uncultivated."[4] Wilson did not exclusively rely on a political authority that presented the Federalists with serious problems. Irrespective of Montesquieu's predictions, Americans had to choose among a limited set of options:

> At this period, America has it in her power to adopt either of the following modes of government: She may be dissolved into the individual sovereignty of States, and become one consolidated empire; she may be divided into thirteen separate, independent and unconnected commonwealths; she may be erected into two or more confederacies; or, lastly, she may become one comprehensive Federal Republic.[5]

Wilson thereby limited Montesquieu's troubling notion of "empire" to countries that were completely consolidated into one central government. The United States would be a Federal Republic, neither a traditional empire nor a stable, republican city-state like Venice. Thus it would not become the corrupt central power that Montesquieu feared. Wilson also distinguished Montesquieu by pointing out that the new system had novel features. It could not be automatically compared to any prior systems of government or to the political theories that evaluated those systems.[6] Wilson modified Montesquieu's argument that large countries had to be ruled by a single person. Because the proposed Constitution was in some senses a mixed constitution, it combined "all the internal advantages of a republic, at the same time that it maintained the external dignity and force of a monarchy."[7]

During the South Carolina debates, Charles Pinckney did not adopt Wilson's technique of simultaneously embracing and distinguishing Montesquieu. The proposed Constitution was "in some measure but an experiment" which would determine if a republic "is capable of uniting the liberty of a small commonwealth with the safety of a peaceful empire."[8] Pinckney had more confidence in a larger system than in smaller societies. He pointed to Rhode Island's continual recalcitrance and Shay's Revolt in Massachusetts: "We begin now to suppose that the evils of a republic –

---

3 James Wilson (Nov. 20, 1787), *1 Elliot*, op. cit., *supra* Intro., n.10, at 421.
4 Ibid.
5 James Wilson (Nov. 24, 1787), *3 Farrand*, op. cit., *supra* ch. 1, n.178, at 140.
6 James Wilson (Nov. 26, 1787), *1 Elliot*, op. cit., *supra* Intro., n.10, at 422.
7 James Wilson (Nov. 24, 1787), *3 Farrand*, ibid., at 139.
8 Charles Pinckney (Jan. 16, 1788), *2 Elliot*, 262.

dissension, tumult, and faction – are more dangerous in small societies than in large confederate states."[9] Furthermore, external threats justified a powerful central government: "Let us, therefore, be careful in strengthening the Union. Let us remember that we are bounded by vigilant and attentive neighbors, who view with a jealous eye our rise to empire."[10]

Although he had initially refused to endorse the Constitution as a Virginia delegate, Governor Randolph became one of its most formidable advocates. Turning to the issues of national size and character, he rejected Montesquieu's assumption that republics were inherently pacific. If the country were divided into several republican confederacies, commercial and political rivalries would soon lead to war: "History will show that as much barbarity and cruelty have been committed upon one another by republican borderers as by any other."[11] A republic could be of any size so long as the people elected the President and the court system "administer[ed] the laws with justice."[12] History also taught that a Republic needs a powerful chief executive: "Recur to the history of Holland, and you will find that country could never have resisted Spain, had it not been for the stadtholder. At those periods when they had no stadtholder, their government was weak and their public affairs deranged."[13] Turning directly to Montesquieu, Randolph set forth basic distinctions between a republic, a monarchy, and a despotism: "[A] republican government is that in which the body, or only a part, of the people is possessed of the supreme power; a monarchical, that in which a single person governs by fixed and established laws; a despotic government, that in which a single person, without law and without rule, directs every thing by his will and caprice." Randolph then observed that those differences had nothing to do with "extent of boundaries." To confirm the point, Randolph noted that Montesquieu elsewhere considered republics "governments of law," instead of "governments of men."[14] Randolph's Virginia ally Francis Corbin observed that the argument against large republics questioned the legitimacy of all the existing State governments except for Delaware and notorious Rhode Island. There was no limit to a republic's size: "A government of this kind may extend to all the western world; nay, I may

---

9 Charles Pinckney (May 14, 1788), ibid., at 326-27.

10 Ibid., at 331.

11 Gov. Randolph (June 10, 1788), *1 Elliot*, ibid., at 197.

12 Ibid., at 199.

13 Ibid., at 200.

14 Gov. Randolph (June 16, 1788), ibid., at 84. A few sentences later, Randolph demonstrated the multiple meanings of the word "empire" by integrating it with republicanism: "The empire or government of laws... is that in which the laws are made with the free-will of the people; hence, then, if laws be made by the assent of the people, the government may be deemed free." Ibid.

say, *ad infinitum*."[15] During New York's Constitutional Convention, Gouverneur Morris explained how large size would "filter out" inappropriate Presidential candidates: "It cannot be possible that a man shall have sufficiently distinguished himself to merit this high trust, without having his character proclaimed by fame throughout the empire."[16] John Rutledge explicitly linked empire with expanding influence: "As we are laying the foundation for a great empire, we ought to take a permanent view of the subject, and not look at the present moment only. He reminded the House of the necessity of securing the West India trade to this country."[17]

The Federalists explained why Congress must control foreign commerce and diplomatic issues to ensure the republic's continued growth. James Wilson condemned the current system because several States had passed laws preventing British creditors from collecting their debts. This local interference with the international economic system prevented westward expansion. When the United States complained to the British about their refusal to surrender their western outposts pursuant to the Treaty signed at the end of the Revolution, Lord Camarthen replied: "The treaty under which you claim those possessions has not been performed on your part; until that is done, these possessions will not be delivered up."[18] John Adams argued that the States could never obtain a good commercial treaty with England so long as they separately pursued their own interests: "Our ambassador at the court of London is considered as a mere cipher, instead of the representative of the United States."[19] Writing many years later, James Madison emphasized the felt need for a concerted effort to combat Great Britain's "monopolizing policy injurious to trade."[20] Madison also explained why Congress should have the power under the commerce clause to regulate all commercial and political relationships with Native-Americans. Congress needed to prevent States like Georgia from violating federal authority by making their own treaties and warring with Indians.[21] Congress also had to regulate interstate commerce to prevent trade wars, which would disrupt the empire and dissolve the adhesive formed by mutual interest through exchange and credit (both public and private).[22]

Similar arguments abounded in the pamphlets advocating ratification of the proposed Constitution. In *The Federalist*, John Jay argued that the

---

15 Francis Corbin (June 7, 1788), ibid., at 108 (italics in original).
16 Gouverneur Morris (July 19, 1787), *2 Elliot*, ibid., at 335.
17 Madison, *Notes*, op. cit., *supra* ch. 1, n.40, at 551.
18 Quoted in Wilson (Dec. 7, 1878), *1 Elliot*, op. cit., at 490.
19 John Adams (Jan. 30,1788), ibid., at 124.
20 Madison, 'Preface', *3 Farrand*, op. cit., *supra* ch. 1, n.178, at 547.
21 Ibid., at 548.
22 Ibid., at 547-48.

greater extent of territory gave the country more choices for leadership: "One government can collect and avail itself of the talents and experiences of the ablest men, in whatever part of the Union they may be found."[23] Such unity would also strengthen the military, making them far more efficient than dividing the armed forces into separate state militias or several distinct confederacies.[24] The pamphleteer Americanus dismissed small republics for having the "inherent properties" of "faction, instability, and frequent revolutions."[25] Republicanism resolves the problem of insensitivity at the national capital by making the central government aware of "the sense of the people" and by requiring it to treat each of its parts equally.[26] Furthermore, the States and the Federal governments would watch each other carefully for abuses.[27] Hamilton went so far as to argue that it would be easier for dissidents to organize their opposition: "The great extent of the country is a further security. * * * If the federal army should be able to quell the resistance of one State, the distant States would have it in their power to make head with fresh forces."[28] Writing under the pseudonym "Fabius," John Dickinson asserted that liberty would remain on the "firmest basis" as long as "frequent recurrence of elections," based upon proportionality, took place, and Congress remained limited to legislative action, having no direct power to interfere with the Executive parts of the government.[29] Fabius concluded that the new egalitarian structure among the States created an imperial system preferable to Rome's attempts to grant limited citizenship and sovereignty to its colonies. The States will serve as "civil and military stations, conveniently planted throughout the empire, with lively and regular communication. A stroke, a touch on any part, will be immediately felt by the whole."[30] In *The Federalist*, James Madison emphasized the Constitution's egalitarian structure to reassure the small states that they would be safe "under a general government pervading with equal energy every part of the empire, and having an equal interest in protecting every part from every other part."[31]

---

23 'The Federalist Number Four' (John Jay), op. cit., *supra* ch. 1, n.20, at 47.

24 Ibid., at 48-50.

25 John Stevens, Jr., 'Americanus III', *1 Bailyn*, op. cit, *supra* Intro., n.7, at 439.

26 Ibid., at 440.

27 Ibid.

28 'The Federalist Number Twenty-eight' (Hamilton), op. cit, *supra* ch. 1, n.20, at 181.

29 Stevens, 'Americanus III', *1 Bailyn*, op. cit, *supra* Intro., n.7, at 440-41.

30 'Fabius' [John Dickinson], 'Observations on the Constitution Proposed by the Federal Convention VIII', *2 Bailyn*, ibid., at 427.

31 Madison, Notes, op. cit., *supra* ch. 1, n.40, at 146.

The risk of partition, and ensuing civil war, permeated the Federalists' public and private thinking. In a letter to Governor Edmund Randolph, Thomas Jefferson feared "[Unless] the Union be organized efficiently on Republican principles, innovations of a much more objectionable form may be obtruded, or, in the most favorable event, the partition of the empire into rival and hostile confederacies will ensue."[32] Alexander Hamilton's letter to George Washington was characteristically blunt: "I fear we shall let slip the golden opportunity of rescuing the American empire from disunion anarchy and misery..."[33] In *Federalist Number Thirteen*, Hamilton publicly discussed the consequences of "the dismemberment of the empire." Although some opponents thought there would be three confederacies, Hamilton predicted a greater number of rival groups. The overall cost of government for all Americans would increase because each of the confederacies would duplicate necessary federal functions and would need to spend more money on military establishments to protect themselves from their neighbors.[34] He mocked the Anti-Federalists' fear of large governments. Under their "misunderstood" reading of Montesquieu, the State of New York was already too large.[35]

At least in less public settings, Hamilton never completely rejected Montesquieu's concerns. During his lengthy speech at the Constitutional Convention that praised the British system, he pointed out that the country's vast size may prevent any form of effective government: "I have great doubts whether a more energetic government can pervade this wide and expansive country."[36] In particular, he doubted that a purely republican form of government would survive: "This view of the subject almost led him to despair that a republican government could be established over so

---

[32] Letter from James Madison to Thomas Jefferson (April 8, 1787), *2 Elliot*, op. cit, *supra* Intro., n.10, at 108. A few months later, Madison could reassure Jefferson: "No proposition was made, no suggestion was thrown out, in favor of a partition of the Empire into two or more confederacies." Letter from James Madison to Thomas Jefferson (Oct. 24, 1787), *3 Farrand*, op. cit., *supra* ch. 1, n.178, at 131.

[33] Letter from Alexander Hamilton to George Washington (July 3, 1787), quoted in David McGowan, 'Ethos in Law and History: Alexander Hamilton, The Federalist, and the Supreme Court', 85 *Minnesotta Law Review* 755, 784 (2001).

[34] 'The Federalist Number Thirteen' (Hamilton), op. cit, *supra* ch. 1, n.20, at 97-99. Oliver Ellsworth made a similar argument during the Connecticut Convention: "It is easy for hostile nations to sweep off a number of separate states, one after another. Witness the states in the neighborhood of ancient Rome." Oliver Ellsworth (Jan.4, 1788), *1 Elliot*, op. cit., *supra* Intro., n.10, at 185.

[35] Alexander Hamilton (June 27, 1788), ibid., at 352.

[36] Alexander Hamilton (June 19, 1787, evidently a mistake for June 18, 1787), *1 Farrand*, op. cit., *supra* ch. 1, n.178, at 295.

great an extent."[37] The British system was more preferable to an unstable, purely republican system: "I believe the British government forms the best model the world ever produced... This government has for its object public strength and individual security."[38] A powerful, disinterested executive was a crucial component: "See the excellency of the British executive – He is placed above temptation – He can have no distinct interests from the public welfare."[39] All of this talk of "empire" did little to hurt the Federalists (*The Federalist* used the word thirty-five times in a variety of contexts). Many other American citizens had similar hopes for their country's future.

B. Anti-Federalist Views On Empire

As mentioned in the preface, one of the traditional tests of any historical thesis is its capacity to generate interesting questions and plausible answers. In this case, why were the Anti-Federalists unable to exploit the Federalist's imperial rhetoric and proposals even though they initially won majorities of delegates to several state Constitutional Conventions? Aside from underlying public opinion, which is difficult to measure during this period, the Anti-Federalists' failure is attributable, at least in part, to their inability to achieve consensus over this basic issue.[40] The imperial question reveals several competing ideologies within the Anti-Federalist movement.

While many Anti-Federalists opposed any conception of empire, others did not fear size or expansion. Such pro-growth Anti-Federalists dreaded governmental "consolidation" at the national level, which they believed would cripple the States, enhance aristocratic power, and lead to the oppression of the common man. They envisioned a different structure for their growing "republican empire," a loose confederation of States retaining most of their sovereignty. For this group of "anti-consolidation" Anti-Federalists, their opposition was over the means, the proper distribution of public power, not the goals of empire.

---

[37] Alexander Hamilton (June 18, 1787), Madison, Notes, op. cit., *supra* ch. 1, n.40, at 134.

[38] Hamilton (June 18, 1787), *1 Farrand*, ibid., at 299.

[39] Ibid.

[40] For a wide-ranging discussion of Anti-Federalist dissent, *see* Saul Cornell, *The Other Founders: Anti-Federalism & the Dissenting Tradition in America* 1788-1828 (Chapel Hill, 1999). In his discussion of size, Cornell emphasizes the "elite Anti-Federalist" beliefs that virtue and liberty could only survive in a small republic, ibid., at 72. This book proposes an additional distinction beyond Cornell's "elite" and "plebian" Anti-Federalism: Many Anti-Federalists did not oppose to a large republic structured by the proposed Constitution once they believed their individual rights would be adequately protected by a Bill of Rights.

Other Anti-Federalists primarily worried about the absence of a Bill of Rights to protect individuals from the more powerful federal government.[41] State Constitutional Conventions addressed the issues of a Bill of Rights by ratifying the Constitution while simultaneously recommending the prompt inclusion of a Bill of Rights. This compromise enabled many Anti-Federalists, including such influential men as New York's Melancton Smith, and Massachusetts's Samuel Adams, and John Hancock, to change their views and support the proposed Constitution. In other words, those Anti-Federalists who were concerned about the lack of textual protection of individual citizens' fundamental rights held a wide range of views about "empire." Some preferred a vast regime headed by a powerful central government, once individual rights were guaranteed. Other Anti-Federalists claimed the Constitution was unnecessary because the existing governmental debts could be paid off by the sale of more Western lands,[42] hardly the position of a group opposed to national growth or large size. Finally, Anti-Federalists never publicly sought to dissolve or reduce the power of the existing Union, which both sides already conceived of as a large country destined for greatness. These fault lines reveals some major differences among the Anti-Federalists: differences that help explain their eventual defeat. Just as the Federalists had to combine republicanism with empire building, so the Anti-Federalists had to resolve their dilemmas. The Federalist Edmund Randolph caustically summarized the Anti-Federalists' problem:

> The extent of the country is objected, by the gentlemen over the way, as an insurmountable obstacle to the establishing a national government in the United States. It is a very strange and inconsistent doctrine, to admit the necessity of the Union, and yet urge this last objection, which I think goes radically to the existence of the Union itself. If the extent of the country be a conclusive argument against a national government, it is equally so against a union with the other states.[43]

Finally, many Anti-Federalists were overtly committed to some vision of "empire." In a concluding group statement, the dissenting minority of Anti-Federalists delegates at the Maryland convention proclaimed that the proposed Constitution was dangerously defective, a threat to the people's happiness, liberty, and safety. Nevertheless, they ended with an imperial prayer: "May the all-wise and omnipotent Being, who made us masters of

---

[41] Jackson Turner Main, *The Anti-Federalists: critics of the Constitution 1781-1788* 130 (New York, 1961).

[42] 'Dissent of the Minority of the Pennsylvania Convention' (Dec. 18, 1787), *1 Bailyn*, op. cit., *supra* Intro., n.7, at 298.

[43] Gov. Randolph (June 6, 1788) *1 Elliot*, op. cit., *supra* Intro., n.10, at 71.

a fair and fruitful empire, inspire us with wisdom and fortitude to perpetuate to posterity that freedom which we received from our fathers!"[44]

Whatever their private beliefs, Anti-Federalists continued to support the existing Union, which already covered a vast expanse of territory. Even Patrick Henry praised the Union a few minutes after damning the Federalists imperial quest: "The first thing I have at heart is American liberty: the second thing is American union; and I hope the people of Virginia will endeavour to preserve that union."[45] Henry frequently worried about the fate of the Mississippi, hardly a narrow, nonexpansionist concern.[46] James Monroe,[47] Benjamin Harrison,[48] and Governor George Clinton[49] were other notable anti-Federalists who opposed the new Constitution while continuing to support the Union. At the New York debates, John Lansing rejected the argument that his fellow anti-Federalists were against Union and that their arguments should be interpreted as anti-Union positions in disguise: "Sir, I know not any gentleman who wishes for a dissolution of the Union."[50] Melancton Smith, who argued eloquently against the Constitution at the New York Convention before reluctantly deciding to vote for it, explained that a union was absolutely necessary.[51] Luther Martin offered an equally conflicted response. On the one hand, he argued that there was no rush to form a new system to regulate this "extensive continent."[52] There was ample time to include a Bill of Rights and other needed protections to create an effective, safe, and free central power. But the proposed Constitution was a "misshapened heterogeneous monster of ambition and interest":

> I most sacredly believe [the Federalists'] object is the total abolition and destruction of all state governments, and the erection on their ruins of one great and extensive empire, calculated to aggrandize and elevate its rulers and chief officers far above the common herd of mankind, to enrich them with wealth, and to encircle them with honours and glory, and which according to judgment on the maturest reflection, must inevitably be attended with the most

---

[44] 'Address to the People of Maryland' (April 21, 1788), *1 Elliot*, ibid., at 556.

[45] Patrick Henry (June 5, 1788), ibid., at 57.

[46] Madison thought that Henry boycotted the Constitutional Convention to keep "himself free to combat or espouse the result of it according to the result of the Mississippi business..." Letter from James Madison to Thomas Jefferson (March 19, 1787), *2 Eliott*, ibid., at 107.

[47] James Monroe (June 10, 1788), ibid., at 209.

[48] Benjamin Harrison (June 25, 1788), ibid., at 629.

[49] Governor George Clinton (June 21, 1788), ibid., at 268.

[50] John Lansing (June 25, 1788), ibid., at 325.

[51] Melancton Smith (June 20, 1788), ibid., at 223.

[52] Luther Martin (March 21, 1788), *3 Farrand*, op. cit., *supra* ch. 1, n.178, at 292.

humiliating and abject slavery of their fellow citizens, by the sweat of whose brows, and by the toil of whose bodies, it can only be effected.[53]

Virginia Anti-Federalists criticized the new government for being so strong that it would threaten the growth and cohesion of the nation. During the Constitutional Convention, John Dawson set forth the basic constitutional distinction that would last until the end of the Civil War; he was a "warm friend of a firm, federal, energetic government" but feared a "consolidated government."[54] "Authority" and "experience of all ages" demonstrated "that no government formed on the principles of freedom can pervade all North America."[55] Yet such Anti-Federalists could rarely maintain their localism. Later in the same speech Dawson feared that the new Constitution would not protect Western settlers' claims to use the Mississippi River, which was controlled by Spain at New Orleans: "The President, with the concurrence of two thirds of the Senate present, may make a treaty, by which any territory may be ceded, or the navigation of any river surrendered."[56] Thus, a relatively small group could engage in the "highest act of sovereign authority," the "dismemberment of empire."[57] Sometimes, the Anti-Federalists expressed dreams as vast as Jefferson's vision of Anglican republicanism throughout the hemisphere. Patrick Henry argued they were attempting to "secure the happiness of one half of the human race," leaving the other hemisphere to its fate.[58]

Another group of Anti-Federalists were not so concerned about the proposed increase in the federal government's power. They wanted to increase the United States' power, prestige, and size. They criticized the Constitution's failure to protect their individual fundamental rights by not having a Bill of Rights. Their fears were legitimate, because the federal government's coercive powers were to be aimed primarily at individuals, not the States. Initially, Federalists like James Wilson opposed a Bill of Rights as unnecessary or even dangerous: "[T]hat very declaration might have been construed to imply that some degree of power was given since we undertook to define its extent."[59] But as the debate wore on and State Convention votes remained uncertain, the Federalists capitulated by agreeing to draft a Bill of Rights soon after Constitutional ratification. The new Congress would consider the numerous suggested Amendments

---

53 Ibid., at 291.

54 John Dawson (June 24, 1788), *1 Elliot*, op. cit., *supra* Intro., n.10, at 606.

55 Ibid., at 607.

56 Ibid., at 610.

57 Ibid., at 609.

58 Patrick Henry (June 24, 1788), ibid., at 625.

59 James Wilson, James Wilson's Speech at a Public Meeting (Oct. 6, 1787), *1 Bailyn*, op. cit., *supra* Intro., n.7, at 64.

offered by several State conventions. Although Anti-Federalists like Patrick Henry claimed that the new system could not be trusted to honor that commitment, enough wavering voters in critical States like Massachusetts and Virginia changed their mind and supported the new Constitution. Some of the proposed Amendments addressed constitutional structure, not individual rights, a movement that eventually led to the Ninth and Tenth Amendments. But even those efforts only signified disputes over the proper distribution of governmental power, not over the basic commitment to a strong central government that would supervise the growth of an empire.

There still remained a large segment of Anti-Federalists, including some of their most eloquent advocates, who opposed the new "empire," whether defined in terms of size or expansion. Montesquieu was their main authority. Large, expanding countries invariably degenerated into centralized governments, led by a single person, permeated with militarism, courtiership, and corruption. Similar views had long been expressed in America. In 1778, Phillips Payson preached: "[I]t is obvious to observe that a spirit of liberty should in general prevail among a people... The inhabitants of large and opulent empires and kingdoms are often entirely lost to a sense of liberty, in which case they become easy prey to usurpers and tyrants."[60] Like their rivals, this group of Anti-Federalists turned to history: "All the exertions of the most potent emperors of Rome were not capable of keeping that empire together, which in extent was far inferior to the dominion of America."[61] Where Madison saw widespread, diverse interests as an impediment to majority tyranny, Luther Martin feared that a powerful group of States representing one interest would oppress other States.[62] During the Ratification Debates, one Anti-Federalist worried that the central government would not be able to extend its power effectively: "[I]f all the United States were to be swallowed up by the great mass of powers given to Congress, the parts that are more distant in this great empire would be governed with less and less energy."[63] In the first of his many brilliant salvoes against the Constitution, "Brutus" summed up these fears of inefficiency and danger:

---

[60] Phillips Payson, 'A Sermon', *1 Political Writings*, op. cit., *supra* ch. 1, n.86, at 525.

[61] 'Dissent of the Minority of the Pennsylvania Convention' (Dec. 18, 1787), *1 Bailyn*, *supra* Intro., n.7, at 536.

[62] Luther Martin, 'The Genuine Information 2' (Jan. 1, 1788), *2 Bailyn*, ibid., at 644.

[63] Mr. Spencer, 'Five speakers Debate Congressional Control of Congressional Elections' (July 25, 1788), ibid., at 855. During the original Constitutional Convention, John Dawson invoked Montesquieu to predict that despotism was the only possibility for an extensive country, John Dawson (June 24, 1788), *1 Elliot*, op. cit., *supra* Intro., n.10, at 607.

> In a republic of such vast extent as the United-States, the legislature cannot attend to the various concerns and wants of its different parts. It cannot be sufficiently numerous to be acquainted with the local conditions and wants of different districts, and if it could, it is impossible it should have sufficient time to attend to and provide for all the variety of cases of this nature, that would be continually arising.[64]

In so extensive a republic, the great officers of government would soon become above the control of the people, and abuse their power to the purpose of aggrandizing themselves, and oppressing them."[65]

"Agrippa" warned his readers that political power would gravitate toward the Federal Capitol: "[I]n a very large empire, as the whole states consolidated must be, there will always be a desire of the government to increase the trade of the capital, and to weaken the extremes."[66] The national leadership would invariably exploit those who lived far away; the new federal District would soon turn into another London, dominating the entire nation.[67] In addition, the voters should reject the Federalists' argument that they ought to "look beyond local interests, and judge for the good of the empire."[68] But even Agrippa implicitly conceded that, at least for some purposes, the existing Union already was an "empire": "It is actually under the pressure of such an absurd government, that the Spanish provinces have groaned for near three centuries; and such will be our misfortune and degradation, if we ever submit to have *all the business of the empire* done by one legislature."[69] Applying the principle "that the powers of Congress over the citizens should be small in proportion as the empire is extended,"[70] Agrippa concluded that Congress should only have "limited revenue" and "the limited powers of managing foreign concerns."[71] Congress could pay the interest on its debt from limited impost taxes and sell Western public lands to reduce the principal.[72] Commerce is the appropriate adhesive, not power.[73] Otherwise, "the extremities of the empire will, like Ireland and Scotland, be drained to fatten an overgrown capital."[74]

---

64 'Brutus' I, *1 Bailyn*, op. cit., *supra* Intro., n.7, at 174.

65 'Brutus I' (Oct. 18, 1787), *1 Bailyn*, ibid., at 174.

66 'Agrippa' [James Winthrop] III' (Nov. 30, 1787), ibid., at 444. *See also* 'Agrippa IV' (December 4, 1787), ibid., at 449.

67 'Agrippa VI' (Dec. 14, 1787), ibid., at 518-19.

68 'Agrippa XII' (Jan. 18, 1788), ibid., at 771.

69 Ibid., at 763 (italics added). *See also* 'Agrippa XVIII', ibid., at 156.

70 'Agrippa IX' (Dec. 28, 1787), ibid., at 629.

71 Ibid., at 630.

72 'Agrippa X' (Jan. 1, 1788), ibid., at 674.

73 Ibid., at 674.

74 'Agrippa XII' (Jan. 15, 1788), ibid., at 768.

The Anti-Federalists were as worried about class conflict as their opponents. But many of them saw the Constitution as a subterfuge that would solely benefit the wealthy: "These lawyers and men of learning and moneyed men that talk so finely and gloss over matters so smoothly to make us poor illiterate people swallow the pill, expect to get into Congress themselves! They mean to get all the money into their hands, and they will swallow up all us little folk, like the Leviathan, Mr. President; yea, just as the whale swallowed up Jonah."[75]

Although many voters were influenced by such arguments, electing anti-Federalist majorities to several State Constitutional Conventions, the Federalists ultimately prevailed without compromising the commitment to empire. At the important, contentious New York ratification debates, Hamilton bluntly dismissed anti-Federalist provincialism with a sweeping principle of national power: "The local interests of a state ought in every case to give way to the interests of the Union."[76]

---

[75] Quoted in 'Dominant Forces in Western Life,' Turner, op. cit., *supra* ch. 1, n.19, at 240.

[76] Alexander Hamilton, 'Alexander Hamilton Defends the Senate: A Small, Independent, Discerning Body to Check the Passions of the People,' *1 Bailyn*, op. cit., *supra* Intro., n.7, at 797.

4 The Struggle Over the Form, Character, and Direction of the New Empire

As soon as the Constitution supplanted the Articles of Confederation, James Madison undermined residual Anti-Federalist opposition to the Constitution by shepherding The Bill of Rights through the First Congress and subsequent State ratification. The Ten Amendments addressed Anti-Federalist concerns over for such important individual rights as freedom of conscience, free speech and press, property, and a right to jury in civil cases as well as genuflecting toward States' rights via the generalities of the Ninth and Tenth Amendments. Although the Bill of Rights encountered resistance in Virginia because critics believed the text in the Ninth and Tenth Amendments were insufficient to stop the federal government's "necessary tendency to consolidated empire,"[1] it did satisfy enough Anti-Federalists to gradually turn the Constitution into a "sacred text," an unquestionable premise for subsequent political controversy. For several decades, the "contest for dominion – for empire"[2] that Patrick Henry had warned about during the ratification debates focused on competing interpretations of the Constitution, not its basic authority.

The ensuing split between the Federalists and the Republicans during the Washington Presidency can be partially explained as a struggle between rival conceptions of empire. Led by Alexander Hamilton, the Federalists sought a powerful central government, supported by a strong army, massive public debt, powerful private creditors, a central bank, an independent federal judiciary, a strong President, political pageantry, tariffs to support manufacturing, and a commercially based economy that looked to Europe, particularly England, for support and inspiration. It is easy to document

---

1 Elkins and McKitrick, op. cit., *supra* ch. 1, n.148, at 135.

2 John Grayson (June 14, 1788), *1 Eliott*, op. cit., *supra* Intro., n.10, at 365.

Hamilton's personal quest for glory as part of his goal of creating a glittering national power. In 1799, he wrote several letters envisioning his leading a powerful army either to take over Louisiana and Florida or even to "detach South America from Spain which is only the Channel, through which the riches of *Mexico* and *Peru* are conveyed to France."[3] Nor would the Republicans ever forget Hamilton's long speech at the Constitutional Convention favoring Britain's mixed constitution based upon a constitutional monarch.

In response to Hamilton's actions as Secretary of the Treasury to implement his nationalist system, Thomas Jefferson and James Madison created the Republican Party to fulfill their vision of a renowned agrarian empire of independent, virtuous yeoman farmers, stretching for thousands of miles. The poet Philip Freneau, whom Jefferson chose to edit a Republican paper that would harshly criticize the Federalists' administration, described this ideal in an ode to Thomas Paine's *Rights of Man*:

> A vast republic, fam'd thro' every clime,
>
> WITHOUT A KING, TO SEE THE END OF TIME.[4]

The Jeffersonian Republicans wanted the States to be the primary governmental institution, pursuing the two primary obligations of maintaining the peace and providing decent public education. The federal government would not be corrupted by such institutions as a national bank, public debt, a powerful national judiciary, an aggressive President, urban centers, factories that turned citizens into dependent laborers, luxurious formalities, and a large military force. They did not believe such institutions were necessary to fulfill their goal of developing greater commercial and political ties with the revolutionary French Republic at the expense of Great Britain, whose navy dominated the oceans and international trade. They expected that an embargo's "economic coercion" of English trade would force Britain to end its discriminatory trade practices. Americans could temporarily forgo their English luxuries, but the British would still desperately need American staples and trade.

As Richard Hofstadter made clear in his famous study of the evolution of the party system, the two parties' hatred was exacerbated by a common ideological flaw; none of the politicians at that time accepted the notion that there could be a rival political party that established its enduring legitimacy through loyalty to the country. Both sides believed that their rival was a

---

[3] Elikins and McKitrick, ibid., at 616 (italics in original).

[4] Ibid., at 240.

dangerous, illegitimate faction that had to be annihilated, not just defeated. To the Federalists, the Republicans were disloyal Jacobins, eager to betray the country to France and anarchistic democracy. The Federalist Fisher Ames equated the Federalists with proper government, portraying the Republicans as the dangerous, illegitimate "Jacobin faction."[5] The Republicans replied, with some justification, that many Federalists were not committed to a republican form of government. Ames' consistently gloomy warnings explicitly assumed the inherent frailty of republics, particularly those that are very "democratic."[6] The Republicans believed creation of such anti-Republican institutions as a bank, national debt, and an army were precursors to transforming the government into a monarchy or at least an aristocracy. The Federalists frequently reinforced these images. John Adams' proposal to create fancy titles for various federal officials was successfully derided as a pretentious attempt to adopt Europe's aristocratic mores. In other words, both sides were committed to an American empire, but many Federalists were tentatively committed to republicanism, much less to the particular ideologically and institutional form of republicanism that the Virginia Republicans demanded. These festering tensions did not prevent the First Congress from establishing many of the basic structures of America's political system, most notably the Bill of Rights and the Judiciary Act.

The political conflict exploded when Secretary of the Treasury Alexander Hamilton decided that the federal government should satisfy its outstanding debts by paying all the proceeds to the current holder of the paper. Hamilton's plan was not a "neutral" commitment premised upon some abstract theory of property and justice. He believed that the country could never become powerful unless it concentrated a great deal of capital in the hands of relatively few people who would then support the national government that had helped enrich them.[7] Thus, he was not troubled that speculators, knowing that public debts would be reimbursed at face value, spread through the backcountry and fraudulently bought up federal debts from uninformed citizens. His plan accomplished four interrelated goals: (1) It resolved the debt crisis and revived the national government's credit; (2) It created a class of even wealthier men; (3) It created a class of wealthy men who would continue to support the national government, not so much out of gratitude as out of concern for their loans to that government; and (4) It created a pool of capital that the government and the private sector could use to create Hamilton's powerful government. Most of the Framers and ratifiers did not foresee that the Constitution could create such a

5 'The Republican I', *1 Ames*, op. cit., *supra* ch. 1, n.61, at 89.

6 'The Dangers of American Liberty,' ibid., at 124.

7 Elkins and McKitrick, op. cit., *supra* ch. 1, n.148, at 117.

consolidation of power and energy within the Executive Branch, but Hamilton hoped to develop a facsimile of the British Constitution through aggressive and creative uses of the limited powers granted to the Presidency and Congress.

Hamilton's proposal outraged Madison because most of the money would go to Hamilton's allies, who had directly or indirectly purchased much of the debt from the citizen-soldiers who fought the Revolutionary War and truly deserved to be compensated for their sacrifices. The Republicans were shocked because they believed that the Constitution must reflect their more communitarian conception of republicanism, which they believed was the animating "spirit" behind the constitutional ratification process. No decent society would be so ungrateful to those citizens who aided their country during its agonizing Revolutionary War.

Hamilton correctly perceived that such general powers as "commerce" and "war" were sufficiently vague, broad, and important to justify his creation of numerous means, such as national banks and debts. The Constitutional text set out the basic structure of empire; politicians (and later judges) would formulate and validate the actual imperial system. Hamilton's perception demonstrates that much of our constitution is significantly created and regulated by unwritten "constitutional conventions," not just by constitutional law as formulated by the United States Supreme Court. Just as one needs to look behind the text to find the two constitutional purposes of protecting the wealthy and empowering the empire, so one needs to look beyond the text to perceive that the political branches primarily resolve many constitutional issues, not solely the judiciary. Although Jefferson would bitterly complain about these developments, particularly before he became President, he concluded that it was too late to alter these changes once he reached office. Fisher Ames, in turn, dismissed many of Jefferson's reservations as bitter jealousy of his political rival Alexander Hamilton.

The Washington administration's negotiations with the British after the Revolutionary War revealed both the consensus over the future of the nation and the limits of that consensus. The British violated the Treaty ending the Revolutionary War by maintaining their forts along the Western frontier in land they had formally ceded to the Americans. They claimed, with quite a bit of justification, that the Americans were not honoring their reciprocal Treaty obligation to protect British creditors and loyalists from State and local confiscation.[8] When George Hammond sailed from England to attempt to negotiate a treaty that would concede the forts in exchange for protection of British property rights in America, Thomas

---

[8] Ibid., at 246-47.

Jefferson relentlessly snubbed him. Hammond's very presence refuted Jefferson's prediction that the haughty English would never send a representative.[9] Jefferson's Anglophobia appalled Hamilton; he readily contacted Hammond, agreeing that the British creditors should be protected, but liberated slaves would not be returned. Hamilton was not too concerned about the British creditors because he foresaw that the new federal court system would effectively protect them. He saw little hope for the British Loyalists' prewar claims. Hamilton also sought to open American trade with the West Indies, but Hammond followed his instructions by refusing to discuss that possibility. On the most important issue, the status of the western lands, Hamilton was as firm as Jefferson would have been had he deigned to negotiate with Hammond. Hamilton informed the British representative that the United States would probably not "consent to a dereliction of any part of its territory acquired in the Treaty."[10] Jefferson's stalling techniques frustrated Hammond, dragging out negotiations indefinitely. Four years later, James Monroe, another of Jefferson's allies, envisioned a military solution: "[B]y our embarking this Government with full zeal in our behalf, and striking terror into England, it will be necessary to lay hold of her property within the United States, take the posts, and then invade Canada."[11]

The political debate between the Federalists and Republicans did not include the ultimate fate of Native-Americans. In a letter to George Washington, Jefferson endorsed military force: "As to myself, I hope we shall give the Indians a thorough drubbing this summer."[12] His fellow Southerners were equally aggressive. Citizen Genet began his ultimately abortive tour of duty as France's ambassador by helping to organize privateers against Spain after landing in Charlestown, South Carolina, a scheme the South Carolinians enthusiastically embraced.[13] Genet later tried to foment insurrections in Louisiana and Canada. Although Secretary of State Jefferson formally stated that such efforts were ill advised, he did nothing to stop or expose these plots.[14]

Jefferson's stalling tactics ultimately failed to prevent the Washington administration from conducting successful negotiations with England. The Treaty ending the revolutionary war had left many important issues unresolved. The British were most concerned about Loyalists' properties and preexisting American debts, while the Americans wanted the removal

---

9 Ibid., at 249.
10 Ibid., at 251.
11 Ibid., at 502.
12 Ibid., at 272.
13 Ibid., at 335.
14 Ibid., at 349-50.

of British troops and forts established in the West after the abortive invasion of Canada, freer trading with England, and the return of all slaves freed by the British Army. In 1795, John Jay returned from England with a proposed treaty that would eliminate the British forts in the Northwest but would make no inroads into Great Britain's rigorous limitations on neutrality rights. It also explicitly conceded that many important products such as cotton could not be re-exported from the West Indies.[15] The Republicans, who had been condemning the Treaty even before they read it, quickly generated widespread opposition. Although public opinion about the Treaty radically shifted to a favorable disposition during the following year, the debate sufficiently polarized the elites and their followers to create two rival parties, the Republicans and Federalists.

Economic and demographic forces overwhelmed the Republicans' arguments that England had not treated America with adequate respect. Despite all the treaty's constraints on international commerce, American shipping exploded during this crucial year. Spurred by a surge in European prices, American shipping soared to 100,000 tons and shipping profits increased by fifty percent.[16] Furthermore, General Wayne defeated the Indians at The Battle of Fallen Timbers in 1774 and then negotiated a favorable treaty. The British "assisted" Wayne by refusing to let fleeing Indians hide in their fort. When Spain signed its treaty finally opening the Mississippi to navigation, the entire Western frontier opened up. Settlers could safely move in, unimpeded by Indians and British, and send their goods down the Mississippi. No longer could British forts, Indians, or Spanish New Orleans prevent the coming explosion of western immigration. Ohio's population would swell to 45,000 within seven years.[17] Although the Whiskey Rebellion in Western Pennsylvania is correctly perceived as a backwoods resistance to federal power, that perception only covers the immediate controversy. When federal officials talked to local citizens after the Rebellion had been suppressed, they discovered that the Westerners were as angry about the absence of federal power as they were about the federal taxes. They wanted more assistance to expand further West: "the General Government has been inattentive to the execution of the treaty of peace respecting the western posts." They also wanted better enforcement of the Treaty's rights to navigate the Mississippi. They also hated Northern speculators who were buying up much of the land.

Madison attributed his party's defeat to the machinations of "The Banks," but it is more likely that prosperity and opportunity meant more to

---

15 Ibid., at 412.
16 Ibid., at 441.
17 Ibid., at 439.

most Americans than British insults and trading constraints that did not effectively limit an explosion in shipping. Britain would continue to seize American ships that were delivering goods to France, but it would reimburse the American shippers for the expense. Madison did not yet understand that the Westerners had their own imperial agenda. Although the country was now divided into two parties reflecting two different ideologies, it was gradually becoming even more sectionalized. The immigrants pouring into States like Ohio would identify neither with Southern slave-owners nor Northern bankers. For the Republicans to prevail, they would need to gain the trust of the pivotal West, which sought continued federal subsidies in violation of strict Old Republican norms that frowned on any expansion of federal authority. The continuing distrust of Northern commercial power throughout the rest of the country facilitated an uneasy alliance between the West and the South.

George Washington's final public statements opposed such fault lines. In his draft of his Farewell Address, he combined patriotism with deification of the Constitution, praying "that their union and brotherly affection be perpetual; that the free Constitution which is of their own hands, may be sacredly maintained..."[18] The revered President emphasized many adhesives: common Country, common sufferings, common successes, and similar interests. The diverse interests created by different climates and soil create opportunities for exchange and mutual growth. So long as the country remained united, with every citizen taking "pride in the name of an American," it would not be "prey to foreign Intriegues and internal discord." Nor would the country pursue War, at least until it became stronger. Just as Washington had defeated the British by refusing to engage in major actions, he now recommended that the country bide its time before asserting itself internationally:

> That we may be always prepared for War, but never unsheath the sword except in self-defence so long as Justice and our essential rights, and national respectability can be preserved without it; for without the gift of prophecy, it may safely be pronounced, that if this country can remain in peace 20 years longer: I devoutly pray that it may do so to the end of time; such in all probability will be its population, riches, and resources, when combined with its peculiarly happy and remote Situation from the other quarters of the globe, as to bid defiance, in a just cause, to any earthly power whatsoever.[19]

---

[18] 'Draft of the Farewell Address', Washington, op. cit., *supra* ch. 1, n.46, at 942.

[19] Ibid., at 945.

The actual Farewell Address, which Burton Kaufman described as a "statement of empire,"[20] developed these themes (with the notable omission of any limitation of the use of force to self-defense). Unity was the primary means to a great future:

> The Unity of Government which constitutes you one people is now also dear to you. It is justly so; for it is a main Pillar in the Edifice of your real independence; the support of your tranquility at home; your peace abroad; of your safety; of your prosperity; of that very Liberty which you so highly prize.[21]

Trade would be the major adhesive. The South would produce agricultural staples that would enhance Northern trade and manufacturing. Internal improvements would permit the West to trade with the East and benefit from the country's ever-increasing maritime power.[22] Washington dismissed any argument favoring state autonomy; only the entire people could change the Constitution through the amendment process.[23] The best way to protect the Union was to educate the populace so public opinion would remain enlightened. In his last Message to Congress, Washington spelled out his means in more detail. Congress should create a National University and a Military Academy to learn the "art of war." It should fund a strong navy to protect international commerce. Local institutions should be funded to provide needed information to farmers to improve agriculture. Differing from Hamilton, Washington recommended that the Country eliminate its debts as quickly as possible while maintaining its public credit.[24] Washington reminded his listeners that the greatest threats to the Union were internal. Reflecting the ideology of the era, he equated "party" and "faction," perceiving both as dangerous threats to unity. He warned against false patriotism or excessive loyalty to other countries, a clear signal to Federalists that they should not be too eager to court England's support and to Republicans that they should not glorify France. Most presciently, he dreaded sectional politics.

No longer shackled by the British or the Spanish, the new nation faced three fractures: party divisions, regional rivalries, and the festering slavery controversy. Within twenty years, Americans were able to resolve the problem of partisanship by accepting the legitimacy of two rival parties.

---

[20] Burton I. Kaufman, 'Washington's Farewell Address: A Statement of Empire', *To the Farewell Address: Ideas of Early American Foreign Policy* (Felix Gilbert, ed., Princeton, 1961).

[21] 'Farewell Address', Washington, op. cit., *supra* ch. 1, n.46, at 964.

[22] Ibid., at 965-66.

[23] Ibid., at 968.

[24] 'Eighth Annual Message to Congress', ibid., at 984.

The other party was not a venal faction, but merely a coalition to be defeated at the polls. During that same period, sectional rivalries would diminish because of widespread support for every section's expansionist agendas. But the slavery issue, an issue that cast a shadow over the Constitutional Convention and which appeared with some frequency during the Constitutional debates, would prove politically intractable. Thanks to the cotton gin and increased European demand, the South would also have its economic boom, ending the once widespread hope that slavery would eventually fade away.

Jefferson's triumph in purchasing Louisiana from Napoleon tends to overshadow his numerous other efforts to extend the nation's boundaries at the beginning of the Nineteenth Century. In a typically literary passage from his marvelous book on Jefferson's administration, Henry Adams described the relentless pressure of the average Western settler, a force that Jefferson continually encouraged. These families were not motivated by high ideals like the earlier Pilgrims of Plymouth, Puritans of Boston, and Quakers of Pennsylvania: "From Lake Erie to Florida, in long, unbroken line, pioneers were at work, cutting into the forests with the energy of so many beavers, and with no more express moral purpose than the beavers they drove away."[25] Jefferson knew that the steady increase in well-armed settlers was America's guarantee of ultimate success. Over the coming decades, none of the European countries could resist that combination of demographic, economic, and military force.

At the same time, the country quickly turned toward a more egalitarian political culture, rejecting the prerogatives of the gentlemen who had led the revolution.[26] The "shape" of the republic was altered from a mixed pattern of suffrage to a growing commitment to universal suffrage. At long last, the limited republicanism of Athens and England had been improved upon by a presumption of equality of full citizenship (at least for white males). Jefferson was not completely exaggerating when he described his electoral victory in 1800 as a second American revolution.[27] But overall, Jefferson's revolution was not very revolutionary. Henry Adams concluded that Jefferson's First Inaugural Address sounded like a speech by George Washington.[28] Most importantly, Jefferson retained many of Hamilton's Federalist institutions that he previously had condemned, most notably the National Bank and a powerful Treasury. Nevertheless, he sought to diminish the national debt and federal taxes by reducing the army and navy

---

[25] Adams, *Jefferson*, op. cit., *supra* Intro., n.14, at 121.

[26] Gordon S. Wood, *The Radicalism of the American Revolution* (New York, 1992), 271-86.

[27] Adams, *Jefferson*, op. cit., *supra* Intro., n.14, at 141.

[28] Ibid., at 139.

and avoiding war. His party eliminated the lower federal court judiciary that had been packed with Federalists, but failed in its effort to dominate the Supreme Court when the Senate would not impeach Justice Chase for many alleged improprieties, including fulminating to a grand jury about the dangers of universal suffrage. At least during his first Term, Jefferson's selective incorporation of Federalist principles overwhelmed the Federalist Party and left it fatally damaged. Jefferson's republican expansionism captured the mood and actions of the country far more than the New England Federalists' embittered caution, which feared that America's evolving form of republicanism was degenerating into a hopelessly unstable "democracy."[29]

Three months after his Inauguration, Jefferson was at war with Barbary pirates in North Africa. Ever willing to twist the knife into his ancestor's rival, Henry Adams noted that Jefferson used the same naval frigates to defeat the pirates that he had previously opposed while in Republican opposition.[30] This success, however, did not convince Jefferson to alter his Constitutional vision. He never supported a powerful seafaring navy, preferring instead local gunboats, a decision that would cost the Americans during the War of 1812.

In 1802, Ohio joined the Union as an equal State, but with a uniquely important condition. Jefferson's Secretary of State, the Pennsylvanian Albert Gallatin, included a contract obligating both the State of Ohio and the national government to raise money for public schools and internal improvements.[31] The Virginia Republicans did not impose their rigid States' rights theory on the Western Republican Gallatin, who sought to develop his State with the federal assistance. To a significant degree, Pennsylvania was the crucial swing state in national elections. The Virginians needed to keep the State in the Republican column. This law created two important "constitutional conventions." First, Congress did not have the power to admit new States as unequal partners but could place some conditions on their admission. In a few decades, anti-slavery members of Congress would rely on this precedent to attempt to exclude slavery from new States seeking to enter the Union. Second, Congress could authorize and fund internal improvements, a power Congress used to start constructing the Cumberland and National Road.[32] In other words, the

---

29 'Dangers', *1 Ames*, op. cit., *supra* ch. 1, n.61, at 141-44.

30 Adams, *Jefferson*, op. cit., *supra* Intro., n.14, at 165.

31 Ibid., at 205.

32 This decision did not create a stable constitutional convention. In 1817, James Madison vetoed a bill authorizing massive internal improvements even though he and Jefferson had overseen the construction of the National Road, James Madison, *Mind*, op. cit., *supra* ch. 1, n.39, at 307-09.

South was willing to compromise basic constitutional principles to form an alliance with the West which would so effectively isolate New England that its Federalist leaders eventually contemplated secession. According to Adams, the pivotal State of New York, another swing state, remained unruffled by these constitutional/political twists and turns because the New Yorkers had no constitutional principles at all: "New York was indifferent whether the nature of the United States was single or multiple, whether they were a nation or a league."[33] New York's wealth, size, and superior location guaranteed its future economic success and political power under virtually any system.

More ideologically intense Republicans such as the Virginians John Randolph and John Taylor of Caroline were not initially concerned about such compromises as national banks or Congressional support of internal improvements in newly admitted Ohio, because they were as eager to extend the Union as their Northwestern neighbors. They faced the rickety kingdom of Spain, whose control of the Floridas and Louisiana sealed off the rivers to the Gulf of New Mexico from the Americans by its control of Pensacola, Mobile, and New Orleans. Equally importantly, Spain held vast territory to the South and West.

Preaching the virtues of "liberty of commerce," "self-government," and castigating violations of "natural law," the Americans relentlessly pressured the Spanish and Indian occupants at both the national and local level: "Against Indians and Spaniards the Western settler held loose notions of law; his settled purpose was to drive both races from the country, and to take their land."[34] Once again, Henry Adams provided a vivid metaphor that demonstrates that one of the glories of the art of history is that it has not improved very much over time:

> In the end, far more than half the territory of the United States was the spoil of Spanish empire, rarely acquired with perfect propriety. To sum the story up in a single word, Spain had immense influence over the United States; but it was the influence of the whale over its captors, – the charm of a huge, helpless, and profitable victim.[35]

Lurking behind Spain was the far more serious threat of France, led by Napoleon. Although France had formally ceded control of Louisiana to Spain in 1763, it retained tremendous influence over both Spain and the colony. France's Minister for Foreign Affairs, Talleyrand, hoped to create French colonies that would simultaneously increase French power and

---

33 Adams, *Jefferson*, op. cit., *supra* Intro., n.14, at 79.

34 Ibid., at 230.

35 Ibid., at 231.

prevent American expansionism.[36] He bluntly described America's vast ambitions in terms that could be equally applied to his own actions: "[T]heir conduct ever since the moment of their independence is enough to prove this truth: the Americans are devoured by pride, ambition, and cupidity."[37] Talleyrand recommended to the Spanish Crown that it give France the Floridas and Louisiana to prevent further American depredations.[38] Fortunately for the Americans, Napoleon would continually get bogged down in European conflicts, running short of funds. Fortune also favored the Americans. Napoleon sent thousands of troops to their deaths in an exhausting effort to suppress the black revolution in Haiti.[39] Before a combination of yellow fever and guerilla warfare annihilated off his army,[40] Napoleon had planned to use Haiti as a springboard to send the army to Louisiana.[41] But this military failure did not completely deter Napoleon; he quickly forced a treaty on Spain that transferred Louisiana back to France. Although Jefferson initially "looked on with folded arms"[42] at Napoleon's savage[43] efforts to return slavery to Haiti, he quickly changed his mind once he accurately perceived that Napoleon threatened his continental vision. The possibility of formal French control of Louisiana evaporated Jefferson's pacifism: "The day that France takes possession of New Orleans fixes the sentence which is to restrain her forever within her low-water mark. It seals the union of two nations, who in conjunction can maintain exclusive possession of the ocean. From that moment we must marry ourselves to the British fleet and nation…"[44] Thus, just as Hamilton never considered returning any land to the British after the Revolution, so Jefferson was willing to form a British alliance to fight his beloved France. Jefferson even considered giving Louisiana to the British to cement the alliance.[45] Washington's fears that one party/faction would become the pawn of another country never materialized. A rumor that Spain had closed New Orleans to Mississippi trade raised tensions even higher. Tennessee and Kentucky predictably clamored for war. Many New England Federalists supported war, if only to embarrass the despised Jefferson into fighting France.[46]

---

36 Ibid., at 238-40.
37 Ibid., at 240.
38 Ibid., at 241.
39 Ibid., at 266.
40 Ibid., at 279.
41 Ibid., at 269.
42 Ibid., at 263.
43 Ibid., at 267.
44 Ibid., at 277.
45 Ibid., at 301.
46 Ibid., at 284.

Jefferson continued to pursue a peaceful resolution (just as Adams had refused to go to war against France during his Presidency). He sent James Monroe to Paris to purchase the land around New Orleans (as well as the Floridas, if France had actually obtained them from Spain) to guarantee Western access to the Mississippi River. Madison's instructions to Monroe reflected the Republican leadership's Enlightenment view of republican empires: All inhabitants would immediately be granted their basic civil rights to property and freedom of conscience.[47] Complete equality would soon follow: "To incorporate the inhabitants of the hereby ceded territory with the citizens of the United States on an equal footing, being a provision, which cannot now be made, it is to be expected, from the character and policy of the United States, that such incorporation shall take place without unnecessary delay."[48]

Every person has an imagined ranking of norms to help define his or her personal identity and provide guidance. Nobody is likely to know the actual set of priorities until several major norms collide in the course of resolving an important problem. Jefferson faced such a dilemma when Napoleon offered to sell to the United States a vast tract of land west of the Mississippi (far surpassing Jefferson's instructions to Monroe to purchase land around New Orleans and to gain the Floridas). Jefferson's quick confirmation of Monroe's bold decision revealed that his enduring desire to expand the country invariably prevailed over some of his most cherished constitutional and his republicanism beliefs. He justified the Purchase because he believed that expanding into new lands could only lengthen the American republic's existence; the alternative was population stagnation and concentration which would lead to anti-republican urbanization, misdistribution of wealth, corruption, and poverty.[49] For Jefferson, republicanism and expansionism were completely intertwined. Heavily influenced by the grim economist Malthus, who believed that the species would always consume its way into disastrous shortages, both Jefferson and Madison had a tragic conception of their empire. Their republic might last for two or three centuries, but it would inevitably corrode. The threat was not empire per se, but urban and industrial empire. At that point, the Constitution's structure could not prevent the average citizen, driven off the farm, from losing his independence and becoming a desperate pawn of the rich and powerful.

---

[47] 'Instructions to Robert B. Livingston and James Monroe' (March 2, 1803), Madison, *Mind*, op. cit., *supra* ch. 1, n.39, at 287.

[48] Ibid.

[49] *See, e.g.*, Drew R. McCoy, *The Elusive Republic: Political Economy in Jeffersonian America* (Chapel Hill, 1980).

Jefferson had little compunction in dealing with Napoleon, whom Jefferson believed to be a vicious tyrant who had subverted the inspiring political culture of France.[50] This opportunity bothered Jefferson because it clashed with his persistent advocacy of "strict construction" of federal powers under the Constitutional: The text failed to expressly provide the President and Congress with the power to buy (or even conquer) new Territories. As he explained in a letter: "our peculiar security is in possession of a written Constitution. Let us not make it a blank paper by construction."[51] Nevertheless, such "metaphysical subtleties" did not prevent Jefferson from "seizing the fugitive occurrence which so much advances the good of the country..."[52] He hoped that the People would amend the Constitution to provide such power in the future but concluded that such an amendment was not necessary since "the good sense of our country will correct the evil of *construction* when it shall produce ill effects."[53] He had widespread support from the more ideological wing of his party. John Randolph, who usually favored a very strict construction of federal powers, asserted during the debate over the Purchase that the Union had the right to annex Louisiana, Texas, Mexico, and even South America.[54]

At his third annual message to Congress, Jefferson proudly discussed the Louisiana Purchase,[55] despite bitter Federalist Party grumblings that he was being hypocritical in his constitutional interpretation of Executive Power. Three years later, he informed Congress that he had authorized Lewis and Clark to "survey" the Continent all the way to the Pacific. This "survey" was part of his plan to eventually extend the United States' sovereignty to the Pacific Ocean.[56] His instructions to Lewis about how to handle the Native Americans that Lewis would encounter effortlessly commingled self-interest, cultural superiority, and smug generosity:

> And considering the interest which every nation has in extending & strengthening the authority of reason & justice among the people around them, it will be useful to acquire what knowledge you can of the state of morality,

---

[50] Nor did he seem bothered about gaining title from an Emperor whose title was based upon the illegitimate doctrine of discovery, which violated the Native-Americans' natural rights.

[51] Letter from Thomas Jefferson to Wilson Cary Nicholas (Sept. 7, 1803), Jefferson, op. cit., *supra* ch. 1, n.29, at 1140.

[52] Letter from Thomas Jefferson to John C. Breckinridge (Aug. 12, 1803), ibid., at 1138-39.

[53] Letter from Thomas Jefferson to Wilson Cary Nichols (Sept. 7, 1803), ibid., at 1141.

[54] Adams, *Jefferson*, op. cit., *supra* Intro., n.14, at 308.

[55] 'Third Annual Message', Jefferson, ibid., at 511-12 (Oct. 17, 1803).

[56] 'Sixth Annual Message', ibid., at 527 (Dec. 2, 1806).

religion & information among them, as it may better enable those who endeavor to civilize & instruct them, to adapt their measures to the existing notions & practices of those on whom they are to operate.[57]

Upon completion of the Louisiana Purchase, Jefferson needed to create some form of provisional government for the huge Territory, which doubled the size of the United States. With broad Congressional permission, Jefferson appointed a governor and created a non-elected council, called "The Assembly of Notables."[58] He distrusted the large number of Creoles, mulattos, and other non-Anglicans then living in the vast new Territory.[59] His non-representative form of government eventually "would make the majority American, & make it an American instead of a French State."[60] When a delegation of citizens came to Washington to complain about this completely nonrepublican mode of government, Jefferson told a correspondent: "our new fellow citizens are as yet incapable of self-government as children, yet some cannot bring themselves to suspend [republican] principles for a single moment."[61] Four years later, he discussed "enlisting 30,000 volunteers, Americans by birth, to be carried at the public expense & settled immediately on a bounty of 160 acres each, on the west side of the Mississippi..."[62] In other words, Jefferson's cherished belief in equal, republican governments throughout an empire, a position he and Franklin had turned into the major constitutional premise justifying the American Revolution, was sacrificed to his desire to expand Westward and his fear of non-Anglicans. The fundamental doctrine of taxation without representation could be delayed until a region became sufficiently "homogenous," that is, until Anglo-Americans had supplanted Creoles as the majority in the new Territory.[63] The American Revolutionary model was altered, at least for several years, into the Athenian-Anglican system of double standards for different parts of an

---

[57] Jefferson, 'Instructions to Captain Lewis' (June 20, 1803), ibid., at 1128.

[58] Quoted from Joseph J. Ellis, *American Sphinx: The Character OF Thomas Jefferson* (New York, 1997), 210.

[59] Ibid., at 211.

[60] Letter from Thomas Jefferson to John Dickinson (Jan. 13, 1807), Jefferson, op. cit., ibid., at 1170. Jefferson never wanted massive immigration, particularly from countries like France: "Is it not safer to wait with patience 27 years and three months longer, for the attainment of any degree of population desired, or expected? May not our government be more homogeneous, more peaceable, more durable?" 'Notes on the State of Virginia', ibid., at 212.

[61] Quoted in Ellis, op. cit., *supra* ch. 4, n.58, at 211.

[62] Letter from Thomas Jefferson to John Dickinson (Jan. 13, 1807), Jefferson, op. cit., ibid., at 1170.

[63] Ellis, op. cit., ibid., at 211.

empire, a system premised upon assumptions of racial and ethnic superiority.

Many Federalists predictably opposed the Purchase. Fisher Ames caustically described the amount of discretion Jefferson provided for himself:

> The Romans, in the days of their degeneracy and corruption, set no more bounds to their favor than to their resentments. While Pompey was their idol, they conferred unlimited authority upon him over all the Mediterranean sea, and four hundred stadia (about forty-five miles) within land. We in like manner devolve on Mr. Jefferson the absolute and uncontrolled dominion of Louisiana. It was thus the Romans were made by their own vote familiar with arbitrary power.[64]

For Ames, Jefferson's maneuver was a classic example of Executive corruption: "[Jefferson's administration] has unconstitutionally annexed to the United States an empire, as a fund for patronage, and in which executive despotism is established by law."[65] In one of those ironic twists of position that makes one wonder what role abstract, ideological beliefs actually play in most political disputes, Ames, the Federalist, sounded like an Anti-Federalist relying upon Montesquieu: "Our country is too big for union, too sordid for patriotism, too democratic for liberty."[66] The New England Federalists understood that the expansion would benefit the South while providing nothing for them. This regionally based dispute raised the first serious threat to the Union. At the Hartford Convention, three groups of New England, Federalist State legislators met but refused to act. Along with many other senior Federalist leaders, Alexander Hamilton consistently opposed such efforts: "Dismembering our empire will be a clear sacrifice of great positive advantages, without any counterbalancing good; administering no relief to our real disease, which is *democracy*, – the poison of which, by a subdivision, will only be more concentrated in each part, and consequent more virulent."[67] The most immediate effect was to tarnish many of the Federalists' patriotism, just as their opposition to the Purchase had weakened the country's faith in their judgment. There were a few tentative reservations with Jefferson's own party, even in the South. John Taylor of Caroline, a Republican theorist who maintained a vibrant correspondence with Jefferson, wrote a pamphlet, *A Defence of the Administration of Thomas Jefferson*, that praised the expansion for its benefits to republicanism but found constitutional problems in Jefferson's

---

64 'Monitor', *1 Ames*, op. cit., *supra* ch. 1, n.61, at 225-26.
65 'The Republican I', ibid., at 87.
66 Quoted in Adams, *Jefferson*, op. cit., *supra* Intro., n.14, at 59.
67 Ibid., at 428.

purchase and in the conditions Jefferson established for controlling Louisiana after the purchase.[68]

Jefferson's double standard extended beyond republicanism to racism. He proposed two Constitutional Amendments. The first standard declared "the provinces of Louisiana is incorporated into the United States and made part thereof." The second limited citizenship in the new land to white inhabitants only: "Its white inhabitants shall be citizens, and stand, as to their rights and obligations, on the same footing as other citizens in analogous situations."[69] Jefferson's commitment to goals other than republicanism had immediate consequences. Jefferson's unwillingness to create a republican form of government in newly purchased Louisiana infuriated many powerful Westerners, particularly the elite in New Orleans. Other Westerners, such as Andrew Jackson, impatiently wanted to resolve remaining Native-American problems by moving them West of the Mississippi. They had none of Jefferson's reluctance to use force, internally or externally. Where Jefferson periodically saw noble Indians, Jackson perceived dangerous obstacles to future white supremacy. This unsettled atmosphere enticed Aaron Burr to attempt to lead a revolution in the West against Jefferson,[70] a ludicrous effort that oddly attracted Jackson's sympathy, if not direct engagement. Jefferson's reaction was almost whimsical. At first, he did nothing to stop Burr's conspiracy, but later became enraged when Chief Justice John Marshall baited him by dismissing the federal government's treason charges against Burr on the ground of prosecutorial incompetence.

Jefferson was not completely hypocritical about his republicanism. His Northwest Ordinance of 1787 had not immediately granted legislative rights to American citizens living in the newly settled lands; each State must first reach a certain level of population. Nor did he want these new lands to remain in perpetual subordination. They would become equal states as soon as they had an adequate Anglo-American population. Republicanism would protect not only Americans, who were steadily increasing in numbers, but also Indians. Ever the Deist, Jefferson did not turn to religion to justify his pursuit of empire. Nor did he seek war, with its attendant strains on Republican virtues. He preferred to purchase property at bargain prices from the Native-Americans and countries like France and Spain. The new lands could grow and then enter the Union as new, equal States via compact.

Jefferson's method of expanding the empire through purchase was quite consistent with his Enlightenment norms and Revolutionary ideology,

---

68 M.E. Bradford, 'Introduction', in John Taylor, *Arator* 24-25 (Indianapolis, 1977).

69 Quoted in *Downes v. Bidwell*, 182 U.S. 244, 253 (1900).

70 Adams, Jefferson, op. cit., *supra* Intro., n.14, at 526-27.

if not with his belief that the Constitution's grants of federal power should be strictly construed. In 1789, the year the Constitution was ratified, David Ramsay explained that the Revolution could be understood as a dispute over who had ultimate title to the New World.[71] After the discovery of the New World, all the European Kings claimed the two continents through the doctrine of "discovery," which held that only Christian Kings held proper title to their lands.[72] Consequently, these Kings could legally extend their authority over all Heathens. The "divine right of kings" thus not only legitimated domestic power but also the use of force abroad. Under this doctrine, the English King (and later the King-in-Parliament) had complete authority over all the lands. The colonists did not have any independent property rights, simply because they did not completely own the property that they controlled and cultivated.

According to Ramsay, the American Colonist maintained that the doctrine of discovery was contrary to the natural rights of all mankind: "He believed that God made all mankind originally equal: That he endowed them with the rights of life, property, and as much liberty as was consistent with the rights of others."[73] The Colonists obtained original title by purchasing these lands from the Native-Americans, who had pre-existing, valid natural rights to their property: "[P]olicy as well as justice led the colonists to purchase and pay for what they occupied."[74] Consequently, the King's charters did not provide full title; they only gave the Colonists permission to buy the lands from the natives.[75] The relationship between the Colonies and King was fundamentally contractual, not subordinate. According to the colonial theory of title, the Americans had the vested property right in the land, not the King (much less Parliament, which gained most of its power long after the New World was claimed, seized, and settled). Because the colonists had developed their lands on their own, they had exclusive title via purchase or conquest. From this perspective, the American Revolution was a legal/political/military debate over land titles: "The slavish doctrine of the divine right of kings, and the corruptions of christianity, by undervaluing heathen titles, favored [the English position]."[76]

---

71 Although Ramsay's history had been criticized for excessive bias, it does reflect American beliefs at the time of the Constitution, and, to a lesser extent, before and during the Revolution.

72 Ramsay, *1 History*, op. cit., *supra* ch. 1, n.92, at 3-6.

73 Ibid., at 30.

74 Ibid., at 17.

75 Ibid., at 16.

76 Ramsay, *2 History*, ibid., at 312.

Although Ramsay did not mention Locke, he also implicitly rejected the Lockean argument that the King or any other European had title in these lands simply because the Native Americans had not cultivated them. Under Locke's theory, Indians had no landed property rights because they were primitive savages who lived in a "waste." Locke conceded that the Indian who "knows no enclosure," has a right to any "fruit or venison" he might find, but has no right to landed property rights because one can only gain property rights through labor and cultivation.[77] Whatever its theoretical validity, Locke's theory did not apply to the actual facts. Ramsay noted that Native-Americans had extensively cultivated land,[78] echoing the delight expressed by a Virginian in 1622 after they savagely suppressed an Indian uprising: "wee shall enjoy their cultivated places... Now their cleared grounds in all their villages (which are situate in the fruitfullest places of the land) shall be inhabited by us, whereas heretofore the grubbing of woods was the greatest labour."[79] More importantly to the Revolutionaries, the Lockean view conflicted with their ambitions and ideals. As with the doctrine of "discovery," the English King would remain the ultimate property-owner because the indolent Indians would have had no property rights when the Crown first claimed these lands. The colonists would not have gained their fully vested rights by purchase or conquest.

Thus, the Americans used Locke selectively to justify their shift in political allegiance. Although Locke's basic theory did not determine original title, the Americans invoked him as authority for their revolution to protect the property rights that they had properly (and exclusively) gained from the Native-Americans through their land deals (that were often marred with swindling or double-dealing with selected, compliant Indians at the expense of others).[80] That revolutionary ideology/history also omits much. In colony after colony, the colonists relied on armed violence, poison, the destruction of crops, and even dogs to destroy local Native American communities.[81] Contemplate the following description of a massacre of hundreds of Pequot Indians, later remembered by Cotton Mather as a "barbeque":

---

[77] John Locke, *The Second Treatise of Government* 288, 290 (Peter Laslett, ed) Cambridge (1988).

[78] Of course, it is possible that Ramsay did not accurately describe the Revolutionary debate and/or that Jefferson did not hold these particular views. Nevertheless, Ramsay's book was well received, a popular interpretation of the American Revolution, which favored national unity.

[79] Quoted in Jennings, op. cit., *supra* Intro., n.19, at 26.

[80] Ibid., at 38.

[81] Stannard, op. cit., *supra* ch. 1, n.7, at 104-118.

> It was a fearful sight to see them thus frying in the fire and the streams of blood quenching the same, and horrible was the stink and stench thereof; but the victory seemed a sweet sacrifice, and they gave the praise thereof to God, who had wrought so wonderfully for them, thus to enclose their enemies in their hands and give them so speedy a victory over so proud and insulting an enemy.[82]

De Tocqueville summed up this peculiar American blend of law and violence: "[T]he conduct of the United States toward the natives is characterized... by a singular attachment to the formalities of law... It was impossible to destroy men with more respect for the laws of humanity."[83] As usual, he captured the uniquely democratic aspects of American imperial expansionism: "[I]t is the misfortune of Indians to be brought into contact with a civilized people, who are also (it must be owned) the most grasping nation on the globe..."[84] Although the federal government was generally not as ruthless as the Southern States,[85] "the rapacity of the settlers is usually backed by the tyranny of the government."[86] Two examples of the federal government's relatively humane approach were sections in the 1817 and 1819 treaties with the Cherokee Indians granting land rights to those "who may wish to become citizens of the United States."[87]

Jefferson was not satisfied with his dazzling geopolitical triumph in Louisiana, an achievement that the American people validated at the polls by reelecting Jefferson and crippling the Federalist Party. Jefferson continued his grand design to expand the American empire through purchasing territory (with the threat of force lurking in the background) from other sellers in dire straits. He consistently looked south to Florida:

> We have some claims, to extend on the sea cast Westwardly to the Rio Norte or Bravo, and better to go Eastwardly to the Rio Perdido... These claims will be a subject of negociation with Spain, and if, as soon as she is at war, we push them strongly with one hand, holding out a price in the other, we shall certainly obtain the Floridas, and all in good time.[88]

---

82 Ibid., at 114.

83 De Tocqueville, *1 Democracy*, op. cit., *supra* ch. 1, n.192, at 369.

84 Ibid.

85 Ibid., at 366.

86 Ibid., at 364.

87 James Kettner, *The Development of American Citizenship, 1680-1870* (Chapel Hill, 1978).

88 Letter from Thomas Jefferson to John C. Breckinridge (Aug. 12, 1803), Jefferson, op. cit., *supra* ch. 1, n.29, at 1137.

Napoleon's willingness to sell any residual Spanish interests to Louisiana whetted Jefferson's appetite for the Floridas, which still remained under Spanish control. Bonaparte made it clear that he would once again betray Spain, just as he had by pocketing all the money from the Louisiana Purchase. A frustrated Talleyrand, who had wanted to colonize Louisiana, intimated French indifference to Livingston about the scope of the purchase: "You have made a noble bargain for yourselves, and I suppose you will make the most of it."[89] Livingston wasted no time, arguing that the Americans had bought the Floridas as well as Louisiana, even though both France and the United States knew their agreement did not include the Floridas.[90] Livingston offered a simple solution should Spain not agree with this aggressive interpretation of the Louisiana Purchase: "The moment is so favorable for taking possession of that country that I hope it has not been neglected, even though a little force should be necessary to effect it."[91] Monroe, Madison, and Jefferson were all receptive to Livingston's claims. Jefferson soon publicly demanded the Floridas. He hoped to move when Spain would again become embroiled in European conflict.[92] He accused Spain of acting in bad faith when it protested that the French had no authority to transfer the Floridas to the United States via the Louisiana Purchase, even though everyone knew that the Floridas had been explicitly excluded.[93] Their Southern allies eagerly supported the three leading Virginians, all of whom would be President. Once again, John Randolph discarded any Old Republican inclinations toward strict constitutional construction and nonviolence. Always flamboyant, Randolph made a speech that could not have been more insulting to Spain: "We have not only obtained the command of the mouth of the Mississippi, but of the Mobile, with its widely extended branches, and there is not now a single stream of note rising within the United States and falling into the Gulf of Mexico which is not entirely our own, Appalochicola excepted."[94]

Charles Pinckney, the South Carolinian minister in Madrid, bullied Spain so aggressively that he embarrassed Jefferson into recalling him. The continual American arrogance provoked a counteraction. Louis Marie Turreau, the new French minister to the United States, wrote back to Talleyrand: "These people here have been well spoiled; it is time to send

89 Adams, *Jefferson*, op. cit., *supra* Intro., n.14, at 350.
90 Ibid., 331.
91 Ibid., at 350-51.
92 Ibid., at 469.
93 Ibid., at 473.
94 Ibid., at 473-74.

them back to their proper place."[95] Talleyrand expressed similar concerns in a response to Turreau, by observing that the Americans would stretch the uncertain western boundaries of the Louisiana Purchase to "the American coast that lies north of California," thereby aggressively construing the doctrine of "contiguity"[96] to create another threat to Spain.[97] Bonaparte, who once again needed Spanish support for his imperial plans, effortlessly shifted his support back to Spain.[98] Although the French switch effectively blunted Jefferson's goal of immediately gaining the Floridas, the French support was luke-warm. Talleyrand explained to the Spanish that the Louisiana Purchase arguably included the entire region of Texas.[99]

Jefferson's policies and statements never created a completely coherent pattern at the tactical level, only at the grand level of the pursuit of empire. Angered by Napoleon's duplicity, which, of course, was no different in kind than his own, and distressed by Napoleon's transformation of the French Republic into an Empire, Jefferson next turned to England. He first reassured the English diplomat that he was not interested in Canada, only the Spanish territories. Although the English impressment of American sailors was a problem, he conceded that Americans had exacerbated the problem by hiring so many sailors from the English navy. For example, Virginia passed a law authorizing the death penalty against any magistrate who returned English deserters or criminals, a particularly provocative law because many of the impressed sailors had been recent deserters from English ships. Without impressment, England's navy would deteriorate.[100] Jefferson would threaten France with force and with the possibility of an English alliance, but he never was willing to fight Napoleon. While some of his Virginia colleagues would became quite bellicose, Jefferson retained his Enlightenment commitment to peace (as well as the Washingtonian assessment that time was on the side of the United States). He was unwilling to spend the money and change the country's political culture to expand the army and navy. Indeed, at the very moment he contemplated war with France, he proposed laying all seven frigates up in dry-dock.[101] He began his second administration by recommending to the Cabinet that the Federal Government actively support internal improvements and set up a "war fund" that would allow the government to fight large wars without

95 Ibid., at 487.
96 Ibid., at 505.
97 Ibid., at 501.
98 Ibid., at 489.
99 Ibid., at 504.
100 Ibid., at 535.
101 Ibid., at 558.

borrowing money.[102] In 1805, he anticipated using a reserve fund for "canals, roads, colleges, etc."[103]

After continuing French and Spanish resistance to obtain the Floridas for the United States frustrated Jefferson, he turned to Texas, where his country's claim to title under the Louisiana Purchase was stronger. Once again, his subordinates did not share his reluctance to use war as a tool of diplomacy. Jefferson's emissary to France, John Armstrong, suggested a straightforward solution to a sympathetic James Monroe just before Monroe sailed to Madrid to commence negotiations: "It is simply to take a strong and prompt possession of the northern bank of the Rio Bravo, leaving the eastern limit *in status quo*. A stroke of this kind would at once bring Spain to reason, and France to her rescue, and without giving either room to quarrel. You might then negotiate, and shape the bargain pretty much as you pleased."[104] Jefferson refused to take their advice in August of 1805, preferring to write self-righteous complaints to his next envoy to Spain, James Bowdoin. These grumblings suggest that Jefferson either had a terrible memory and could not recall his efforts to extend the Louisiana Purchase to the Floridas or that he could effortlessly slip from cool calculation to sentimental bombast:

> Our relations with [Spain] are vitally interesting. That they should be of a peaceable and friendly character has been our most earnest desire. Had Spain met us with the same disposition, our idea that her existence on this hemisphere and ours should have rested on the same bottom, should have swum or sunk together. We want nothing of hers, and we want no other nation to possess what is hers; but she has met our advances with jealousy, secret malice, and ill-faith. Our patience under this unworthy return of disposition is now on its last trial, and the issue of what is now depending between us will decide whether our relations with her are to be sincerely friendly or permanently hostile.[105]

A few months later, Jefferson cheerfully described the outcome of any war with Spain to the British. After the United States strengthened its navy, it could easily conquer the Floridas and Cuba.[106] Jefferson's admiration for Indians was equally conditional. In 1807, he ordered his Secretary of State to meet any resistance to white expansion with force:

> And… if we ever are constrained to lift the hatchet against any tribe, we will never lay it down until that tribe is exterminated, or is driven beyond the

---

102 Ibid., at 604-605.
103 Ibid., at 615.
104 Ibid., at 628.
105 Ibid., at 641.
106 Ibid., at 673.

> Mississippi * * * [I]n war, they will kill some of us; we shall destroy all of them.[107]

A rightfully cynical Talleyrand saw through the bluster and the false pieties without minimizing the effects of ever-increasing American power. Because the Americans had a weak "military constitution," they could not and would not presently go to war. One might initially think that such a pacific policy would fail, but the United States would ultimately rule the continent: "To conquer without war is the first fact of their politics."[108] His correspondent Turreau was even more blunt: "France has, and will ever have, nothing to hope from the dispositions of a people that conceives no idea of glory, of grandeur, of justice; that shows itself the constant enemy of liberal principles; and that is disposed to suffer every kind of humiliation, provided it can satisfy both its sordid avarice and its projects of usurpation over the Floridas."[109] Jefferson would continue this policy throughout the remainder of his second administration. Because the French and Spanish continued to call his military bluffs and Spain refused his offer to purchase the Floridas and concede that the Louisiana Purchase extended to Colorado,[110] Jefferson's territorial ambitions were never fulfilled after the initial success of the Louisiana Purchase. Perhaps the closest Jefferson came to another diplomatic victory was when Napoleon once again betrayed Spain by offering Jefferson the Floridas if he would go to war against Britain.[111]

Of course, Jefferson and his countrymen did not know that they would have no more expansionist victories after the Louisiana Purchase. Sectional rivalries resurfaced, creating another roadblock to further effective action. Jefferson's easy reelection in 1804 confirmed the Louisiana Purchase, and demonstrated that a vast majority of Americans endorsed westward expansion (as if there were anything they could have done in opposition to the continued massive migration).

In 1806, Jacob Crowninshield, a Federalist Massachusetts member of the House of Representatives, expressed both outrage and aggressiveness when complaining about continuing English impressment of American sailors (many of whom had deserted from the English navy). Were the practice to continue, America should consider war. Great Britain would back down: "Our trade is too valuable to her. She knows, too, that in such an event she will lose her eastern provinces; the States of Vermont and

---

107 Quoted in Stannard, op. cit., *supra* ch. 1, n.7, at 120.
108 Adams, *Jefferson*, op. cit., *supra* Intro., n.14, at 661.
109 Ibid., at 1023.
110 Ibid., at 676.
111 Ibid., at 1129.

Massachusetts will ask no other assistance than their own militia to take Canada and Nova Scotia. Some of her West Indian islands will also fall."[112] Reflecting the views of many Southern Republicans who were uneasy with Jefferson's continual drift toward a more centralized form of government, an inflamed John Randolph used more provocative rhetoric than usual to repudiate Crowninshield's militarism: "It is mere waste of time to reason with such persons; they do not deserve anything like serious refutation. The proper arguments for such statesmen are a strait-waistcoat, a dark room, water-gruel, and depletion."[113] But Randolph did not stop there. He dramatically broke with Jefferson, who still tended to favor Napoleon, because Randolph believed that Napoleon, not England, had become the real threat to "the human race."[114] Compulsively opposed to Jefferson, the New England wing Federalist Party continued to assert its reservations about the Louisiana Purchase, much less Jefferson's relentless pursuit of the Floridas.

Despite these growing party and sectional differences, the Jefferson administration never vacillated in its commitment to a continental empire. When relations with England deteriorated even more during 1807, the Pennsylvanian Albert Gallatin described to his wife the plan formulated at a Cabinet meeting. The governors of the States would raise one hundred thousand militia to "have the portions of the sea-coast ready for any emergency; and for those in the North we may look to a winter expedition against Canada."[115] According to a French envoy, Jefferson was even more blunt: "If the English do not give us the satisfaction we demand, we will take Canada, which wants to enter the Union; and when, together with Canada, we shall have the Floridas, we shall no longer have any difficulties with our neighbors."[116] In short, the way to eliminate problems with neighbors is to conquer them. Similar tensions with Spain once again drove Jefferson to seek an alliance with Napoleon: "We expect, therefore, from the friendship of the Emperor that he will either compel Spain to do us justice or abandon her to us. We ask but one month to be in possession of the city of Mexico."[117] Machiavelli's warnings to those who live near powerful republics were being consistently verified.

Jefferson was also a Machiavellian Republican in his commitment to global republicanism. Although the Declaration of Independence had been addressed to all mankind and Jefferson and his country had justified many

---

[112] Ibid., at 711.
[113] Ibid.
[114] Ibid., at 713.
[115] Ibid., at 949.
[116] Ibid., at 952.
[117] Ibid., at 904.

of their actions based upon the "self-evident" justice of republicanism, Jefferson felt no obligation to support reform abroad. When the Spanish people revolted against Napoleon, gaining support throughout Europe, America remained the Emperor's most loyal ally.[118] Indeed, the revolution weakened Spain even more, increasing the Americans' hopes that they would gain the Floridas at the least possible cost.[119] More often than not, Presidents Jefferson and Madison based their foreign policy hopes on a victorious Napoleon. Even when Napoleon posed a threat before the Louisiana Purchase, most Southerners supported his genocidal efforts to suppress the slave rebellion in Haiti. The "empire of freedom" was for white Americans only.

Finally, two technological changes facilitated the Jeffersonian vision of a continental power. First, the cotton gin rejuvenated the slave economy, encouraging the Southerners to look South and West. Second, Robert Fulton's steamboat enabled Americans to extend their culture far more deeply into the continent.[120] Soon they would be able to ship goods up the Mississippi against its powerful current. Where Jefferson once dreamed of a hemisphere of related republics, it was now possible to imagine a far larger single nation. Protecting, regulating, taxing, trading, and communicating with outlying areas would not be insurmountable barriers.

---

118 Ibid., at 1134.
119 Ibid., at 1141.
120 Ibid., at 1019.

5 The Republican Empire of Conquest

A. Madison's Gradual Shift to a Hamiltonian Constitution

James Madison, never as ideological or sentimental as his close friend Thomas Jefferson, was far more willing to use force to achieve his country's objectives. Jefferson's Republican/Enlightenment constraints of "compact and purchase," limits that Jefferson would have been willing to waive if necessary, quickly became dated. A wave of religious enthusiasm, which changed the belief structure of many Americans, provided another justification for expansion: Americans had an obligation not just to civilize Native Americans, but also to save their souls and spread righteous Christianity throughout the hemisphere. Of course, those who did not want their souls saved might need to be dispensed with. God (or at least Providence) was particularly supportive of the American cause; the "divine right of kings" became the "divine right of Americans." Nor did the country retain its republican squeamishness about war and glory. The political movement that would in a few decades be known as "Manifest Destiny"[1] supplanted Jefferson's Republican Empire premised upon Enlightenment values. Many other Americans did not want to save the souls of Jefferson's "noble savages"; they sought to eliminate the race. Continued expansion in the West enhanced the political power of the Scotch-Irish, whom David Hackett Fisher has described as a particularly crude and violent group whose basic consciousness was formed by the constant wars along the borders of England and Scotland. Andrew Jackson emerged as their leader, eventually supplanting the Virginian gentlemen's Enlightenment norms with his much more ruthless imperial vision.

---

[1] John O'Sullivan coined the phrase "Manifest Destiny" in 1845, Anders Stephanson, *Manifest Destiny: American Expansion and the Empire of Right* (New York, 1995), xi. Another famous phrase, Horace Greeley's "Go West, Young Man," also came centuries after the fact.

One of James Madison's first Presidential actions was to disavow Jefferson's well-known desire for additional territory. The French Minister Turreau reported to his superiors what he heard from Madison's representative, Albert Gallatin: "We are and we wish to be strangers to all that passes in the Floridas, in Mexico, and also in Cuba. You would be mistaken if you supposed that Mr. Madison wishes the possession of Florida. That was Mr. Jefferson's hobby..."[2] Gallatin explained that the new administration did not wish to become entangled in French and Spanish politics. Subsequent events, particularly the American invasions of the Floridas, demonstrate that Madison's disclaimer was designed to gain desperately needed maneuvering room during the Napoleonic Wars. First of all, he and Jefferson continued their friendship and correspondence; Madison was not about to repudiate Jefferson's ambitions. But such plans could wait, partially because the two Virginians still preferred France to England, a political prejudice that can be traced back to the American and French Revolutions. In addition, Madison and Jefferson's favorite foreign policy tool, commercial "coercion" via an embargo, had been very unpopular at home and had not stopped either the French or the English from continually seizing and even burning American ships. Yet neither Jefferson nor Madison was willing to take the next obvious step: significantly increasing the navy and army to prevent these depredations and increase options for expansion.

One of the great ironies of this period of American history is that Jefferson and Madison, who disliked northern industry, created the opportunity for that industry to develop through their unpopular, sporadically effective embargo against England to force England to repeal its oppressive trade regulations.[3] This burst of manufacturing so strengthened the northern economy that it attracted most of the country's specie capital, adding yet another source of power. Although the remaining Federalists gloated over the eventual collapse of the embargo and the Pennsylvania legislature even authorized their Governor to use state troops to block the enforcement of a Supreme Court decree,[4] the country was slowly coalescing into a more unified force. The "era of good feelings" began when all three sections recognized that there was enough for everyone. For many years, most Americans spoke reverently of the Union and its Founders.[5] Henry Adams marked Senator Henry Clay's maiden speech to the Senate on February 22, 1810, as the "beginning of an epoch":

---

2 Quoted in Henry Adams, *History of the United States of America During the Administration of James Madison* (Earl N. Harbert wrote notes, New York, 1986), 30.

3 Ibid., at 19.

4 Ibid., at 14-15.

5 Ibid., at 135.

> The conquest of Canada is in your power. I trust I shall not be deemed presumptuous when I state that I verily believe that the militia of Kentucky are alone competent to place Montreal and Upper Canada at your feet... The withered arm and wrinkled brow of the illustrious founders of our freedom are melancholy indications that they will shortly be removed from us. Their deeds of glory and reknown will then be felt only through the cold medium of the historic page; we shall want the presence and living example of a new race of heroes to supply their places, and to animate us to preserve inviolate what they achieved...[6]

Henry Clay did not have to wait for "a new race of heroes" to make the transition[7] from shrewd Jeffersonian negotiations to military aggression. The founder James Madison, who once argued in *The Federalist* that that the Federal government would remain small because there was little likelihood of war, invaded Western Florida a few months after Clay spoke. Madison thereby demonstrated that he also enjoyed Jefferson's "hobby" of American expansionism. Revolutions and unrest from Mexico to Venezuela battered the Spanish Empire, a "friend" of the United States at the time.[8] It had a miniscule military presence in the colony. A group of American settlers in Western Florida easily overran the main Spanish fortress at Baton Rouge. They then announced to the world that they were a "free and independent State."[9] The rebellious Americans asked the Madison administration to be admitted into the Union, but only on the condition that they retain title to all public lands because they were "the people of this Commonwealth, who have wrested the government and country from Spain at the risk of their lives and fortunes."[10]

Madison had several alternatives: doing nothing, aiding the rebels, aiding Spain, seizing West Florida, or waiting until Congress could meet in six weeks and declare War.[11] In a letter to Jefferson, Madison acknowledged that he was violating a general understanding, a "constitutional convention" that had been part of the United States' military constitution, that the Executive could not start a war except during an emergency.[12] In addition, the Constitution failed to explicitly give the Executive the right to begin a war for conquest. Furthermore, the United States and Spain had previously agreed to resolve peacefully the ultimate status of this land. Despite these constitutional and ethical constraints,

---

6 Ibid., at 144.
7 Ibid., at 215.
8 Ibid., at 213.
9 Ibid., at 215.
10 Ibid.
11 Ibid.
12 Ibid., at 217.

Madison redefined and expanded Executive power within the "military constitution" by ordering William Claiborne, Governor of the Territory of Orleans, to use the Federal Army to take permanent control of West Florida. Madison ignored the victorious rebels' claims that they had created an independent State, which gave them title to public lands. Claiborne was instructed to defeat all local resistance while avoiding direct conflict with any Spanish forces.[13] The Spanish futilely protested the seizure. Madison did not fear the French because Napoleon had recently waved the entire Western Hemisphere in front of him: "I am in no way opposed to the Floridas becoming an American possession; that I desire, in general, whatever can favor the independence of Spanish America."[14] The Americans explained to the French that they needed to invade Florida to prevent the English from seizing it: "whether our pretensions are well-founded or not, your interest, like ours, requires us to oppose the enterprises of England in that country."[15] The British, not widely renowned for their punctilious foreign policy, piously queried:

> Would it not have been worthy of the generosity of a free nation like this, bearing, as it doubtless does, a respect for the rights of a gallant people at this moment engaged in a noble struggle for its liberty, – would it not have been an act on the part of this country dictated by the sacred ties of good neighborhood and friendship which exist between it and Spain, to have simply offered its assistance to crush the common enemy of both, rather than to have made such interference the pretext for wresting a province from a friendly Power, and that at a time of her adversity?[16]

When one English diplomat asked Secretary of State Monroe how much Spanish territory the United States planned to obtain, Monroe simply laughed.[17]

The invasion of West Florida was the first of several decisions that James Madison and a majority of Republican Congressmen made over several years that so altered the federal government's form, choice of means, and methods of constitutional interpretation that Henry Adams concluded they created a "new Constitution."[18] The Republican Congressmen were as eager to change constitutional traditions as Madison. In a secret session, the Eleventh Congress ratified both the transition from expansion through purchase to expansion through military aggression and

---

13 Ibid., at 218.
14 Ibid., at 266.
15 Ibid., at 219.
16 Ibid., at 220.
17 Ibid., at 322.
18 Ibid., at 227.

the new assertion of Executive Power by giving the President discretion to enter East Florida either with the consent of local authority or upon invasion by a foreign power.[19] Congress then passed a secret law that gave George Mathews latitude in determining when to take territory in East Florida, particularly Mobile and Fernandina, a town on Amelia Island that attracted British smugglers who sought to avoid the Non-importation Act. Mathews observed that the Eastern Floridians, unlike their Western counterparts, did not have enough arms to start a revolt. On March 19, 1812, he solved this problem by sending two hundred "insurgents," supported by American gunboats, to take over Amelia Island.[20] The Spanish commander of the garrison capitulated once he was told the gunboats would join in any conflict. After "independence" was declared, the local residents asked to become part of the Union.[21] Mathews was surprised when the Madison administration criticized his victory as an action beyond the scope of his authority; Mathews understandably could see no significant difference between the conquest of West and East Florida. In another secret session, Congress authorized Madison to take control of both Floridas, but Madison decided on a more fictional approach. In a public letter, Secretary of State Monroe ordered the governor of Georgia to dismiss Mathews and return all of East Florida to Spain. But in a separate letter to the governor, Monroe ordered him to keep "the ground occupied" to protect the troops' safety, which the governor properly interpreted as a mandate to retain complete control of Amelia Island to prevent additional British smuggling.[22] Thus the American Republic became more monarchical in spirit and form; Presidents and even individual generals could start offensive wars without public debate or Congressional authorization.

Madison's latest thrusts for empire did not go unopposed. Disenchanted with the evolutionary Jefferson-Madison republicanism which more and more resembled the Hamiltonian vision, the Virginian John Randolph reverted to "Old Republican" strict constructionism. According to Randolph, the Federal government did not have the constitutional power to invade Florida. Randolph's opposition would prove to be a rare example of a leading politician's opposing the expansion of empire in an area that would benefit his region (even though Randolph had earlier supported other aggressive actions). The resistance from some diehard New England Federalists was more widespread, revealing once again how the Federalists' abiding hatred of the Virginian Presidents drove

---

19 Ibid., at 228.
20 Ibid., at 459.
21 Ibid., at 418-19.
22 Ibid., at 461.

them into constitutional irrelevance. In an infamous speech that revived thoughts of previous Federalist threats to withdraw from the Union, Josiah Quincy claimed that America could not expand beyond its initial size of thirteen States without violating those States' basic rights under the original constitutional contract: "If this bill passes, it is my deliberate opinion that it is virtually a dissolution of this Union; that it will free the States from their moral obligation; and, as it will be the right of all, so it will be the duty of some, definitely to prepare for a separation, – amicably if they can, violently if they must."[23] In other words, each State, as an original, equal member of the compact, must concur before any new members could be admitted. Aside from the fact that Quincy's argument flew in the face of overwhelming historical forces and massive popular support, it was not very persuasive on its own terms. Original, individual members of a club rarely retain a unilateral veto over new members. Even Quincy's home state of Massachusetts supported the administration.

Madison's continuing negotiations with Napoleon angered his political opponents, who argued that supporting such a dictator was not only immoral, but also would lead to war with England. When Madison entered into a formal agreement with Napoleon, based upon the assumption that Napoleon had repealed a set of Decrees that the Americans believed violated their neutrality rights on the high seas, the huge majority of Republicans in the House of Representatives once again used ruthless legislative tactics. Not satisfied with stifling debate through their silence, the Republicans rejected a basic assumption of republican democracy – that the legislature should have open, deliberate debate before entering into actions that may well lead to war – by passing a gag rule precluding their opponents from discussing Madison's negotiations. Foreign policy aspirations led the Republican leadership to jettison both substantive and procedural constitutional norms, ranging from strict construction of federal powers to the right to open legislative debate and deliberation, creating in their place constitutional conventions of executive supremacy in foreign affairs and majority tyranny in legislative deliberations. The aggressive "military constitution" prevailed over the discursive "republican constitution." Assuming that Madison had good strategic reasons to be angrier about English naval depredations than French ones (which continued even after Napoleon made his agreement), Madison's tactics were questionable because he chose his favorite means, an embargo, even though Jefferson's earlier embargo had been such a disaster. Aside from ancient prejudices, Madison probably preferred to support the French because they were not interfering with the Southern expansion, including

---

[23] Ibid., at 226-27.

the invasion of the Floridas. Napoleon offered the Americans everything in the hemisphere.[24] In 1812, against the wishes of those white Anglicans who lived there, Congress passed a law annexing part of West Florida to Louisiana while merging the rest of West Florida into the Mississippi Territory.[25]

Alongside these foreign policy efforts, all of which eventually lead to an embarrassing war with England in 1812, Western Americans continued to pressure Native-Americans along the frontier. While Jefferson had hoped that the Indians would be squeezed into agriculture pursuits as their capacity to hunt for game was constrained by the legalistic enclosures of white civilization, Kentucky settlers simply trespassed on Indian territory and slaughtered so many animals that there was little wild game left for anyone.[26] Whenever there was a murder involving the two races, Native Americans complied with their treaties by handing over Indian suspects. White juries then convicted and hung any Indians, but never found any white defendants guilty of murdering Indians.[27] Thus, even the hallowed republian institution of the jury became an institutional tool of imperial growth. Even the ever-ambitious Governor William Henry Harrison, who had all but guaranteed war in 1809[28] by grabbing most of the best land East of the Mississippi through alleged "purchases" of vast amounts of land from small Indian tribes, was appalled by this discrimination.[29] As would be the case throughout this tawdry history, average white American males took advantage of their citizenship rights to exploit the other races.

Harrison's compassion did not go very far. Responding to efforts by Tecumseh and "The Prophet" to form a national Indian confederation in 1811, Harrison informed Tecumseh that his Native Americans had initiated hostilities by seizing five barrels of salt. Whatever his ultimate plans, Tecumseh bravely came to Vincennes to try to settle these differences peacefully. But Harrison refused to negotiate; he wanted to fight the Indians before they might receive significant aid from the English. Several racially motivated murders on both sides further aggravated the situation. Despite President Madison's express wishes for continued peace,[30] Harrison organized a military expedition. After a sentinel was shot and wounded, he launched his attack on November 2, 1811. Although the battle of Tippecanoe was not a clear-cut victory, Harrison seized enough land and

---

24 Ibid., at 266.
25 Ibid., at 456.
26 Ibid., at 343-46.
27 Ibid., at 347.
28 Ibid., at 354-55.
29 Ibid., at 347.
30 Ibid., at 361-62.

showed enough aggression to become the popular leader of Western expansion, a popularity that culminated with his becoming President. Madison did not punish his wayward, aggressive Territorial Governor.[31] After Harrison's attack, Tecumseh resisted full-scale war until he and his people were dragged into the War of 1812, which forced them to side with the British.[32] Harrison's unilateral aggression thereby created yet another grim constitutional convention in America's evolving "military constitution": American leaders on the frontier, isolated from direct control by the President, could initiate their own military actions to extend the empire and/or defeat its enemies. The American electorate consistently endorsed these changes by sending such aggressive generals as Harrison and Andrew Jackson to the White House. While the telegraph would bring the army back under direct civilian control, the tradition of military aggression remained.

B. The War of 1812 and its Immediate Aftermath

Although sectional rivalries, biases, and differences constantly strained and divided the emerging republic, most major politicians initially embraced war with England in 1812.[33] Henry Clay's flamboyant maiden speech to the Senate in 1810 captured the emerging consensus that nobody could stop the Americans from taking as much land as they wanted. There would be enough for the North, West, and South. The South Carolina Senator John C. Calhoun started his career as a nationalist War Hawk thirsting for a "mighty empire."[34] In 1811, Calhoun defended the policy of expanding the army, despite the argument from old Republicans like John Randolph that such a plan created a dangerous, anti-Republican "standing army." Calhoun excoriated the argument that the people would be unwilling to pay additional taxes for military forces needed to protect foreign trade:

> Sir, I here enter my solemn protest against this low and "calculating avarice" entering this hall of legislation. It is only fit for shops and counting-houses; and ought not to disgrace the seat of sovereignty by its squalid and vile appearance. Whenever it touches sovereign power, the nation is ruined. It is too short-sighted to defend itself. It is a compromising spirit, always ready to

---

31 Ibid., at 370.

32 Ibid., at 373.

33 Clay and Calhoun led Congressional support for the war efforts, Merrill D. Peterson, *The Great Triumverate: Webster, Clay, and* Calhoun (Oxford, 1987), 39. Reflecting widespread New England opposition, Daniel Webster first gained national recognition through his opposition, ibid., at 37.

34 'Speech on the Resolution of the Committee on Foreign Relations' (December 12, 1811), Calhoun, op. cit., *supra* ch. 1, n.185, at 294.

> yield a part to save the residue. It is too timid to have in itself the laws of self-preservation. It is never safe but under a shield of honor. There is, Sir, one principle necessary to make us a great people – to produce not the form, but the real spirit of union – and that is, to protect every citizen in the lawful pursuit of his business. He will then feel that he is backed by the government – that its arms are his arms; and will rejoice in its increased strength and prosperity. Protection and patriotism are reciprocal. This is the way which has led nations to greatness.[35]

The United States had sufficient justification to go to war against either France or England. Indeed, some people advocated fighting both countries. Up to very moment of formal declaration of War, France and England flagrantly assaulted neutral American shipping. Madison claimed that Napoleon had suspended his edicts even though Napoleon continued to enforce them. Probably to garner popular support,[36] the Madison Administration finally began seriously protesting the English impressment of sailors on American ships into the English Navy. Henry Adams mordantly summarized the shift in foreign policy: "[A]s late as the close of 1811, neither the President, the Secretary of State, nor Congress had yet insisted that the person of an American citizen was as sacred as his property."[37] Aside from the continuing split between the Federalists and the Republicans over England and France, the deciding factor was Canada. Once Napoleon seemingly lost interest in the Western Hemisphere and encouraged the Americans to plunder Spain, there was little to be immediately gained from a war with France. Indeed, James Monroe sought French aid:

> But in order to go further, to bring us to great resolutions, the Emperor must aid us; private and public interest must make the same demand. The President does indeed hold the rudder of the Ship of State; he guides, but it is public opinion which makes the vessel move. On France depends the winning of public opinion; and we wish for it, as you can well conceive in our position we should.[38]

Monroe and Madison had important allies in their battle for public opinion. In an early display of "yellow journalism," an eager press inflamed the public with invented injustices and constant temptations of a supine Canada.[39]

---

35 Ibid., at 291.
36 Adams, Madison, op. cit., *supra* n.421, at 377.
37 Ibid., at 376.
38 Ibid., at 379.
39 Ibid., at 376-77.

Both the West and the South foresaw benefits, particularly for the North. During the War Debates, Felix Grundy of Tennessee rhapsodized:

> This war, if carried on successfully, will have its advantages. We shall drive the British from our continent. ... I am willing to receive the Canadians as adopted brethren. It will have beneficial political effects; it will preserve the equilibrium of the government. When Louisiana shall be fully peopled, the Northern States shall lose their power; they will be at the discretion of others; they can be depressed at pleasure; and then this Union will be endangered. I therefore feel anxious not only to add the Floridas to the South, but the Canadas to the North of this empire.[40]

Grundy conceded that America's "republican institutions" would have to weather "the shock of war," but was willing to run the risk on the hope that after the war ended, Americans would resume their "peaceful attitude" and keep their liberties.[41] Thus, republics could have large, powerful armies, so long as those armies were used for external purposes, not domestic suppression.[42] Many New England Federalists, who had been advocating such an approach for decades, were easily persuaded, particularly since Canada was the anticipated spoil. Almost half of them joined the War Republicans to defeat their more pacific opponents from both parties, one of many indications that old party polarities were breaking down. These Federalists combined with the militant Republicans to pass a bill expanding the army, even though Madison opposed the proposal.[43] The anti-war Republican John Randolph summarized the debates in his typically acrid way: "Ever since the report of the Committee on Foreign Relations came into the House, we have heard but one word, – like the whippoorwill, but one monotonous tone, – Canada, Canada, Canada!"[44] Those who opposed war with England would have had even stronger grounds if Madison had fully disclosed how he had been consistently misled by Napoleon after they entered into their neutrality agreement. A bare majority of the Federalists joined Randolph.

Randolph opposed the war on pragmatic as well as constitutional grounds: "Go to war without money, without men, without a navy! Go to war when we have not the courage, while your lips utter war, to lay war taxes! When your whole courage is exhibited in passing Resolutions! The people will not believe it!"[45] Randolph's forebodings proved accurate.

---

[40] Ibid., at 392.
[41] Ibid., at 390.
[42] Ibid., at 390-91.
[43] Ibid., at 400.
[44] Ibid., at 395.
[45] Ibid., at 440.

War mongering was premised upon delusions of military grandeur. The United States was completely unprepared to fight defensively, much less offensively. The Eleventh Congress had let the National Bank expire, leaving in its place a variety of State banks of varying degrees of quality. Still adhering to many Old Republican norms, Jefferson and Madison never wanted a standing army or a powerful navy, preferring disorganized State militia and tiny gunboats that supposedly could guard waterways. Congress refused to allocate sufficient money to fight the upcoming war. Madison chose elderly, incompetent generals, including the perpetually discredited General Wilkinson, who had been deeply involved with Burr's treasonous conspiracy, to direct the campaign.

Calhoun claimed Randolph far too pessimistic: "So far from being unprepared, sir, I believe that in four weeks from the time that a declaration of war is heard on our frontiers the whole of Upper and part of Lower Canada will be in our possession."[46] Developing its appalling constitutional precedent, Congress did not hold these debates in public, perhaps because the War Party knew it had to act as summarily and quickly as possible. Henry Adams estimated that up to eighty percent of the population initially wanted to avoid war with England.[47] The issue split the country sectionally; the South and the West supported the war but not a single New England State voted for war. Madison could safely ignore such views. As the Revolutionary War historian David Ramsay had previously pointed out, the Constitution had been designed to make the President into an emperor-like figure, largely immunized from political or legal constraints in his conduct of foreign policy, capable of using all the traditional tools of empire to strengthen the new country. Thus insulated from immediate republican pressures, Madison launched the war against England, relying on the previously underemphasized issue of impressments. Tragically, England had already decided to repeal its most oppressive laws authorizing interference with American shipping, but that news did not reach North America until after the war had begun.[48]

From both England and America's perspective, the military campaigns were a deluge of errors, echoing the incoherent diplomacy that helped start the war in the first place. Napoleon's abortive invasion of Russia left the Americans without an ally to fight England.[49] But the Americans did not hesitate. Just as the Continental Congress had authorized invasion of Canada a year before the Declaration of Independence, Madison ordered General Hull to invade Canada. Trying to avoid conflict, Hull issued a

46 Ibid.

47 Ibid., at 449.

48 Ibid., at 491.

49 Ibid., at 476.

proclamation to the Canadians in July that combined American aggression with American virtue:

> You will be emancipated from tyranny and oppression, and restored to the dignified station of freemen... I have a force which will break down all opposition, and that force is but the vanguard of a much greater... The United States offer you peace, liberty, and security, – your choice lies between these and war, slavery, or destruction. Choose then; but choose wisely.[50]

From their point of view, the Canadians chose wisely, first rejecting the Americans' offer and then crushing Hull near Detroit. British military power once again plunged deep into the United States.[51] Although they did not lose any land, Generals Van Rennselear and Smyth led their troops, who were outnumbered because of minimal enlistments, to equally bloody defeats when the United States twice tried to invade Canada along the Niagara River. Politicians like Henry Clay had promised many thousands of volunteers to reinvade Canada, but those volunteers never materialized.[52] On the other hand, the American navy was able to establish, much to the horror of England and to the delight of the American populace, that it could stand up to the vaunted British navy.[53]

Early setbacks did not deter the Madison Administration. Monroe rejected English overtures to negotiate, making the basic argument that American leaders would use for the next two centuries: "When our honor shall be avenged, when you shall have recrossed the rivers, when our generals shall occupy the best part of your Canada, then I shall be disposed to listen, and to treat of peace."[54] Monroe quickly retreated from this ultimatum, only to encourage another Canadian invasion the following year.[55] Madison also turned to the south to consolidate and extend gains in the Floridas. Quite simply, it made no difference to the Americans whether they were invading the colonies of a country against which they were formally at war or the colonies of a putative "friend." Andrew Jackson enthusiastically described the motives of the Tennessee volunteers called up to "defend" their region by marching to Natchez:

> I have the pleasure to inform you that I am now at the head of two thousand and seventy volunteers, the choicest of our citizens, who go at the call of their country to execute the will of the Government; who have no constitutional scruples, and if the Government orders, will rejoice at the opportunity of

50 Ibid., at 503.
51 Ibid., at 527.
52 Ibid., at 570.
53 Ibid., at 559.
54 Ibid., at 584.
55 Ibid., at 644.

> placing the American eagle on the ramparts of Mobile, Pensacola, and Fort St. Augustine.[56]

But Madison was unable to send a clear message because the Senate only authorized him to keep West Florida, not East Florida. He ordered Jackson to dismiss his volunteers and Pinckney to withdraw the troops in East Florida. Madison faced opposition in his own Cabinet, particularly Albert Galatin. He also needed to placate a powerful alliance recently formed by Russia, Spain, and England.[57]

Andrew Jackson complied with the orders. But he then turned his fury toward that other source of resistance to American expansionism, the Native Americans. Jackson led three thousand troops on a campaign to "exterminate" a tribe of Creeks who were holed up in a fort. These Creeks had previously committed an atrocity that serves as a grim reminder that genocide knows no racial barriers. Inspired by Tecumseh, who raged "Let the white race perish!," they overwhelmed the fortified residence of Samuel Mims. Their leader, Red Eagle, failed to prevent the slaughter of 250 people, who "were butchered in the quickest manner, and blood and brains bespattered the whole earth. The children were seized by the legs, and killed by batting their heads against the stockading. The women were scalped, and those who were pregnant were opened, while they were alive, and the embryo infants let out of the womb."[58]

With the help of Cherokee allies and the use of heavy artillery, Jackson's force wiped out nine hundred males, allowing only twenty to escape, with only 32 killed and 99 wounded. Jackson was not as genocidal as his opponents. He lamented "two or three women and children were killed by accident."[59] After being rewarded with an appointment as a major general in the regular army, Jackson forced a treaty on the Creeks, seizing so much of their land for indemnification for the costs of the war that they were isolated from any Native-American allies. Although only a few Creeks agreed to this treaty while the rest continued to fight the war for some time, Jackson had established sufficient "legal authority" for the whites to gain much more valuable land.[60]

The Federalist Party more than failed to take advantage of Madison's many blunders, highlighted by the British army's burning down the capitol

---

[56] Ibid., at 764.

[57] Ibid., at 766-67.

[58] Albert J. Pickert, 2 History of Alabama... 275 (Charleston, 1851), quoted in Robert V. Remini, *1 Andrew Jackson: The Course of American Empire 1767-1821* (Baltimore, 1998), 190. Peter Fitzpatrick is skeptical about the truth of these facts, given the source.

[59] Adams, *Madison*, op. cit., *supra* n.421, at 797.

[60] Ibid., at 800-01.

of Washington, D.C. Already divided by the war and discredited by their opposition to the Louisiana Purchase, the most aggressive New England members of the Federalist Party struck back at Madison's pathetic military adventures by committing political suicide. Having already considered leaving the Union because of the Louisiana Purchase, they steadily escalated their anti-war efforts during the War. They certainly had sufficient provocations. In addition to the numerous military blunders and disasters, the Republicans committed a serious domestic outrage that both emboldened and enraged the Federalists. A Republican mob broke into a Baltimore jail, savagely beating dissenting Federalists who had volunteered to stay there after earlier bloodshed. The mob would not let the beaten men be rescued for many hours, preferring instead to cut and burn the bodies to see if they were still alive. One of the Federalists died.[61] Madison then revived the hated embargo,[62] once again damaging the New England economy over the short term but making it ultimately stronger and more independent. For instance, the number of cotton mill spindles increased from 8000 in 1807 to one half million eight years later.[63] Another was that they saw no end to the war with England, which they vastly preferred for religious, cultural, economic, and political reasons to the tyrant Napoleon. The Massachusetts Senate passed a resolution that made them sound like pacific Jeffersonian Republicans: "[A] war like the present, waged without justifiable cause, and prosecuted in a manner which indicates that conquest and ambition are its real motives, it is not becoming a moral and religious people to express any approbation of military or naval exploits which are not immediately connected with the defence of our sea-coast and soil."[64] Governor Strong of Massachusetts refused to send his powerful militia to help fight the British in Canada, another example of the United States' decrepit military constitution. In 1813, Governor Chittenden of Vermont recalled his troops from national service, noting that "in his opinion the military strength and resources of this State must be reserved for its own defence and protection exclusively, excepting in cases provided for by the Constitution of the United States, and then under orders derived only from the commander-in-chief."[65] By 1814, Pickering was openly advocating disunion in letters and a pamphlet: "I believe an immediate separation would be a real blessing to the 'good old thirteen States' as John Randolph once called them."[66] Cultural as well as political differences animated New

---

61 Ibid., at 579.
62 Ibid., at 873-76.
63 Malone and Rauch, op. cit., *supra* ch. 2, n.28, at 405.
64 Adams, *Madison*, op. cit., ibid., at 664.
65 Ibid., at 873.
66 Ibid., at 909.

England's alienation. President Dwight of Yale College conveyed his impressions of a travel to the West: "The class of pioneers cannot live in regular society. They are too idle, too talkative, too passionate, too prodigal, and too shiftless to acquire either property or character. They are impatient of the restraints of law, religion, and morality, and grumble about the taxes by which the Rulers, Ministers, and Schoolmasters are supported..."[67] Finally, economics motivated many New England leaders to oppose expansion, as best expressed by Secretary of the Treasury Richard Rush in 1827: "It is a proposition too plain to require elucidation that the creation of capital is retarded rather than accelerated by the diffusion of a thin population over a great surface of soil."[68] Other New England leaders were more ambivalent. Responding to numerous local communities' complaints about the Jefferson administration, the General Court of Massachusetts revived the Jefferson/Madison arguments opposing the Alien and Sedition Laws: "Whenever the national compact is violated and the citizens of this State are oppressed by cruel and unauthorized laws, the legislature is bound to interpose its power and wrest from the oppressor his victim." Although it recommended a convention of New England States, the General Court sought to remedy the problem through Constitutional amendments, not formal separation.[69] In 1814, at the very moment that England became far more powerful due to the defeat of Napoleon at the battles of Leipzig and Vittoria, Daniel Webster argued that the United States should never go on the offensive: "Give up your futile projects of invasion. Extinguish the fires that blaze on your inland frontiers. * * * The enemy, as we have seen, can make no permanent stand in any populous part of the country. Its citizens will drive his forces to the line; but at that line where defence ceases and invasion begins, they stop."[70]

The continuing war enraged the New Englanders, particularly the Puritan clergy. Peace in Europe so strengthened England's hand that the United States could not possibly conquer Canada, the main temptation for many New Englanders. Military defeats accumulated, peaking at the Madison Administration's flight from the British Army that sacked Washington, D.C. Although the initial call for New England States to meet in Hartford for a Convention only drew delegates from the States of Massachusetts, Connecticut, and Rhode Island, the Federalists pounded the

---

[67] Turner, 'Contributions of the West to American Democracy', Turner, op. cit. *supra* ch. 1, n.19, at 251.

[68] Quoted in Turner, 'Social Forces in American History', ibid., at 317. Turner noted: "We may trace the conflict between the capitalist and the democratic pioneer from the earliest colonial days," ibid., at 325.

[69] Adams, *Madison*, op. cit., *supra* n.471, at 911-12.

[70] Ibid., at 883.

Republicans in the fall Congressional elections, winning thirty-nine out of forty-one seats in New England.[71] Despite Madison's many weaknesses, the Hartford Convention contained many cautious, senior Federalists who were unwilling to make the final step toward disunion. Instead, they informed their more fervent colleagues "We are going to keep you young hot-heads from getting into mischief."[72] The Convention's final report threatened "imposition" but opposed the destruction of the Union: "A severance of the Union by one or more States against the will of the rest, and especially in time of war, can be justified only by absolute necessity."[73] At the very least, the leading Federalists were unwilling to confront Madison until New Orleans fell to the British.[74] Defeat seemed even more probable after Andrew Jackson acted contrary to orders by invading Spanish Mobile instead of moving quickly to defend New Orleans.[75]

Madison avoided disaster by negotiating an end to the war before the Battle of New Orleans, which instead of leading to more disgrace catapulted the victorious Andrew Jackson to national prominence. But even those negotiations revealed America's continual preoccupation with growth. Secretary of State James Monroe instructed his commissioners "to bring to view the advantage to both countries which is promised by a transfer of the upper parts and even the whole of Canada to the United States."[76] Internal imperial rivalries threatened the treaty process. New Englanders wanted to expand their rights to fish in Canada by giving the British the right to navigate on the Mississippi, a deal that Western politicians like Henry Clay opposed. The two nations were able to resolve the two issues by deferring them to a later date, a maneuver effectively maintaining the status quo.[77]

While the War of 1812 did not significantly alter the external shape of America's empire, it radically changed its internal political culture and relevant constitutional practices, accelerating the transition from nonaggression to militarism, from provincialism to nationalism. During the War, the central government quickly learned that State Militias were unreliable. The troops remained under the control of State governments. This power proved disastrous because the Federalist Governor of Massachusetts, Caleb Strong, who had the richest, most powerful militia at the time, refused to lend his troops to the war effort. Strong interpreted the

---

71 Ibid., at 1068.
72 Ibid., at 1111.
73 Ibid., at 1114.
74 Ibid., at 1123.
75 Ibid., at 1139.
76 Ibid., at 1192.
77 Ibid., at 1216.

Second Amendment to preclude the use of State militia except to repel invasion or quell domestic violence. In particular, he would not join the assault on Canada.[78] In addition, the militia rarely fought very well. America's naval strategy also had to be revamped. Jefferson's gunboat system proved less than useless, while victories by American frigates on the open seas captured the country's imagination and admiration. Even the privateer system, which effectively used privately owned ships to harass for profit English shipping (even in the British Channel and the Irish Sea), was subsidized at great expense. The financial system was a disaster. During the war, gold and silver moved to the Northern States because the English did not enforce their blockade against their sympathetic Federalist allies and the Northern States developed manufacturing goods to sell to the South. The Northern banks, controlled by pro-English Federalists, refused to help finance the War.[79] Thus the Republicans' opposition to a national bank hurt them dearly during the war. Next, the army remained too small and unprofessional until Madison appointed John Armstrong after a long series of military disasters. Even then, it took Jackson's startling victory at New Orleans to soothe the nation's military self-esteem. During the War, Madison continued to aggregate power within the Presidency by defying and ignoring Congressional directives.[80]

Despite all these problems and despite the bland treaty that superficially reaffirmed the status quo, the war was a great success for the Americans. Jackson's victories over the Creeks and the English effectively established American control of the western frontier. In addition, Jackson gained land for the United States because it kept New Orleans and Mobile instead of returning them to Spain.[81]

After the War ended, Madison proposed in his last Annual Message the form of government that he had opposed when Hamilton and Adams were in power: a standing army, a navy, a national bank, protective tariffs to protect local manufacturing, and government paper as national currency.[82] In 1816, for the first time, the country passed a tariff primarily intended to protect infant industries, not to raise revenues.[83] Congress reconfirmed another important "constitutional convention"; it could use its constitutional powers as means to achieve a constitutional end not explicitly in the Constitutional text. By chartering a second national bank that same year, Congress created a means, incorporation, that was not in the

---

78 Ibid., at 575.
79 Ibid., at 574.
80 Ibid., at 461, 466.
81 Remini, op. cit., *supra* n.527, at 298-307.
82 Adams, *Madison*, op. cit., ibid., at 1253-54.
83 Malone and Rauch, op. cit., *supra* ch. 2, n.28, at 405.

text to support the textually based ends of taxation and military support (as well as the nontextually based end of providing great opportunities for additional wealth to those connected to the Bank). With the return of peace, Madison did not become completely Hamiltonian; he vetoed a Congressional bill authorizing internal improvements because the Constitution's text did not provide express authorization. This veto angered Calhoun, who commingled nationalism and sectionalism, a commitment to empire with a fear of large nations, in an ominous speech on behalf of internal improvements, which were the nation's "most powerful cement":[84]

> Let it not be forgotten, let it be forever kept in mind, that the extent of our republic exposes us to the greatest of all calamities, next to the loss of liberty, and even to that its consequence, – *disunion*. We are great, and rapidly – I was about to say fearfully – growing. This is our pride and danger, our weakness and strength. Little does he deserve to be entrusted with the liberties of this people, who does not raise his mind to these truths. We are under the most imperious obligation to counteract every tendency to disunion...If...we permit a low, sordid, selfish and sectional spirit to take possession of this House, this happy scene will vanish. We will divide, and in its consequences will follow misery and despotism.[85]

Others foresaw equally fundamental changes. Where John Randolph saw a "great consolidated nation,"[86] Henry Clay predicted perpetual war: "That man must be blind who cannot see that we are destined to have war after war with Great Britain, until, if one of the two nations cannot be crushed, all grounds of collision shall have ceased between us." Clay explained that those grounds included both North and South America.[87]

Overall, both Republicans and Federalists made major contributions to the evolution of America's Republican empire. Under the Washington administration, Hamilton broadly interpreted the Constitutional text to create a political culture and supporting institutions very different from what the Virginians thought they had formulated. But once the Republicans seized power and could determine how that power would be used in the future, they found Hamilton's powerful means to be irresistible. By focusing on the two American continents, not Europe, the Republicans adapted Hamiltonian means to their different ends. Quite simply, the empire's Western direction would be Republican, its form primarily Hamiltonian. With the notable exception of internal improvements, the

---

84 Ibid., at 412.

85 Adams, Madison, op. cit., *supra* n.471, at 1282-83.

86 Ibid., at 1257.

87 Ibid., at 1256.

political, economic, and military constitutions had become more Federalist in form, doctrine, and content.

C. War And Peace Under the Monroe Administration

Although the Monroe administration is primarily remembered for the Monroe Doctrine, the dramatic assertion of the United States supremacy throughout the Americas, that Doctrine had far less immediate importance for the growth of the republic than several technical diplomatic victories. Monroe's Ambassador to England/Secretary of State, John Quincy Adams, followed in his father's footsteps by working closely with the British Empire. Through a variety of steps, of which the Monroe Doctrine was only one, the English and the Americans carved up both continents. The resulting peace was uneasy at times, notably during the Civil War when the English elite favored the South, but proved enduring.

The English were willing to negotiate because they feared European rivals more than the Americans. Although England initially joined the Quadruple Alliance, thereby helping determine European boundaries created by the 1815 Congress of Vienna, they never entered the Holy Alliance, a group of European emperors dedicated to promoting religion and eliminating republicanism (demonstrating how monarchies can create their own mixture of virtue and self-interest to justify aggression). In terms of the Americas, the English preferred to rely upon their potent navy to maintain economic control of South America and Canada and prevent other Europeans from reasserting themselves. Fortunately for Adams and his English counterparts, the Americans and English ended the War of 1812 by agreeing to return to the status quo before the conflict began. In 1815, Adams first negotiated a four-year trade agreement that eliminated many of the prior sources of tension. The two countries gave each other trading rights equal to whichever third country was their "most favored nation," thereby opening up British markets to American foodstuffs and raw materials.[88] After Lord Castlereagh complained of "the great and growing military power of the United States," Adams and Monroe eliminated a potentially dangerous naval arms race on the Great Lakes by convincing the British to accept mutual disarmament in 1817. This pacifism was selective; Monroe sent the sloop-of-war *Ontario* to the Pacific to threaten force against British fur traders who had settled at the mouth of the Columbia River.[89] The following year, after Adams was promoted from British ambassador to Secretary of State, he settled most lingering disputes. The

---

88 Malone and Rauch, op. cit., *supra* ch. 2, n.28, at 392.

89 Ibid., at 394.

British agreed to relinquish their claim of exclusive sovereignty over the Oregon lands, which instead would be jointly occupied by both countries. To obtain the Red River Valley, the British effectively conceded any rights to navigate on the Mississippi River by agreeing to a Canadian border above the Mississippi's headwaters.[90] Assisted by the display of naval force and a Congressional law excluding British merchant ships in retaliation for Britain's continuing prohibition of American ships in the West Indies, Adams obtained New England perpetual fishing rights in selected Canadian waters in exchange for renewing the earlier Commercial Convention accepting England's mercantile policies in the West Indies. Thus, at long last, the United States had enough power to enable Adams to satisfy both the West and South by gaining complete control of the Mississippi while also pleasing the North with greater access to Canadian fisheries. No longer would American diplomats face Jay's dilemma of choosing between fisheries and the Mississippi, thereby angering and aggravating sectional politics. Most importantly, the United States no longer had to worry about its Northern flank as it drove toward the Pacific.

Only feeble Spain stood in its way in the South. Like Madison before him, Monroe turned to armed aggression. In 1817, troops seized Amelia Island near the coast of Georgia.[91] The next year, Monroe unleashed Andrew Jackson against the Seminoles.[92] Once again exceeding his authority, Jackson seized St. Marks and Pensacola. He caused a diplomatic spat by court martialling and executing two British subjects, but Lord Casterleagh was unwilling to turn the executions into a major controversy.[93] When Spain complained about Jackson's adventures, Adams defiantly informed the Spanish that they needed to indemnify the Americans not only for the costs of previous Seminole raids, but also for the expenses of Jackson's invasion. Spain capitulated, giving up title to both Floridas and to all territory north of a line beginning at the Sabine River on Louisiana's western border, extending to the 42nd parallel, and then moving directly westward to the Pacific. For consideration, the Americans recanted their dubious claim to Texas under the Louisiana Purchase.[94] Now that the United States' southern flank to the Pacific was protected, with only a relatively few Native Americans standing in its way, the only remaining question was its ultimate size.

These more aggressive tactics did not receive complete public support. Even Henry Clay, one of the original War Hawks who had envisioned an

---

[90] Ibid., at 395.

[91] Ibid., at 397.

[92] Remini, op. cit., *supra* n.527, at 351-77.

[93] Ibid.

[94] Ibid., at 398.

easy conquest of Canada and would soon be complaining about the "loss" of Texas,[95] criticized Jackson's actions.[96] Of all the leading American politicians, Clay seemed the most concerned about the rights and opportunities of those people living south of the border.[97] But even if Clay was primarily piqued by jealousy of the popular successes of a potential Presidential rival, his opposition demonstrates that no one factor, be it expansionism, greed, or decency, can fully explain the motives and actions of any individual, much less those of an entire region or country over a protracted period of time.

Having secured control of its westward expansion through North America, the Monroe administration turned to the rest of the hemisphere, reviving Jefferson's dreams of an Anglican republic throughout the two continents. As Adams explained in a Cabinet meeting, the world "must be familiarized with the idea of considering our proper dominion of the continent of North America."[98] The European monarchs thinking about recapturing the revolutionary republics in South America and turning them back into colonies: Tsar Alexander, one of the most aggressive members of the Alliance, issued a ukase in 1821 extending Alaska's jurisdiction deep into the Oregon territories.[99] Adams bluntly rejected Alexander's maneuver, setting forth one of the principles that would soon appear in the Monroe Doctrine: "We should contest the right of Russia to *any* territorial establishment on this continent, and that we should assume directly the principle that the American continents are no longer subjects for any new European colonial establishments."[100] Thus, Adams must have been particularly pleased two years later when Britain's new Foreign Secretary, George Canning, proposed that the two countries join together to ban any further European incursions. France's invasion of Spain had raised British and American concerns that the French and/or the Holy Alliance would next reconquer Spain's old colonies that had successfully revolted.[101] This was one "entangling alliance" that neither Monroe nor Jefferson, whom he consulted, would pass up. But Adams shrewdly recommended that the Americans not make a joint statement with the British, else they "come in as a cock-boat in the wake of the British man-of-war."[102] Far more than prestige was at stake. Canning wanted the United States to declare that

---

95 Ibid.

96 Ibid., at 397.

97 Peterson, op. cit., *supra* ch. 5, n.33, at 52-55.

98 *Quoted from* Perkins, op. cit., *supra* ch. 1, n.109, at 29.

99 Malone and Rauch, op. cit., *supra* ch. 2, n.28, at 400.

100 Ibid.

101 Perkins, op. cit., *supra* ch. 1, n.109, at 42.

102 Malone and Rauch, op. cit., ibid., at 401.

neither country would ever annex any Spanish-American territory. In its proposal, England stated not only "that she aimed at the possession of no portion of the colonies for herself," but also "that she could not see the transfer of any portion of the Americas to any other power, without indifference."[103] Such a principle was unacceptable to the Americans because it would apply to them. Speaking to Congress, Monroe's formal statement contained no diplomatic subtlety. He set forth two major foreign policy principles, opposing European colonial expansion and European transfers of existing colonies (which pressured weak Spain to keep Cuba).[104] He threatened any European power that would attempt to create new colonies or extend existing colonies in either North or South America: "The political system of the allied powers is essentially different ... from that of America ...We should consider any attempt on their part to extend their system to any portion of this hemisphere as dangerous to our peace and safety."[105] Like Thomas Jefferson, Monroe effortlessly combined republican virtue with self-interest. The United States would protect the rest of the hemisphere from Europe's "essentially different" political systems, while also insuring its national security, which now reached far beyond its formal borders to include its future capacity to extend those borders as it saw fit.

There was a streak of sincere support for republicanism. James Monroe and his Secretary of State John Quincy Adams had some hopes that the Latin American revolutionaries would establish their own republics. In the course of defending the Neutrality Act of 1818, Adams told Henry Clay, who strongly supported the rebels: "So far as they were contending for independence, I wished well to their cause; but I had seen and yet see not prospect that they would establish free or liberal institutions of government."[106] Nor did Adams expect America to profit commercially as a result of this policy of maintaining the status quo.[107] Thus the commitment to republicanism, unlike the drive toward hemispheric dominance, stopped at America's borders. Spain could continue to suppress those living within its existing South American empire but could not rely on its allies, particularly the French, in the Holy Alliance.[108]

---

103 Perkins, op. cit., ibid., at 37.

104 Malone and Rauch, op. cit., ibid., at 401.

105 James Monroe, 'The Monroe Doctrine', quoted in Perkins, op. cit., *supra* ch. 1, n.109, at 28.

106 Quoted from Samuel Eliot Morison and Henry Steele Commager, *1 The Growth of the American Republic* 453 (New York, 1958).

107 Ibid.

108 Ibid., at 452-56.

The Latin Americans quickly learned that the Doctrine's primary beneficiary was the United States. When Mexico and Columbia considered liberating Cuba from Spanish control to make it part of a larger republic, the Monroe administration explained that the doctrine applied to all South American countries as well. Only one country could be permitted to expand anywhere in the two hemispheres.[109] Although it was enthusiastically received at home, the Doctrine seemed to have little effect on European behavior, which was far more likely to be deterred by British ships and the risks and costs of counter-revolution. The United States did nothing when the British invaded the Falkland Islands a few years later. In fact, the Doctrine disappeared from public discourse for many years[110] while the United States consolidated and extended its more immediate gains.

The "era of good feelings" lasted for so short a time that it can hardly be characterized as an "era." In 1819, the brewing political tensions and personal rivalries that are part of any body politic were reduced to trivialities by the first public debate over the role of slavery in the United States. As would be the case for the next forty years, the formal growth of the empire was the aggravating factor, hopelessly exacerbated by the slavery problem. The Missouri Territory's request to be admitted as an equal State guaranteed conflict because the Territory straddled the Mason-Dixon Line, which had evolved into an important informal division between the Free and Slave States. The Northern ex-Federalists, dismayed at their declining power, angry about excessive Southern representation in the House because of the "three fifths" rule that cynically counted slaves as part of the body politic,[111] morally and/or pragmatically opposed to slavery, and eager to divide the Republican political monolith, launched the opening salvo. New York Representative James Tallmadge, Jr. proposed that Congress not admit Missouri unless it amended its proposed State constitution to prohibit new slaves from being brought into the land and guarantee that all slaves born after Statehood would eventually become free.[112] Ex-Federalist leader Rufus King, "who had a reputation for opposition to western growth and development,"[113] successfully led the plan through the United States House of Representatives. The Northerners relied upon on the Pennsylvania precedent as authority for the "constitutional convention" that Congress could condition Territorial entries into Statehood. This desperate Northeastern gasp to prevent the growth of

[109] Malone and Rauch, op. cit., *supra* ch. 2, n.28, at 403.

[110] Perkins, op. cit., *supra* ch. 1, n.109, at 65.

[111] Peterson, op. cit., *supra* ch. 5, n.33, at 59.

[112] Malone and Rauch, op. cit., *supra* ch. 2, n.28, at 419.

[113] Ibid.

empire, which diluted its power, threatened the flank of the Southern slave economy.

Many moderate Southerners, including Jefferson, thought the anti-slavery advocates acted in bad faith:

> But nothing has ever presented so threatening an aspect as what is called the Missouri question. The Federalists compleat put down, and despairing of ever rising again under the old division of whig and tory, devised a new one, of slave-holding, & non-slave holding states, which while it had a semblance of being Moral, was at same time Geographical, and calculated to give them ascendancy by debauching their old opponents to a coalition with them.[114]

Jefferson explained that their moral claim was pretextual, because their recommended policy would not reduce the number of slaves by a single person.[115] This argument, like most of Jefferson's observations about slavery, is quite feeble. Slavery is less likely to grow if it is not permitted into new lands, which provide further economic demand for existing and future slaves. He also exacerbated self-righteousness on both sides by characterizing anti-slavery as a Federalist plot to gain Northern supremacy, a charge that ruffled both sides because there was some truth in it.[116]

Kentucky's popular Henry Clay, a large slave owner who nevertheless believed that slavery was immoral, cared far more about westward expansion and unity than slavery. He did not think that the Constitution gave Congress any power to regulate slavery in the Territories. As each Territory matured from undeveloped land to a sizable population, the people of that Territory had sufficient sovereignty to determine if they wanted slavery. Otherwise, the new Territories would not have been permitted to evolve in ways similar to the earlier States. This "constitutional convention," which combined popular sovereignty with State equality, is theoretically consistent with Jefferson's theory that each new Territory should be able to enter the Union as a State via "compact and equality." After all, slave states constituted a large majority of the original thirteen colonies; slavery still existed in New York and other Northern States at the time of the Constitution's ratification. Subsequent Territories should have "equal rights" to enter the Union under similar conditions. The Constitutional requirement that Congress ensure "Republican forms of government" in the States showed that the Framers did not consider slavery to be an "anti-Republican" aspect of government. Consequently, Congressional power under the Constitution to regulate the Territories did

---

[114] Letter from Thomas Jefferson to Albert Gallatin (Dec. 26, 1820), Jefferson, op. cit., *supra* ch. 1, n.29, at 1448-49.

[115] Ibid., at 1449.

[116] David B. Davis, *Slavery in the Age of Revolution, 1770-1823*, 184 (Ithaca, 1975).

not carry any implicit authority to require, forbid, or condition slavery. On a more practical level, delegating the contentious issue of slavery to the Territories reduced the likelihood of national conflict. Just as the Sixteenth Congress convened in 1820 to resolve the Missouri controversy, Clay expressed his fears: "It is a most unhappy question, awakening sectional feelings, and exasperating them to the highest degree. The words, civil war, and disunion, are uttered almost without emotion."[117]

In an extremely persuasive speech, Clay asked Congress to rescind the Tallmadge restrictions, arguing that the growth of the republic would eventually destroy slavery by diffusing slaves throughout the country. Because no new slaves could be imported into America, the number of existing slaves would be dwarfed by the steady increase in the white population. Furthermore, the country's economy and its moral commitment to freedom would gradually erode that peculiar institution. Clay transformed the expansion of the nation, which put continual strains on the Union by periodically reviving the slavery issue, into the best means to protect the nation and even gradually eliminate slavery! Like Madison in *The Federalist*, Clay relied on large size to simultaneously resolve several constitutional issues and interests. Clay's diffusion argument, which may have reassured humanitarian slave owners like himself who hoped that the problem would easily but slowly fade into a more just future, did not convince his opponents. After all, it was easy to make the counter-prediction that diffusion would strengthen slavery by increasing the demand for slave labor. As President of the American Colonization Society, which sought to free slaves and send all blacks back to Africa, Clay must have sensed that diffusion would not solve by itself the country's race problems, particularly since many white Americans throughout the nation were virulently opposed to spread of free black labor.

As is usually the case, grand constitutional theory framed the public debate with noble sounding principles, providing moral sustenance to each side and generating allegedly inevitable conclusions to the particular problem. The North relied on the principles of liberty and national power; the South on property, equal rights, and state sovereignty; and the West on popular sovereignty within the territories. But if Congress were to avoid stalemate, it had to create a compromise that, by definition, gave each side immediate benefits at the expense of their more abstract, deeply held beliefs. Although he had resigned as Speaker of the House, Clay pushed through an amendment by an Illinois Senator that admitted Missouri as a slave state but forbade slavery above the Mason-Dixon Line. Thus, Jefferson's ban on slavery in the Northwest Ordinance was now extended

---

[117] Ibid., at 60.

to future states deeper into the Midwest. The South gained another Slave State, but only by conceding that Congress had the authority to prohibit slavery in other Territories. Although the South might gain one or two more States above the Mason-Dixon line, the North could soon expect to add several additional Free States, populated by anti-slavery New England pioneers. While John Randolph predictably fought this crippling of States' rights and Southern slave interests to the bitter end, John Calhoun accepted the compromise to preserve the Union, just as he would later not publicly side with the South Carolina Nullifiers against President Jackson's enforcement of the 1832 Tariff when he was Vice President.[118] But such an awkward, unpopular solution could only reassure the naïve. In perhaps his most famous letter, Jefferson wrote that this "momentous question" terrorized him "like a fire bell in the night." Culture, ideology, interest, economics, and race all convened: "I considered [the issue] at once as the knell of the Union. It is hushed, indeed, for the moment. But this is a reprieve only, not a final sentence. A geographical line, coinciding with a marked principle, moral and political, once conceived and held up to the angry passions of men, will never be obliterated; and every new irritation will mark it deeper and deeper."[119] His rival/friend's son, John Quincy Adams, was equally forlorn: "I take it for granted that the present question is a mere preamble – a title-page to a great, tragic volume."[120] The West would eventually determine the outcome of this "Cold War" that turned into the United States' bloodiest conflict.

Aside from the Missouri Compromise, the political branches did little to define or change the internal structure of the constitution during Monroe's presidency; Chief Justice Marshall's Supreme Court was playing an ever-greater role in transforming the Constitution. The Cumberland and National road, which had begun construction with federal support during Jefferson's administration, was finally usable by 1818. But because of Madison's veto, the States led the country in improving transportation lines. Baltimore and Pennsylvania built turnpikes while New York began constructing the Erie Canal.[121] Monroe proved not to be as formalistic as Madison about internal improvements. Although no new federal projects began during his era, he signed a Survey Bill in 1824 planning for future improvements.[122] When John Quincy Adams followed Monroe to the Presidency in 1817, the federal government went through its most

---

118 Ibid., at 61-62.

119 Letter from Thomas Jefferson to John Holmes (April 22, 1820), Jefferson, op. cit., *supra* ch. 1, n.29, at 1434.

120 Malone and Rauch, op. cit., *supra* ch. 2, n.28, at 422.

121 Ibid., at 413.

122 Ibid., at 406.

aggressive period of funding internal improvements. In the 1830s, Congress would periodically fund parts of the Cumberland road, which eventually reached as far as Vandalia, Illinois.

These subsidies were not enough for Adams to defeat Andrew Jackson four years later. Aside from Jackson's inherent popularity as "The Hero" of the Battle of New Orleans and other conflicts, Adams angered many Southerners by threatening to use force to protect the Creeks from Georgian aggression.[123] Jackson's victory signified not only the political ascension of the more egalitarian culture of the West, but also the triumph of a more militaristic, racist, and aggressive conception of the Constitution. Jackson's pervasive popularity was based upon a mixture of his personal dignity and his many military victories. It did not matter that he had frequently disobeyed orders; he had won. His ruthless treatment of Native Americans and other foreigners during these forays did not dishonor him; it enhanced his support. The Virginia aristocracts' commitment to Enlightenment values, best reflected by their relatively decent treatment of the native population and a reluctance to go to war, quickly became memories. Jackson easily rebuffed the Virginians' last effort by refusing to enforce Chief Justice John Marshall's attempt to protect the Cherokee Nation from Georgian depredations in *Worcester v. Georgia*. Instead, he enthusiastically used the federal government to assist the States in removing all Indians who lived East of the Mississippi River.[124] Jackson thereby transformed the Constitution from a document endorsing race slavery to a system totally oppressing all people of color. Jackson's widespread support, which lasted beyond his death, is a grim reminder that many of the United States' most appalling traits are attributable not just to the country's ruling class, but also to its citizenry.

Like Madison before him, Jackson utilized the Presidential prerogative to use the veto power to interpret the Constitution as he saw fit. Where Madison had vetoed a Congressional law authorizing internal improvements because there was no textual authority for that power, Jackson vetoed the third attempt to create a National Bank. For the first time, an American leader questioned some of the rights of the wealthy. In his famous veto message, Jackson explained: "But when the laws undertake to add to these natural and just advantages, artificial distinctions...to make the rich richer and the potent more powerful, the humble members of society... have a right to complain of the injustice to the government."[125] To solve this problem, Jackson believed in a strict construction of "formal equality" that would protect the property rights of

---

123 Ibid., at 436.
124 Ibid., at 468.
125 Ibid., at 451.

rich and poor without creating special favors for the rich. Jackson thereby used the veto not just to further some abstract theory of constitutional interpretation, but also to implement a particular political ideology. By using the veto far more often and for more reasons than his predecessors, Jackson altered the "constitutional convention" about vetoes, turning it into another tool of partisan politics. Jackson also altered the conventions surrounding civil service. Up to his time, Presidents were reluctant to make massive substitutions within the federal bureaucracy; Jefferson had been castigated for removing a handful of Federalists.[126] But Jackson introduced the "spoils system," purging the federal government of opponents and neutrals and replacing them with political allies.

Although he was not as aggressive in foreign affairs as one might have predicted, Jackson continued his predecessors' commitment to imperial expansion. His administration finally convinced Britain to open up the West Indies to American trade.[127] The French signed a treaty compensating Americans for damage done during the Napoleonic Wars. Looking ever Westward, Jackson secretly authorized the merchant Edmund Roberts to negotiate treaties in the Far East.[128] He also looked approvingly upon the massive immigration of American settlers in Mexico's province of Texas, a demographic transformation which culminated in the Texans' successful revolution, led by his compatriot Sam Houston, from Mexico in 1836. Jackson promptly recognized Texas as a new nation. As has been the case throughout the Republic's history, many average Americans had their own methods of expressing imperial ambition. In the modern era, many American citizens smugly buy running shoes at cheap prices from exploited laborers abroad or make extra profits on their shares through the exploitation of foreign countries; back then, they simply seized other people's lands. Finally, he oversaw the sloppily conducted Second Seminole War in Florida, an expensive and bloody catastrophe that lingered after he retired until 1842.[129]

In terms of Presidential actions, Jackson's most important contribution to the growth and structure of America's republican empire was his strong endorsement of the Union when he repudiated South Carolinian recalcitrance during the Nullification Crisis. The South Carolinians opposed the Tariff of 1832, which Jackson had not vetoed. Jackson conceded their right to pass resolutions but threatened to respond to any

---

126 Adams, Jefferson, op. cit., *supra* Intro., n.14, at 151-55. At the state level, Republicans aggressively replaced Federalist officials, ibid., at 155.

127 Ibid., at 467.

128 Ibid.

129 Robert V. Remini, *3 Andrew Jackson: The Course of American Democracy 1833-1845* (Baltimore, 1984) 304-14.

violence or resistance with hangings. South Carolina reacted by being the only Southern State not to vote to reelect Jackson that same year. Soon after the election, the South Carolina legislature convened a convention passing the Ordinance of Nullification. Not only did the Ordinance declare the Tariff unconstitutional, but it also set forth immediate exclusive remedies, forbade collection of the taxes, required all civil and military officers to submit to a test oath, and precluded any appeal to the United States Supreme Court. It concluded by asserting its right to complete independence should the federal government use coercion. Although the convention claimed that Madison and Jefferson's legislative responses to the Alien and Sedition Acts provided authority, those earlier protests were not as aggressive. First, the Virginian and Kentucky resolutions merely asserted that the Acts were unconstitutional. The Virginia resolution, drafted by Jefferson, vaguely said the State had the right to "interpose," but neither resolution explicitly set up a legal structure that would overtly oppose the federal law, require the use of state coercion against federal officials, or envision secession. Jackson predictably retaliated with his own threats of force, reinforcing Forts Sumter and Moultrie, deploying the navy off the South Carolina coast, and ordering federal officials to collect the tariff. While Jackson conceded that the South Carolinians abstractly had the right to revolt, they could not pick and choose between federal laws while still in the Union. Their refusal to permit appeal to the Supreme Court effectively made them the final interpreters of the Constitution, a system that would soon disintegrate the country. In other words, they had a Lockean "natural right" to revolt, but they could not use force or law to assert any "constitutional rights" while members of the Union. Jackson noted that such a doctrine would have permitted the eastern states to destroy the Embargo and Nonintercourse Acts, Pennsylvania the Whiskey Tax, and Virginia the carriage tax.[130] Jackson shrewdly continued to pursue the possibility of using force while offering South Carolina a compromise by reducing the tariff rates. South Carolina's partial victory of reduced tariffs came at a high price. Jackson's militant, articulate nationalism sparked the loyalties of citizens throughout the country, particularly in the vital Western swing section.[131]

---

[130] Ibid., at 455.
[131] Ibid., at 457.

6 Chief Justice John Marshall's Hamiltonian Empire: Turning Constitutional Conventions into Constitutional Law

Another way to test the imperial ambition thesis is to apply it to a high-quality, contemporary work of legal history. That technique helps determine the proposition's current influence, its ability to illuminate preexisting scholarship, and its capacity to coexist with the other work's insights. G. Edward White's The Marshall Court & Cultural Change 1815-1835[1] combined a thoughtful reading of the dynamic nature of American culture during the early 1800s with a careful analysis of that era's legal beliefs to explore the Marshall Court's internal culture, modes of reasoning, forms of rhetoric, and technical legal doctrine. White showed how the Marshall Court pursued its goal of "Union" by creating an institutional climate of judicial unanimity. Residing in the same boarding-house, the seven Justices casually resolved their differences until they could delegate the writing of their ultimate, usually unanimous decision to one Justice, normally Chief Justice John Marshall in important constitutional law cases. Marshall, in turn, appealed to the country's sense of unity not just through his explicit rhetoric, but also through his jurisprudence, which assumed that as long as judges remained within their appropriate jurisdictional sphere, they could exercise any residual "discretion" without making law or engaging in politics. Under this theory, the Court had no "political discretion" at all; it merely fulfilled its duty to enforce the law. In other

[1] G. Edward White, *The Marshall Court & Cultural Change 1815-1835* (New York, 1991). The amount of Marshall scholarship is prodigious. *See also* Jean Edward Smith, *John Marshall: Definer of a Nation* (New York, 1996), William E. Nelson, 'The Eighteenth-Century Background of John Marshall's Constitutional Jurisprudence', 76 *Minnesota Law Review* 893 (1978).

words, a court acted legally, not politically, whenever it had appropriate legal jurisdiction over a case because that jurisdiction required the court to resolve the issue to the best of its abilities. Although Marshall's opponents never accepted Marshall's conception of his practice, he wrote splendid, sweeping opinions containing a body of law and modes of legal and political thought which have endured to the present day.

White emphasized the Marshall Court's assumption that federal judicial power was coextensive with Congressional power. Under this doctrine, any judicial decision extending federal jurisdiction or validating Congressional power simultaneously expanded both Congressional and Judicial powers at the expense of the States that were subordinated by the Constitution's Supremacy Clause. White divided the Marshall Court's cases into four categories: admiralty jurisdiction, sovereignty and union, property and vested rights under the contracts clause, and natural law and racial minorities. White contrasted the Marshall Court consistent use of nontextual "natural law" arguments to defend the rights of white creditors with its unwillingness to extend similar rights to black slaves and its "diluted" version of natural rights to Native Americans.[2]

Although admiralty is technically not constitutional law, White began his doctrinal analysis in that field to demonstrate the Marshall Court Justices' skill in extending federal court jurisdiction (and thus Congressional power) while simultaneously establishing doctrinal limits to that power. This doctrinally constrained expansionism enhanced the imagery of the Supreme Court as an institution of law and principle. In *DeLovio v. Boit*, a District Court decision that the Supreme Court never reviewed, Justice Story established the basic parameters of admiralty jurisdiction: litigants rely on federal courts to resolve virtually any activity concerning ships while the boats were in waters influenced by the ebb and flow of tide. Thus contracts, insurance policies, and wage disputes of sea-faring vessels could all be litigated in federal courts. But when interstate and international trade extended from the coastline to interior rivers as the country expanded westward, the federal judiciary could no longer rely on tides to establish jurisdiction to preserve uniformity in the United States' trade law. The Supreme Court then interpreted the Commerce Clause (including the derivative "dormant commerce clause" doctrine[3]) to establish Congressional and judicial power over all "navigation" on "navigable waters."[4] Quite simply, the Court used a mix of admiralty law and constitutional law to regulate business on the ocean and rivers, the nation's major arteries of interstate and foreign commerce.

---

2 White, op. cit., ibid., at 706.

3 *Willson v. Black-bird Creek Marsh Co.*, 27 U.S. (2 Pet.) 245 (1829).

4 *Gibbons v. Ogden*, 22 U.S. (9 Wheat.) 1 (1824).

Fairly early in his book, White set forth the constitutional premises that Marshall shared with his Republican opponents: "[F]ew quarreled with the starting premises: America was a republic; property rights were to be protected; commerce was to be encouraged; liberty and virtue were to be furthered; sovereignty was to be divided among the respective spheres of influence."[5] By making a list of assumptions, some of which could and would conflict with each other, White avoided the mistake of reducing the country's goals to a single factor. But he did not include as a "starting premise" the equally universal commitment to the growth of the republican empire. Instead, he emphasized the country's expansion as one of the major forces of "cultural change," an external, background pressure on the existing legal system.

White quoted James Fennimore Cooper's anxieties about the country's explosive growth: "[T]he first impression that strikes the mind is the impossibility that 100,000,000 people should consent to live quietly under the same government."[6] In some detail, he described Cooper's novel *The Pioneers* as a tragic tale of the triumph of the rule of law, often fraudulently implemented by scheming lawyers, over the natural rights of men like the hunter Natty Bumppo, who ultimately had to leave his village for new western wilderness.[7] But most of Cooper's American contemporaries, including those seven Justices sitting on the Supreme Court, did not see their vigorous society as inherently problematic. The Marshall Court was an enthusiastic advocate of national power and expansion. White also discussed Jefferson and Madison's Malthusian belief that the vast land would absorb millions of virtuous agrarians before it would overflow into invariably corrupt cities. Because of its large size, the United States would be able to avoid for many decades the inevitable tendency of republican governments to degenerate into corruption.[8]

So what difference does it make to turn "the quest for empire" into a shared constitutional premise instead of the major background fact of "cultural change?" First of all, the omission generates misconceptions. One perceives expansionism as some external force the Court is responding to, instead of fostering through its constitutional doctrine. Omitting empire-building from constitutional jurisprudence tends to de-politicize the Court and its jurisprudence. One is more likely to see the Court as a fairly autonomous legal unit, independent of one of the country's basic goals, a perspective which in turn can lead to an excessive focus on modes of

---

5 White, op. cit., *supra* ch. 6, n.1, at 52-53.
6 Ibid., at 15.
7 Ibid., at 46.
8 Ibid., at 69.

arguments and theories of interpretations at the expense of analysis of decisions' outcomes.

Next, there is a necessary tendency in legal analysis to separate cases into their doctrines; admiralty law is different in many ways than constitutional law or property law. The concept of "empire" provides some unity between these seemingly unrelated doctrines. The Marshall Court's jurisprudence constitutionalized a particular ideological/political tradition, the imperial vision of Alexander Hamilton. For it was Hamilton, inspired by the British Empire's successful example and David Hume's observations about political economy, who foresaw a strong national republic, dominated by a powerful Executive, but heavily dependent upon and supported by concentrated private power. In his two chapters on the origins of the Marshall Court's jurisprudence, White lucidly, even thrillingly explains the influence of "republicanism" and different conceptions of "common law" on the Court, but only refers to Hamilton in two relatively minor passages.

A. Allocating and Restraining Public Power

Chief Justice John Marshall knew his goal of increasing federal court power (and thus national power in general) to protect private power and Congressional authority at the expense of the States would be extremely controversial. After all, Justice Chase had almost been impeached for excessively deviating from the existing political ethos.

While the Northern commercial economy needed a strong central government to protect its investments and to attract capital from abroad, the Southerners correctly sensed from the very beginning that a dynamic federal government was the most serious threat to their preferred form of capital, slavery. Although many decades would pass before the country fatally divided over this terrible problem, the slavery issue informed constitutional thinking from the beginning. A month into the Convention, Madison warned: "[T]he States were divided into different interests not by their difference of size, buy by other circumstances; the most material of which resulted partly from climate, but principally from (the effects of) having or not having slaves. These two causes concurred in forming the great division of interests in the U. States. It did not lie between the large & small States: it lay between the Northern & Southern..."[9] Having all but completed its work, the Constitutional Convention almost disintegrated over the slavery issue.[10] During the ratification debates, Patrick Henry

---

9 Madison, *Speech* (June 30, 1787), *in* 1 Farrand, op. cit., *supra* ch. 1, n.178, at 486.

10 Ellis, op. cit., *supra* ch. 1, n.17, at 91-96.

warned how Congress might abuse its dangerously vague "implied powers":

> Slavery is detested. We feel its fatal effects – we deplore it with all the pity of humanity. Let all these considerations, at some future period, press with full force on the minds of Congress. Let that urbanity, which I trust will distinguish America, and the necessity of national defence, let all these things operate on their minds; they will search that paper, and see if they have power of manumission. And have they not, sir? Have they not power to provide for the general defence and welfare? May they not that these call for the abolition of slavery? May they not pronounce all slaves free, and will they not be warranted by that power?[11]

This instinctual Southern reaction in favor of State rights lurked behind virtually every constitutional issue. Although they may not have been consciously aware of the linkage, Jefferson and Madison's reliance on State legislatures to protest the Federalist's Alien and Sedition Acts was also an assertion of State authority to protect slavery from federal incursion. The merger might never have taken place but for a strategic miscalculation. The Southern States joined the Union partially because they mistakenly believed that Southern population and wealth would eventually overtake the North.[12]

The young republic's recurrent domestic problem was to avoid making slavery the central political issue. By aggressively protecting private property, whatever its form, Marshall provided continuing constitutional protection to slavery. He thereby sufficiently submerged the issue, protecting the Supreme Court's steadily growing popularity and thus its legitimacy as a major governmental actor. But given the intransigence of his opponents, who feared "consolidation" irrespective of slavery, Marshall needed more than pro-property and pro-slavery doctrine to convince the public that the Court was not a partisan political institution resolving basic political issues, exercising unjustifiable "political discretion" instead of appropriate judicial "judgment."

He employed several rhetorical, analytical, and doctrinal devices that benefited from the widespread nineteenth century jurisprudential assumption that "the essential function of judges was to discover legal principles and apply them to particular situations."[13] In virtually every opinion, Marshall would first separate and state the issues, next turn to the Constitutional text and "general principles" to "find" legal principles, and

---

11 Patrick Henry, *Speech* (June 24, 1788), *1 Elliot*, op. cit., *supra* Intro., n.10, at 590.

12 Letter of James Madison to Thomas Jefferson (March 19, 1787), James Madison, *Writings* (Jack Rakove, ed., New York, 1999), 65.

13 White, op. cit., *supra* ch. 6, n.1, at 198.

then apply them to the particular facts, somehow almost always coming out in favor of central government and private property. Because of his consistent bias toward the federal government, Marshall needed more than the myth that judges do not make law, but only discover law. After all, his opponents were hardly fooled. The Republican theorist Judge Spencer Roane wrote powerful newspaper articles criticizing his major opinions. Thomas Jefferson and Madison frequently condemned Marshall's analysis. These attacks were so effective that Marshall responded with several *in cognito* articles of his own.[14] He also fought back in his legal opinions by twisting the knife. He listed Jefferson and Madison's embargoes, so despised by his fellow Federalists, as precedents for the extension of Congressional Commerce power over "navigation" in *Gibbons v. Ogden*.[15] And he almost gleefully dismissed Aaron Burr's treason charges on technicalities, enraging President Jefferson, who had finally decided to pursue Burr aggressively after initially vacillating over Burr's scheming:

> Several months have elapsed since this fact did occur, if it ever occurred. More than five weeks have elapsed since the opinion of the Supreme Court has declared the necessity of proving the fact if it exists. Why is it not proved? To the Executive government is entrusted the important power of prosecuting those whose crimes may disturb the public repose or endanger its safety. It would be easy in much less time than has intervened since Colonel Burr has been alleged to have assembled his troops, to procure affidavits establishing this fact.[16]

Although Marshall's opinions did not prove sufficiently persuasive to prevent armed conflict, they may have helped delay civil war until the federal government and its Northern supporters had gained sufficient economic and military strength to defeat the South. At the least, Marshall's arguments helped provide the ideological and rhetorical groundwork for the Union nationalists (particularly Daniel Webster).

Marshall developed what he called a "train of reasoning"[17] consisting of arguments, metaphors, and fictions to reinforce the underlying proposition that his Court was not making law, only discovering and applying it. He began some of his most important cases by contemplating the gory alternative of civil war, a choice that effortlessly combined justification,

---

[14] *See generally John Marshall's Defense of McCulloch v. Maryland* (Gerald Gunther ed., Stanford, 1969) and R. Kent Newmyer, John Marshall, 'McCulloch v. Maryland, and the Southern States' Rights Tradition', 33 *John Marshall Law Review*, 875 (2000).

[15] 22 U.S. (9 Wheat.) 1 (1824).

[16] *United States v. Burr*, 25 F. Cas. 2, 15 (C.C. D. Va., 1807).

[17] Marshall first used the term in a Circuit Court decision, *Short v. Skipwith*, 22 F. Cas. 9, 12 (C.C. D. Va., 1806).

fear, finality, and authority. The Supreme Court must decide certain important cases to avert such a conflict, which all reasonable people dreaded. Once the Court resolved a particular case, opponents had only three choices; they must accept the Court's decisions, amend the Constitution, or fight. In the first paragraph of *McCulloch v. Maryland*, Marshall observed that the issue "must be resolved peacefully, or remain a source of hostile legislation, perhaps, of a hostility of a still more serious nature; and if it is to be so decided, by this tribunal alone can the decision be made."[18] In *Cohens v. Virginia*, Marshall rejected the proposition that the Supreme Court could not review State Court decisions upholding state laws against federal constitutional challenges: "They maintain that the nation does not possess a department capable of restraining peaceably, and by authority of law, any attempts which may be made, by a part, against the legitimate powers of the whole; and that the government is reduced to the alternative of submitting to such attempts, or resisting them by force."[19] Marshall acknowledged in *Craig v. Missouri* that the Court's decisions might lead to civil war because a state might become enraged by a "wound" on its sovereign dignity, but replied that such political decisions must be made elsewhere while the Court continued to fulfill its constitutional obligations:

> To these admonitions, we can only answer: that if the exercise of that jurisdiction which has been imposed upon us by the constitution and laws of the United States, shall be calculated to bring on those dangers which have been indicated: or if it shall be indispensable to the preservation of the union, and consequently of the independence and liberty of these states: these are considerations which address themselves to those departments which may with perfect propriety be influenced by them. This department can listen only to the mandates of law; and can tread only that path which is marked out by duty.[20]

In other words, the Court could and would develop the basic structure of the republic, through its "legal" interpretations of the Constitution's text and other relevant legal authorities, until the political culture chose either to amend the Constitution or turn to combat.

Having established the Court's essential role as peacekeeper in the debate over allocation of state and federal power, Marshall used a variety of concepts, including empire, to place the States in a subordinate position. In *Fletcher v. Peck*, he reminded the State of Georgia that "She is part of a large empire; she is a member of the American union; and that the union

---

18 *McCulloch v. Maryland*, 17 U.S. (4 Wheat.) 316, 400-01 (1819).

19 *Cohens v. Virginia*, 19 U.S. at 377 (1821).

20 *Craig*, 29 U.S. at 438.

has a constitution the supremacy of which all acknowledge, and which imposes limits on the legislatures of the several states, and which none claim a right to pass."[21] In a land where most politicians still thought of the "United States" as a plural phrase, reflecting multiple sovereignties, Marshall consistently used words like "nation," and "union" to describe the republic. In *McCulloch*, he asserted that the system was a Union, not a league.[22] In *Cohens*, he followed existing conventions by using the noun "United States" as a plural but conceptualized it in the singular: "[T]he United States form, for many, *and for most important purposes*, a single nation..."[23] Within this sphere of "most important purposes," this singular entity had complete sovereignty: "These States are constituent parts of the United States. They are members of one great empire – for some purposes sovereign, for some purposes subordinate."[24]

To rebut the countervailing argument that the Constitution was merely a compact between the sovereign States, the Marshall Court combined the doctrine of popular sovereignty with the metaphor of social contract. It invoked "the people" as the ultimate authority for its construction of the Constitution's federal structure. For instance, Justice Story set forth the fundamental difference between the Constitution and the Articles of Confederation: "The constitution was for a new government, organized with new substantive powers, and not a mere supplementary charter to a government already existing. The confederation was a compact between states; and its structure and powers were wholly unlike those of the national government. The constitution was an act of the people of the United States to supercede the confederation..."[25] Those who maintained the State compact theory, which placed the States as primary contractors at the center of the constitutional system, were trying to resurrect a system that "the people" had rejected for something profoundly different. Quite simply, they did not want the States to have certain powers.[26] Furthermore, the States had implied that they would accept the people's will when their legislatures authorized separate constitutional conventions to ratify the Constitution. Only the people, acting through their representatives at the Convention, had the capacity to accept or reject the Constitution.[27] Consequently, the people had given the federal courts the legitimate authority to "coerce" the States through their own judges, who had taken an

---

21 *Fletcher v. Peck*, 10 U.S. (6 Cranch) 87, 136 (1810).
22 *Cohens*, 19 U.S. at 354.
23 *Id.* at 413 (italics added).
24 Ibid., at 414.
25 *Martin v. Hunter's Lessee*, 14 U.S. (1 Wheat.) 304, 332 (1816).
26 Ibid., at 325.
27 *McCulloch*, 17 U.S. at 404.

oath to comply with the national Constitution: "It is obvious that this obligation is imperative upon the state judges in their official, and not merely in their private, capacities."[28]

In *Marbury v. Madison*,[29] Marshall turned again to "the people" to justify the assertion of constitutional judicial review over Congress and the Presidency: "That the people have an original right to establish, for their future government, such principles as, in their opinion, shall most conduce to their own happiness, is the basis on which the whole American fabric has been erected."[30] The Supreme Court, bound by its oath, was obligated to enforce these fundamental principles against all violators, be they Secretary of State Madison, who refused to deliver a signed and sealed appointment to Marbury, or Congress, which unconstitutionally expanded the Supreme Court's original jurisdiction to permit Marbury to bring his case directly to the Supreme Court instead of through appeal. The Court was the true and best representative of the people, who had expressed their will only through the written Constitution and who had "assigned to the judicial department" the task of making a "final construction" of the Constitution.[31] Consequently, there was no "countermajoritarian difficulty," because the Court represented "We, the People," a supermajoritarian body politic that could design the Constitution to trump majorities in any way it saw fit. Congress merely represented temporary, often passionate majorities, while the Court alone acted on behalf of "the People." Should other authorities such as the States, the President, or Congress dislike the Court's decisions, they had only one peaceful alternative: Return to the people and ask them to amend the Constitution's text:

> The people made the constitution, and the people can unmake it. It is the creature of their will, and lives only by their will. But this supreme and irresistible power to make or unmake, resides only in the whole body of the people, not in any sub-division of them. The attempt of any of the parts to exercise it is usurpation, and ought to be repelled by those to whom the people have delegated their power of repelling it.[32]

Again and again, the Marshall Court supplemented this analysis with references to the "Union" and the "nation": "The American states, as well as the American people, have believed a close and firm Union to be essential to their liberty and to their happiness."[33]

---

28 *Martin*, 14 U.S. at 340.
29 5 U.S. (1 Cranch) 137 (1803).
30 Ibid., at 176.
31 *Cohens*, 19 U.S. at 377.
32 Ibid., at 389.
33 Ibid., at 380.

Marshall's eloquence could not prevent the country from gradually sectionalizing and the States rights advocates from continuing their counterattack. Although most opponents remained committed to the "state compact" structure, in which the States were the original social contractors who agreed to form a Union and thus remained the ultimate sovereigns, some of the more thoughtful anti-consolidationists supplemented that metaphor with a rival conception of popular sovereignty. The first words of the Preamble of the Constitution do not just read "We, the People," but rather "We, the People of the United States." These States rights advocates contended that the original social contract was between the People of each State, not between the People of the entire nation. The Constitution was not formed by "We the People," a national polity perpetually committed to Union, but was the product of "We the People of the United States," in which the "people of each State" retained their basic sovereignty by entering into a revocable compact with the people of every other State. After all, the Constitution had required ratification by a majority of representatives chosen by the voters of nine separate States, not by a majority or supermajority of the voting population of the entire United States. The people of each State were the ultimate sovereigns because they were the original social contractors. Proving once again that political ideology is more powerful than even the most potent examples of legal reasoning, Justices sympathetic to this view gradually gained control of the Court. For example, dissenting Justice Baldwin stated: "The constitution of the United States was formed, not, in my opinion, as some have contended, by the people of the United States, nor as others, by the states; but by a combined power, exercised by the people, through their delegates, limited in their sanctions, to the respective states."[34]

When it came to interpreting and applying different sections of the Constitution to particular cases, the Marshall Court supplemented its invocations of "the people" with two more abstractions, "The Framers" and "the State Conventions," and one primary source for divining those abstractions' intentions, *The Federalist*. These sources were doubly useful to Marshall because Hamilton played a significant role in the Framing and a major role in writing *The Federalist*, while the Republican James Madison, who had since become a critic of the Court, was the leading Founder and the other major author of *The Federalist*. Marshall could appear to be incorporating the views of both Federalists and Republicans by citing two of their most important leaders, even though Madison had since shifted to a less centralized conception of the republic. Of course, Madison thought

[34] *Worcester v. Georgia*, 13 U.S. (6 Pet.) 515, 569 (1832) (Baldwin, J., dissenting).

Marshall was misconstruing *The Federalist*.[35] Marshall, however, retained the last legal opportunity to interpret that important text which was packed with nationalistic passages (including many references to "empire"). Marshall's interpretive moves also guaranteed that the Constitution would be construed primarily through the ideological prism of the elite Framers who created and defended it, instead of the far more democratic mass of voters that sometimes elected a majority of representatives favoring the proposed Constitution. Overall, Marshall turned to "the people" to justify broad judicial review and to the Framers to construe particular parts of the Constitution. To justify the Supreme Court's protection in *Fletcher v. Peck* of third parties who had bought land from speculators that had flagrantly bribed the Georgia legislature to grant them the land, Marshall invoked both "the Framers" with the "people" to rein in a subsequent State law attempting to regain the land:

> Whatever respect might have been felt for the state sovereignties, it is not to be disguised that *the framers of the Constitution* viewed, with some apprehension, the violent acts which might grow out of the feelings of the moment; *and that the people of the United States*, in adopting that instrument, have manifested a determination to shield themselves and their property from the effects of those sudden and strong passions to which men are exposed.[36]

On the other hand, in that same case Marshall made "the people" disappear from daily operations: "But the real party, it is said, are the people, and when their agents are unfaithful, the acts of those agents cease to be obligatory. It is, however, to be recollected that the people can only act through these agents, and that, while within the power conferred on them, their acts must be considered as the acts of the people."[37] Thus "the people" could express themselves and bind themselves through their elected representatives, but only the Court could speak for "The People" who ratified the Constitution. Except by amending the Constitution, they had no direct effect on the political culture. The Court would ensure that agents stayed within their appropriate sphere, but after that, the elected branches best represented the people on a daily basis while the Court best represented "The People" when it exercised judicial review.

According to Marshall, "the People" did not just want a court that would constrain the States. They also wanted the President and Congress to exercise effectively and aggressively their "important powers." One way the elected branches could best serve the people is through that great

---

[35] Letter from James Madison to Thomas Jefferson (Feb. 8, 1825), Madison, *Mind*, op. cit., *supra* ch. 1, n.39, at 349.

[36] *Fletcher*, 10 U.S. at 137-38 (italics added).

[37] Ibid., at 132-33.

adhesive, interstate commerce: "[W]hen we consider the nature of our Union; that it is intended to make us, in a great measure, one people, as to commercial objects..."[38] Although they had very different forms of private property, Americans could rely upon the Supreme Court to protect that property and to encourage trade between the different regions.

Marshall validated the National Bank in *McCulloch v. Maryland* in part because he did not believe a court had the capacity to determine how "necessary" a corporate bank was as a means to the textually authorized ends of protecting the currency and raising taxes. Only Congress could and should make that discretionary decision. Professor White noted that *McCulloch* was particularly important because its validation of extensive implied Congressional powers all but formally resolved the legal debate over the constitutionality of two even more important and controversial Congressional activities: federal "internal improvements" of roads and canals and Congressional slavery legislation.[39] The decision also made it possible for Congress to create, if it ever wanted, mercantile corporations like the East India Company. After all, the National Bank had been created not just to facilitate public ends, but also to generate private profits. Later Presidents, such as James Madison and Andrew Jackson, would interpret the Constitution to preclude federal internal improvements and a national bank, but their interpretations could only be ratified or rejected in the majoritarian political arena, not the legal forum.

Because Marshall believed that judicial power was co-extensive with legislative power, he played leapfrog with his doctrine. Some cases would extend Congressional authority, thereby expanding judicial authority by implication. Another set of cases would first expand judicial power, creating precedents for later Congressional action. Precedent after precedent accumulated, creating a steadily expanding national government. There were some exceptions to this growth. Marshall was a brilliant lawyer, judge, and politician who could sense how far to push his authority. As has been frequently pointed out,[40] his carefully crafted opinion in *Marbury v. Madison* asserted Supreme Court authority over both the Executive and Legislative branches without requiring any of the three branches to act. By holding that Congress had unconstitutionally given the plaintiff Marbury, who had made a valid claim against the Executive, original jurisdiction in the Supreme Court to bring his writ of mandamus, Marshall could condemn both the Executive and Legislative branches without issuing any order needing subsequent enforcement. Thus, on the surface of *Marbury*, Marshall constrained Supreme Court power by

---

38 *Ogden*, 25 U.S. at 334.

39 White, op. cit., *supra* ch. 6, n.1, at 542.

40 Laurence H. Tribe, *American Constitutional Law* (New York, 1978), 23.

limiting its original jurisdiction, but barely beneath that surface he had made the Court an equal branch of the national government. Given the hostility of the Republican President and Congress, manifested most dramatically in their elimination of lower federal courts filled with Federalist judges and their failed effort to impeach Justice Chase, Marshall knew he must proceed carefully. Furthermore, relentless expansion of federal court jurisdiction would have undercut his argument that he was acting under a duty of law mandated by the Constitutional text and supported his opponents' arguments that he was turning the Court into a political organ.

Finally, Marshall was a judge who took text seriously. The Constitutional text had sought to limit both national and state power. Having set the basic conceptual and doctrinal groundwork in cases like *Marbury v. Madison*, *McCulloch v. Maryland*, *Cohens v. Virginia*, and *Martin v. Hunter's Lessee*, he and his colleagues did not need to be fanatical in subsequent derivative cases which, merely by being subsequent, were less important. For instance, they could unanimously hold that federal courts had no common law jurisdiction to create federal crimes; federal courts could only enforce Congressional laws enacted prior to any alleged violations. They could accept a state-built dam that blocked a navigable river to stop disease;[41] the Court retained jurisdiction over the case and Congress could choose to eliminate the dam through legislation under the interstate commerce clause. Most importantly, Marshall was strongly deferential to State taxing power as long as it was not facially aimed at federal operations. Even when he struck down a State tax on the National bank's operations in *McCulloch*, he held that States could pass general tax laws, covering all related transactions or assets, that would apply to the National Bank. For example, the Bank would have to pay any general State property tax that applied to everyone who owned property in that State.[42]

The Marshall Court deliberately played a less active role in establishing the contours of the United States' "military constitution." By stating in *Marbury v. Madison* that most foreign affairs questions were judicially unreviewable "political" decisions, he allocated responsibility for the implementation of foreign affairs and the war power to the two elected branches.[43] In those areas, the politicians would be primarily constrained by their consciences and the electorate. Thus Marshall helped created a Machiavellian republic, in which the rule of law would apply internally, but not externally. He also implemented David Ramsay's vision of a republic headed by an emperor-like figure who had vast discretion over foreign

41 *Willson v. The Blackbird Creek Marsh Co.*, 27 U.S. (2 Pet.) 245 (1829).
42 *McCulloch*, 17 U.S. at 436.
43 *Marbury*, 5 U.S. at 166.

policy. While making it clear that Congress could somewhat constrain Presidential power/discretion by placing conditions on Presidential appointments,[44] Marshall explained that in the absence of such conditions, the President would have total power, far more power than a British Prime Minister had over his Cabinet: "If, by law, the officer be removable at the will of the president, then a new appointment may be immediately made, and the rights of the officer are terminated."[45] Thus the President could enforce the constitutional convention of "collective responsibility," which requires loyalty throughout the Executive branch, with a vengeance; any Cabinet official who disagreed with him, publicly or privately, could be summarily removed from office. Within the sphere allocated to him by Congress, the President gained the powers of an emperor over his courtiers. In such a case, the President would be exercising his political discretion, not violating any legally protected expectations/rights of an individual.[46] This centralization of force was not limitless. In *Houston v. Moore*, Justice Story held that Congress did not have total control over the State militias. It could "organize, arm, and discipline" them, but the States otherwise retained complete sovereignty until the Congress called them to arms.[47]

In 1823, Marshall directly considered in *American Insurance Co. v. Canter* the questions of the structure and rights within the American empire. In a dispute over title to salvage, the plaintiffs asserted that the Florida Territorial Court had unconstitutionally granted title to a rival because neither Congress nor the Florida Territorial legislature had authority to establish such courts that could deprive individuals of their private property rights. Once again, Marshall, unlike Jefferson, aggressively implied extensive federal powers from a mixture of text and general principles; the Union's powers of making wars and treaties and "the usage of the world" implied the derivative power to acquire additional land, "either by conquest or by treaty."[48] Sounding like Jefferson when he rebuffed the Louisiana leaders who had sought republican government in their Territory after the Purchase, Marshall ruled against the challengers, who were inhabitants of Florida, because they:

---

[44] *Id.* at 167. Marbury's holding and reasoning undercut the contemporary constitutional argument that the Executive must be "unitary," completely under Presidential control. *See* Steve G. Calabresi & Kevin H. Rhodes, 'The Structural Constitution: Unitary Executive, Plural Judiciary', 105 *Harvard Law Review* 1155 (1992) and Cass R. Sunstein, 'The Myth of the Unitary Executive', 7 *Administrative Law Journal* 299 (1993).

[45] *Marbury*, 5 U.S. at 167.

[46] *Id.* at 166.

[47] *Houston v. Moore*, 18 U.S. (5 Wheat.) 1, 50 (1820).

[48] *American Insurance Co. v. Canter*, 26 U.S. (1 Pet.) 511, 542 (1828).

> do not, however, participate in political power; they do not share in the government till Florida shall become a State. In the mean time Florida continues to be a territory of the United States, governed by virtue of that clause in the Constitution which empowers Congress "to make all needful rules and regulations respecting the territory or other property belonging to the United States." Perhaps the power of governing a territory belonging to the United States which has not, by becoming a State, acquired the means of self-government, may result necessarily from the fact that it is not within the jurisdiction of any particular State, and is within the jurisdiction of the United States. The right to govern may be the inevitable consequence of the right to acquire territory. Whichever may be the source whence the power is derived, the possession of it is unquestioned.[49]

In other words, Congress exercised the "the combined powers of the general, and of a state government."[50]

More than any other Marshall opinion, even *McCulloch v. Maryland*, this case would prove to be the greatest threat to the South. The decision could easily be construed to give Congress authority (or at least subsequent Territorial legislative authority) over the slavery issue in all Territories. Because Congress, not the States, had sovereign authority over the Territories, neither the States nor individual citizens had clear constitutional rights to export slaves into new Territories or keep them there should Congress prohibit slavery. Both the North and the South agreed that State governments determined the legality of slavery; this power would now reside in Congress. Although Congress (or its agents the Territorial legislatures and courts) almost certainly could not have taken preexisting slaves away from their owners, it could ban the continuation of slavery within any Territory. The federal government could eventually lock slavery into the existing States until enough new Free Territories entered the Union, thereby upsetting the precarious balance of power between the slave and free States. Unlike so many of his Southern colleagues, Marshall chose to expand national power rather than reduce potential threats to slavery when the choice had to be made. Or, to put the case in terms of the structures of republican empires, he elevated national control of recently seized lands over the egalitarian arguments that all citizens and/or States had equal access to those new lands, an equality that included the right to bring all their preexisting property with them.

This approach clashes with the subsequent views of Calhoun and Taney that each of the States had continuing rights involving the Territories. Also, the decision is virtually impossible to reconcile with *Dred Scott's* holding that the Territories Clause was limited to the lands covered by the

49 Ibid.

50 Ibid., at 546.

Northwest Ordinance. Demonstrating how clever lawyers can turn virtually any precedent until a justification for subsequent action, Taney found support for *Dred Scott* in *Canter* because it held that Congressional power over individuals was not absolute. First of all, individuals retained their preexisting property rights; only the political system had been changed. In addition, Spain's treaty with the United States had stipulated that the Floridians would be incorporated into the United States as soon as possible and would receive "the enjoyment of the privileges, rights, and immunities of the citizens of the United States."[51] Congress then delegated its regulatory power to the Florida Legislature, which would have "legislative powers over all rightful objects of legislation; but no law shall be valid, which is inconsistent with the laws and Constitution of the United States."[52] Thus, the Florida legislature could establish courts regulating the law of salvage, as well as any other property law. According to Taney, Congress had created laws "inconsistent" with the Constitution.

Canter can be read more narrowly without reaching Taney's extremes of denying Congress virtually any powers over the newer Territories. Congress could have undivided sovereignty over the territories yet be precluded from preventing individuals from bringing in new slaves (assuming that one aspect of equal citizenship is the constitutional right to bring all of one's property into Territorial lands held in common). For an analogy, one could easily argue that Congress cannot violate the First Amendment rights of those living in Territories even if Congress has "sovereign authority" over those lands. On the other hand, *Canter* does not necessarily guarantee full constitutional rights to Territorial inhabitants; the Treaty with Spain and the Congressional enabling statute were independent legal sources of constitutional rights. Thus it remained possible to have Territories that did not provide full constitutional rights to their inhabitants, an approach that would make the prohibition of slavery even easier. We shall see later in the book that such a discriminatory doctrine became reality in *The Insular Cases*. The central importance of *Canter*, which Professor White considered only for its jurisdictional implications, reconfirms the utility of emphasizing the role of empire in constitutional ideology. Perhaps some readers think the case for America's imperial republic has been overstated or overemphasized, but is the reader willing to argue that this aspect of *Canter* is not one of Marshall's most important constitutional cases even though it is not even close to being part of the traditional "constitutional canon" that most scholars and students know?

---

51 Ibid., at 542.

52 Ibid., at 543.

B. Defending and Limiting Private Rights and Private Power

Concentrated private power was a crucial institutional component in Hamilton's imperial vision; the federal government would have a symbiotic relationship with a group of wealthy individuals. Chief Justice John Marshall consistently construed the Constitution to protect not just private rights, but also private power and its special relationship with the central government. The States were the focal point of Marshall's attack. Only once, in *Marbury v. Madison*, did Marshall invalidate federal action. But it is worth noting that *Marbury* itself is in part a private property case; the Court chastised the Executive for unconstitutionally violating Marbury's "vested right" to his five year appointment as justice of the peace, a right he gained when Madison refused to deliver a commission previously signed and sealed by the outgoing Adams administration. Marshall primarily relied upon Madison's strategy of protecting the property rights of all, which in effect particularly benefited the wealthy. For example, the protection of creditors assists a relatively poor man who has loaned a small amount of money to his neighbor in the same way it benefits a rich man who has loaned millions to thousands. But overall, the wealthy are predominately going to be the creditors. As a class, they flourish under the neutral application of general rules.[53]

Such general private property rights, which protect everyone while creating a system favoring the wealthy, are not the equivalent of private power – the actual concentration of wealth and influence in the hands of relatively few people. The Marshall Court laid the groundwork for an additional legal institution that would soon become the preferred vehicle of private power: the corporation. In *McCulloch*, the Court deferred to Congressional efforts intermingling public and private power when Congress created a national bank. It permitted private interests to plunder the public in *Fletcher v. Peck*[54] by striking down the State of Georgia's legislative attempt to regain land that companies had purchased very inexpensively by bribing many Georgia representatives.[55]

Just as the Marshall Court Justices had relied upon social contract theory to help define the basic relationships between the People, the States, and the Federal government, they used the same methodology to delineate the role of private property and power in the new republic's constitutional system. They supplemented the metaphor of social contract with concept that was even more vague: natural law. The State of Georgia was

[53] Jean Jacques Rousseau, 'The Second Discourse', *The Discourses and Other Early Political Writings* (Victor Gourevitch, ed., Cambridge, 1997), 173.

[54] 10 U.S. (6 Cranch) 162 (1810).

[55] C. Peter Magrath, *Yazoo: The Case of Fletcher v. Peck* (New York, 1966).

precluded from regaining its land in *Fletcher* from innocent third party purchases "either by general principles which are common to our free institutions, or by the particular provisions of the constitution of the United States."[56] The Constitutional text and more general doctrines constantly commingled to constrain public influence: "[R]ight and power will be found to be measured neither by moral law alone, nor universal law alone, nor by the laws of society alone, but by a combination of the three, – an operation in which the moral law is explained and applied by the law of nature, and both modified and adapted to the exigencies of society by positive law."[57]

The use of abstract principles was not merely a culture-bound methodology of the early Nineteenth Century; it may well have been a necessity. Three major historical events reappeared as cases that could not be easily resolved without returning to political/legal "first principles": The European take-over of the continent at the expense of the Native Americans, the introduction of race slavery, and the American Revolution. To determine the property rights, if any, of Native Americans, the Court consulted not only the Constitution and various Treaties, but also basic theories of title acquisition. To ascertain what property rights, if any, white revolutionaries retained to property they owned before they successfully shattered their social contract with the British Empire, the Court employed both social contract and natural law. Finally, the Court needed to reconcile the flagrant tension between slaves' "natural law" rights to the fruit of their labor with the States' positive laws permitting slavery and the Constitution's all but textually explicit support of slavery. During this era, The Marshall Court never faced the other most glaring systemic violation of social contract/natural law principles (and resulting manifestations of inequality throughout America's republican empire): the subordinate legal status of women.

Having grounded its property jurisprudence in constitutional text, natural law, and social contract, the Court focused on four legal doctrines to define constitutionally protected sources of property: possession, conquest, labor, and governmental grants such as patronage, land transfers, and corporate charters. For all its differences with the Jefferson administration, the Marshall Court's theory and application of private property rights was equally a product of the Enlightenment. The two factions' disputes occurred more frequently over the appropriate distribution of public and private power, not over the basic metaphors that helped formulate their political/legal lives.

---

[56] *Fletcher*, 10 U.S. at 139.
[57] *Ogden*, 25 U.S. at 282.

Despite all their enmities, Marshall and Jefferson had similar Enlightenment preferences about the appropriate means to expand the American empire at the expense of Native Americans. Above all, both men favored negotiation over war. In an unparalleled homage to Jefferson, Marshall lauded him in an opinion for the "magnificent purchase of Louisiana."[58] When Marshall first faced the issue of Native American rights in 1823 in *Johnson v. McIntosh*, he combined the prerogatives of empire and paternalism at the expense of private rights. At stake were the claims of white plaintiffs to lands in the Territory of Illinois; the speculators asserted that Indian chiefs had given them the land before the Revolutionary War. On a practical level, such claims would disrupt the federal government's capacity to regulate the Territories. As usual, Marshall started with first principles. A private individual's right to own land was not based upon "abstract justice"; that right depended "entirely on the law of the nation in which they lie."[59] To divide up the spoils of the two continents among themselves, the European countries had formulated the doctrine of "discovery," which Marshall defined as the "exclusive right to extinguish the Indian title of occupancy, either by purchase or by conquest; and gave also a right to such a degree of sovereignty, as the circumstances of the people would allow them to exercise."[60] The English colonists had primarily created their title east of the Mississippi "by the sword." Fortunately, Anglican decency, manifested through public opinion, fostered a relatively egalitarian relationship: "[H]umanity demands, and a wise policy requires, that the rights of the conquered to property should remain unimpaired; that the new subjects should be governed as equitably as the old..."[61] Thus, "equality of citizenship" could humanely and efficiently absorb diverse, defeated populations.

In the United States, however, neither English whites nor Native Americans wanted to merge into a single body politic. The only way to settle the enduring bloody conflicts between the two races was to rely on the principle that "the Indian inhabitants are to be considered merely as occupants, to be protected, indeed, while at peace, in the possession of their lands, but to be deemed incapable of transferring absolute title to others."[62] This denial of equal citizenship was not as heartless as it may first appear to be. The colonies frequently included provisions in their constitutions prohibiting whites from purchasing lands from Native Americans. After all, the Native Americans faced two threats: the overwhelming force of

---

58 *Johnson v. M'Intosh*, 21 U.S. (8 Wheat.) 543, 587 (1823).
59 Ibid., at 572.
60 Ibid., at 587.
61 Ibid., at 589.
62 Ibid., at 591.

governmental power (from both States and the Federal Government) and the vicious dealings of private individuals, "the encroachments of whites."[63] This doctrine prevented any Indian chiefs, claiming to represent their tribe, from selling their people's land to local speculators. The doctrine also obligated the federal government to protect law-abiding Indians and to rely upon purchase, not conquest to gain the lands the Indians still possessed as occupants.

Marshall's opinion relied upon the English version of the social contract between the colonists and the Crown, not the Revolutionary title theory of David Ramsay. Originally, the Crown had complete title to all the lands under the doctrine of discovery. Private individuals had no particularized, vested rights: "[T]he country becomes the property of the discoverers, so far at least as they can use it. They acquire a title in common. The title of the whole land is in the whole society. It is to be divided and parceled out according to will of the society..."[64] Marshall thereby rejected Ramsay's argument that the Crown never had sovereignty over the land but merely authorized the colonists to purchase or conquer the land for their own exclusive title. This profound shift in basic constitutional premises confirms once again the accuracy of Holmes' aphorism that law consists of "the felt necessities of the time." The Revolutionaries employed every conceivable legalistic argument to legitimate their leaving the British Empire. Marshall was far more concerned about regulating the Territories and protecting the Native Americans from private depredations. Marshall's candid race-based imperial system, tempered by paternalistic humanitarianism, is not the noblest form of constitutional morality.[65] But compared to what would follow, Marshall's views proved to be a high point in the Supreme Court's jurisprudence of empire.

Like Jefferson, Marshall was upset by the plight of Native Americans. Marshall began his opinion in *The Cherokee Nation v. Georgia*, in which the Cherokee Nation sought an injunction preventing the State of Georgia from continuing its invasion of their land and gold mines seemingly protected by Federal Treaty: "If courts were permitted to indulge their sympathies, a case better calculated to excite them can scarcely be imagined. A people once numerous, powerful, and truly independent, found by our ancestors *in the quiet and uncontrolled possession* of an ample domain, gradually sinking beneath our superior policy, our arts, and our arms..."[66] Despite these feelings, Marshall dismissed the claim on the

---

[63] Ibid., at 598.
[64] Ibid., at 594.
[65] *See, e.g.*, Bryan, op. cit., *supra* Intro., n.20.
[66] *Cherokee Nation*, 30 U.S. at 15.

important technical ground that the Supreme Court did not have original jurisdiction over a claim brought by the Cherokee Nation against a State because the Cherokee Nation was not a "foreign state" that could bring original actions in the Supreme Court under Article III of the Constitution.[67] This decision directly echoes his famous *Marbury* holding that Congress could not create original jurisdiction in the Supreme Court for a plaintiff to file a mandamus action against the Executive branch. Marshall relied upon political realities and constitutional text. Militarily defeated, the Indians were "in a state of pupilage," dependent upon the federal government for protection and support.[68] The Commerce Clause of the Constitution placed the Indians in a unique, subordinate position; their status was explicitly distinguished from Congress' power over trade with foreign nations. Marshall ended his opinion with a scintilla of hope for the Native Americans: "If it be true that the Cherokee nation has rights, this is not the tribunal in which those rights are to be asserted."[69]

Justice Johnson's concurrence was even more political in tone. Observing that the Indians had "uncontrolled possession" and were "a race of hunters, connected to society by scarcely a semblance of organic government,"[70] Johnson veered close to the Lockean argument that a people could only gain title by developing land, not by occupying it, without completely endorsing that historically dubious, morally repellant, and legally problematic approach. One did not have to improve land to have a right to it.

With brutal candor, Marshall grounded European title exclusively on violence. The Native Americans had lost a "contest for empire"[71] because of superior force, not law.[72] Sovereignty employs force to trump possession and rights, including any rights that can be derived from the Indians' preexisting "hunter states."[73] At least when it comes to conquest, the State is a Hobbesian creature, above the law: "In the exercise of sovereign right, the sovereign is sole arbiter of his own justice. The penalty of wrong is war and subjugation."[74] When the United States defeated the British Empire, it not only gained any residual title that Empire had to the land, but it also assumed that sovereignty's hunger for Indian lands: "The general policy of the United States… always looked to these Indian lands for future

67 Ibid., at 20.
68 Ibid., at 17.
69 Ibid., at 20.
70 Ibid., at 22 (Johnson, J., concurring).
71 Ibid., at 29.
72 Ibid.
73 Ibid., at 23.
74 Ibid., at 29.

acquisition."[75] Those generalities could not determine if the Cherokee had any particular rights under the Constitution or Congressional treaties. Marshall strongly intimated that his Court did not have the power to forcibly enjoin the State of Georgia from invading the reservation because the claim was "of a political nature altogether."[76]

In his concurrence, Justice Baldwin disagreed that the Cherokees had any legally protected rights. They could hunt the land they occupied but they had no basic property right (either individual or collective) to sell that land. The United States had "full dominion"[77] over any Native American tribes in the territories while the States had "full sovereignty"[78] over Indian tribes that remained within the States' preexisting jurisdiction. To justify this peculiar conception of dual sovereignty, Baldwin briefly described the basic structure of the republic. His premise was the constitutional doctrine of state equality that Madison raised at the original Constitutional convention. The United States had made "a solemn pledge to the inhabitants, that whenever their population and circumstances would admit they should form constitutions and become free, sovereign and independent states on equal footing with old component members of the confederation…"[79] From this general proposition,[80] Baldwin concluded that the States had complete power over Native Americans living within their jurisdiction. The federal courts had no power to "divest the states of rights of sovereignty."[81] The argument has its flaws; equality between old and new states does not imply anything about the textually granted constitutional powers of Congress to negotiate treaties and trade with the Indians, grants that are not limited to the Territories. More plausibly, all states were equally forbidden to interfere with Congressional actions in this area.[82] After all, state sovereignty is no more absolute than federal sovereignty.

Justice Thompson's scathing dissent, joined by Justice Story, lambasted their colleagues' narrow interpretations of Article III. Citing the renowned international lawyer Vatel, Thompson concluded that a dominant country could form a large variety of "unequal alliances" with other States within

75 Ibid., at 25-26.

76 Ibid., at 28.

77 Ibid., at 40 (Baldwin, J., concurring).

78 Ibid., at 39.

79 Ibid., at 40.

80 Baldwin also relied upon Constitutional text and political practices to give the States sovereignty over the Indian tribes within their jurisdiction.

81 Ibid., at 49.

82 Carolyn M. Landever, 'Whose Home on the Range? Equal Footing, the "New" Federalism and State Jurisdiction on Public Lands', 47 *Florida Law Review* 557 (1995).

and without its formal jurisdiction.[83] Having never been completely conquered, the Cherokee tribe was still enough of an independent nation to obtain original Supreme Court jurisdiction under Article III. Because the issue was the legality of Georgia's violation of the tribe's continuing right to occupancy,[84] the Court could not avoid the case by labeling it "political" instead of "legal"; "But when the question relates to a mere right of property, and a proper case can be made between competent parties; it forms a proper subject for judicial inquiry."[85] The Supreme Court has the power to prevent State coercion that threatens any person or any group's rights to property, in this case "the total destruction of the complainants' rights."[86] Marshall's sudden anxieties about judicial coercion seemed misplaced. It is hard to imagine that the Chief Justice would have been equally reluctant to order a State to return property unconstitutionally seized from a private individual or federal official. Thompson chided the majority for not following such cases as *Fletcher v. Peck* to protect the Indians' peculiar property right.[87]

One of the enduring mysteries of law is that legal opinions invariably leave so many issues unresolved that one can never be sure how a judge will decide a subsequent, related case. In *Cherokee Nation*, Marshall was torn between three competing norms: outrage at the treatment of the Indians versus his long-held commitment to strictly limiting the Supreme Court's original jurisdiction and his fear of embroiling the Court in a political conflict it could not win. One year later in *Worcester v. Georgia*, Justice Marshall strongly asserted that the Supreme Court could and should protect rights derived from the status of the Cherokee Nation, thereby firmly planting himself in the David Ramsay/Thomas Jefferson tradition of treating the Native Americans as human beings entitled to legally protected natural rights. The facts could not have been more compelling. A white missionary, sanctioned by the President and invited by the Cherokee, had been sentenced to four years hard labor for violating a Georgia law that created a "high misdemeanor" for any person to enter the reservation "under pretext of authority from the Cherokee Indians and their laws."[88] Some might say that Marshall changed his mind because the victim was white, but Marshall's broad, sympathetic rhetoric on behalf of the Cherokee undermines such racial reductionism. Marshall distinguished *Cherokee Nation* as an "original jurisdiction" case. Worcester had appropriately

[83] *Cherokee Nation*, 30 U.S. at 53.
[84] Ibid., at 54-55.
[85] Ibid., at 59.
[86] Ibid., at 79.
[87] Ibid., at 70.
[88] *Worcester v. Georgia*, 31 U.S. (6 Pet.) 515, 521-22 (1832).

appealed from a Georgia court while the Cherokee had violated *Marbury* and Article III by seeking immediate relief from the Supreme Court. Marshall first found it "difficult to comprehend" how the discovery of one group of humans of another group's lands "should give the discoverer rights in the country discovered, which annulled the pre-existing rights of its ancient possessors."[89] Once again, he grounded the Europeans' title on brute force instead of the historically inaccurate doctrine of "discovery": "But power, war, conquest, give rights, which after possession, are conceded by the world; and which can never be controverted by those on whom they descend."[90] Conquest need not mean the total deprivation of rights any more than revolution necessarily signified the extinction of all pre-existing property rights. The colonies retained the exclusive right to purchase the land, which limited the Indians' capacity to sell it, and the Indians kept both the right of possession and the right to sell to the colonies.[91] Covering some of the same ground as this book, Marshall reviewed the colonies' early charters and constitutions to demonstrate that the Americans had a long-standing commitment to Native American rights: "The charters contain passages showing one of their objects to be the civilization of the Indians, and their conversion to Christianity – objects to be accomplished by conciliatory conduct and good example; not by extermination."[92] The early charters, which extended sovereignty from the Atlantic to the Pacific, were aimed at rival Europeans. Indeed, the colonies' charters only authorized defensive wars against their white rivals: "The power of war is given only for defence, not for conquest."[93] Marshall could have found addition authority in the texts of several Colonial Constitutions, which included passages sheltering Indians from private depredation. He quoted a British superintendent of Indian affairs speaking in Quebec in 1763: "I inform you that it is the king's order to all his governors and subjects, to treat Indians with justice and humanity, and to forebear all encroachments on the territories allotted to them; accordingly, all individuals are prohibited from purchasing any of your lands."[94]

Nevertheless, the opinion bowdlerizes the relevant history. Marshall omitted the American colonists' furious reaction to the 1763 Quebec Proclamation. Not all Native American land was gained by purchase. Nor were all the colonial constitutions and charters limited to defensive wars. It is also difficult to base European title on conquest and then conclude that

---

[89] Ibid., at 543.
[90] Ibid.
[91] Ibid., at 545.
[92] Ibid., at 546.
[93] Ibid.
[94] Quoted ibid., at 547.

the doctrine had minimal effect on Native American rights: "The Indian nations had always been considered as distinct, independent political communities, retaining their original natural rights, as the undisputed possessors of the soil, from time immemorial, with the single exception of that imposed by irresistible power, which excluded them from intercourse with any other European potentate than the first discoverer of the coast of the particular region claimed."[95]

Marshall strengthened his opinion by turning to post-Revolutionary history. Like Justice Thompson in *Cherokee Nation*, he quoted Vatel to place the Indian tribes within the international law of nations: "Tributary and feudatory states do not thereby cease to be sovereign and independent states, so long as self government and sovereign and independent authority are left in the administration of the state."[96] An American treaty with the Delaware Indians in 1778 was written in "the language of equality."[97] He next turned to the Cherokee Nation's treaty, noting that the United States never completely defeated the Cherokee. Both sides entered into that treaty to achieve a desired peace. A major part of the bargain was federal protection: "The Cherokees acknowledge themselves to be under the protection of the United States, and no other power. Protection does not imply the destruction of the protected."[98] Overcoming his prior reservations in *Cherokee Nation* about using federal coercion against the States, his conclusion is a classic demonstration of the eloquence of lucidity:

> The Cherokee nation, then, is a distinct community occupying its own territory, with boundaries accurately described, in which the laws of Georgia can have no force, and which the citizens of Georgia have no right to enter, but with the assent of the Cherokees themselves, or in conformity with treaties, and the acts of congress. The whole intercourse between the United States and this nation, is by our constitution and laws, vested in the government of the United States.[99]

This episode ends bleakly, confirming Marshall's earlier statement in *Cherokee Nation* that sovereignty and force often trump the law. President Andrew Jackson, who had a disturbingly different view of the American Constitution than Virginia aristocrats like Jefferson and Marshall, is said to have replied: "John Marshall has made his decision, now let him enforce

---

95 Ibid., at 559.
96 Ibid., at 561.
97 Ibid., at 549.
98 Ibid., at 552.
99 Ibid., at 561.

it."[100] Georgia continued the cleansing of the remaining Cherokee, forcing them on their "Trail of Tears" to resettle in the Far West. By this single brutal inaction, which proves that it matters which particular person controls the reins of government, Jackson elevated undiluted racism, violence, and lawlessness above the nation's obligations to keep its commitments to its "tributary states."

Hemmed in by the Constitutional text and the South's ever-growing commitment to slavery, Marshall reinforced that vicious institution in *The Antelope* by returning a large number of slaves to the Spanish and Portuguese Consuls.[101] Echoing Locke, he concluded that although slavery "is contrary to the law of nature" because "every man has a natural right to the fruits of his own labor," slavery has long been considered a legitimate spoil of war. He alluded to the Greeks: "But from the earliest times war has existed, and war confers rights in which all have acquiesced. Among the most enlightened nations of antiquity, one of these was, that the victor might enslave the vanquished. This, which was the usage of all, could not be pronounced repugnant to the law of nations..."[102] Up to the current moment, slavery has been a tool of empire: "It has been sanctioned in modern times by the laws of all nations who possess distant colonies, each of whom has engaged in it as a common business which no other could rightfully interrupt."[103] Consequently, the United States must return these slaves, who were being smuggled into the State of Florida contrary to the Federal law prohibiting slave importation, because they were found in the hands of pirates who had stolen them on the high seas. This opinion, like virtually every other important legal decision, was hardly inevitable. Marshall could have held that the Spanish and Portuguese Consuls did not have standing to assert the rights of the original owners (who may well have been American citizens using the foreign ships to evade their own laws). Or, more dramatically, he could have held that when the rights of liberty and property clash, there exists a presumption in favor of liberty, a presumption that particularly includes all attempts to import slaves in violation of Congressional laws. While Marshall was willing to aggravate the South through general, broad assertions of federal power, he was not about to strike directly at the heart of their economic system.

Having established basic property rights through conquest, the British immigrants grounded their particular liberty and property rights in "the rights of Englishmen." Although possession could sometimes generate

---

[100] Leonard Baker, *John Marshall: A Life in the Law* (New York, 1974), 745.

[101] *See, e.g.*, John T. Noonan, Jr., *The Antelope: The Ordeal of the Recaptured Africans in the Administrations of James Monroe and John Quincy Adams* (Berkeley, 1977).

[102] 23 U.S. (10 Wheat.) 66, 120 (1825).

[103] Ibid., at 115.

rights via the technical common law doctrine of "adverse possession," the Marshall Court found authority for the citizenry's rights in the Constitution and natural law/social contract principles. Private individuals could obtain "vested rights" either by a grant from the government or through their own labor that the Court had an obligation to protect. For example, Marbury's "vested property right" to the governmental commission giving him a governmental salary for five years was not a fruit of his labor, but rather a grant. Eager to cover as much ground as possible in *Marbury v. Madison*, Marshall analogized Marbury's "commission" to a "patent for land."[104] Although he must have enjoyed angering the Jefferson administration by validating Marbury's commission, Marshall knew that land grants were a far more important issue. The Yazoo land fraud in Georgia had long been a national controversy.[105] Ten years earlier, Marshall had supported in Congress James Gunn's attempt to compensate Yazoo landholders.[106] The property owners heavily relied upon Alexander Hamilton's 1795 opinion letter: "[T]he revocation of the grant by the act of the legislature of Georgia, may justly be considered as contrary to the constitution of the United States, and, therefore null: and that the courts of the United States... will be likely to pronounce it so."[107] Thus, it hardly came as a shocking surprise when Marshall held in *Fletcher v. Peck*[108] that once "innocent" third party purchasers obtained the land from those who had bribed the Georgia legislature, those third parties had a "vested right" that was protected by the Constitution's prohibition of State impairment of contracts as well as by general principles. Marshall self-consciously expanded the scope of the "impairment of contracts" clause, which historically was a response to state legislative debtor relief laws, by including "grants" as well as "contracts" and by including "contracts" in which the State was a party. Not complying with the Court's norm of total unanimity, but still supporting its outcome through his concurrence, Justice Johnson based the plaintiff's property rights exclusively on metaphysics: "I do not hesitate to declare that a state does not possess the power of revoking its own grants. But I do it on a general principle, on the reason and nature of things; a principle which will impose laws even on the deity."[109]

---

104 5 U.S. (1 Cranch) 137, 171 (1803).

105 Magrath, op. cit., *supra* ch. 6, n.55.

106 Ibid., at 70.

107 Alexander Hamilton, 'Alexander Hamilton's Opinion on the Georgia Repeal Act', Magrath, op. cit., ibid., at 150.

108 10 U.S. (6 Cranch) 87 (1810).

109 Ibid., at 143 (Johnson, J., concurring).

Because the Crown had originally held all the land, all subsequent titles began with grants. Although it was conceptually possible to argue that the American Revolution effectively undercut these property rights, such a holding would have undermined the existing distribution of power. Thus, Justice Story held in *Terrett v. Taylor*[110] that Virginia could not force the Episcopal Church to distribute its lands to help the poor. The churchwardens were a "corporate body" with the power to purchase lands. Once purchased, those lands became "vested" with the Church, which could do what it wanted with them.[111] Although the Revolution obviously changed the political contract, it was constitutionally irrelevant to existing private property rights: "The dissolution of the regal government no more destroyed the right to possess or enjoy this property than it did the right of any other corporation or individual to his or its own property."[112] The common law, which protected the (property) rights of Englishmen, had weathered the Revolution undamaged: "It has been asserted as a principle of the common law that the division of an empire creates no forfeiture of previously vested rights of property." This legal principle is "equally consonant with the common sense of mankind and the maxims of eternal justice."[113] Story also pointed out that such a conclusion was consistent with the Framers' views. He then added yet another element to republican constitutionalism: "[Virginia's law] is utterly inconsistent with a great and fundamental principle of a republican government, the right of the citizens to the free enjoyment of the property regally acquired."[114] In a subsequent opinion, Story went still further, making judicial protection of private property from majoritarian institutions a cornerstone of freedom and republicanism: "That government can scarcely be deemed to be free, where the rights of property are left solely dependent upon the will of a legislative body, without any restraint."[115] In other words, Story's definition of republicanism excluded pure majoritarianism. All of these natural law/general principles arguments strongly suggest that Congress could not reverse these decisions even though Congress was not restricted by the "contract clause," which only constrained the States. The Court was forging a meta-federal common law. If Congress had passed legislation setting aside the holding of one of these cases', the Court may very well have held that it too violated "general principles" as well as the due process clause of the Fifth Amendment. This super federal common law would

---

110 13 U.S. (9 Cranch) 43 (1815).

111 Ibid.

112 Ibid., at 50.

113 Ibid.

114 Ibid., at 50-51.

115 *Wilkinson v. Leland*, 27 U.S. (2 Pet.) 627, 657.

soon fade into the more traditional form of federal common law typified by Justice Story's opinion in *Swift v. Tyson*; the federal courts could create a common law for international and interstate transactions, doctrine that Congress could reverse if it so wished.

Despite his close personal relationship with Justice Marshall, Justice Bushrod Washington decisively broke with Marshall's rigid conception of property in *Ogden v. Saunders*,[116] holding that States could pass prospective bankruptcy laws that would apply to subsequent contracts. Washington simultaneously reduced "natural law" to the "common law of nations" and elevated civil law: "[T]his common law of nations, which has been mentioned, may form in part the obligation of a contract, I must unhesitatingly insist, that this law is to be taken in strict subordination to the municipal laws of the land where the contract is made, or is to be executed."[117] In his concurrence, Justice Trimble used the social contract metaphor to purge natural law, which he characterized as "universal law,"[118] from constitutional legal reasoning. Trimble agreed that men had "natural rights" and "natural obligations" under the "law of nature." However, he took a more Locke/Hobbesian approach: "[W]hen men form a social contract, and organize a civil government, they necessarily surrendered the regulation and control of these natural rights and obligations into the hands of the government."[119] Because the State could regulate, modify, and absolutely restrain property rights, "the right and power of enforcing performance exists... only in the law of the land, and the obligation resulting from this condition is a civil obligation."[120] The State can therefore prospectively change the obligations of future contracts under the proposition that the power to regulate the whole implies the power to regulate such parts as the remedies, to create "only a conditional or qualified obligation."[121] Justice Trimble did not need to make such a strong break to uphold the state insolvency law. Justice Johnson had perpetuated his commitment to natural law by holding that it only precluded retroactive alteration of pre-existing contract rights. So long as people were aware of their rights entering into a contract, the State could change the background rules of obligation. The Court could infer the assent to those laws by anyone who later enters into a contract in that State.[122] Justice Washington and Trimble's shift may well have been a response to the uneasy

---

116 25 U.S. (12 Wheat.) 213 (1827).
117 Ibid., at 259.
118 Ibid., at 318-19 (Trimble, J., concurring).
119 Ibid., at 319.
120 Ibid., at 320.
121 Ibid., at 323.
122 Ibid., at 285.

relationships between natural law, the Contracts clause, state debtor relief laws, and the Congressional power to regulate bankruptcy. To the degree that the Court based creditors' rights on "general principles," Congress arguably would have no more power to alter those rights than the States. But the Constitution gave Congress the power to change/impair creditors' rights by passing uniform bankruptcy laws. In addition, many emerging capitalists opposed the Marshall Court's rigid defense of existing conceptions of creditors' rights. To reduce their risks, these entrepreneurs did not want to be punished with jail and sought insolvency relief from the States for any business failures. Meta-federal common law based upon natural law principles would ossify existing contract law and judicial decisions. To the degree that federal common law would remain necessary, it would make the system more flexible if Congress could reverse such decisions just as a state legislature could pass a statute setting aside ordinary state common law decisions. These two Justices' arguments were early indications of the eventual demise of natural law reasoning on the Court.

Chief Justice Marshall's dissent, joined by Justices Story and Duvall, predictably rejected the majority's reasoning and outcome. He emphasized Locke's theory that men established rights even in "the rudest state of nature" to that which they labor for, acquire, and possess.[123] The individual retains these rights when he enters into the social contract. Although he delegates the "right of coercion" to the government, the government is obligated to furnish a remedy.[124] Marshall grounded these principles in the Constitution; the State has "all the power of society" over contract rights except when restrained by the Constitution.[125] For once, Marshall made an error, assuming that one of his underlying goals was to create constitutional doctrine that would facilitate the growth of private power. He did not fully understand the new capitalist economy, which wanted more protections for risk and less protection of the status quo.

On the other hand, Justices Marshall and Story successfully laid the constitutional foundation for what would turn out to be the preferred mechanism of private power: the corporation. They never hesitated to include this English common law institution within the new American constitutional system. Marshall began his analysis in *Marbury v. Madison* by citing Blackstone's definition of a writ of mandamus, which covered "any person, *corporation*, or inferior court of judicature."[126] One year later, in his first important corporations case, *Head & Armory v. Private*

---

[123] Ibid., at 345 (Marshall, J., dissenting).

[124] Ibid., at 346-47.

[125] Ibid., at 348.

[126] 5 U.S. at 168 (italics added).

Insurance Co., Marshall based the rights of corporations on a mixture of common law and statutory authorization.[127] The Marshall Court's incorporation of traditional "common law" enabled it to utilize English precedents and to establish jurisdiction to create the basic parameters of corporate law in America.[128] Although corporations took many forms – churches, colleges, towns, Territorial governments,[129] the District of Columbia,[130] and banks – they all "appertain to sovereignty."[131] Corporations can either be "public," created "for public and national purposes," or "private...whose principal object is individual trade and individual profit."[132] Both the State and Federal Governments had the implied power to create artificial "beings,"[133] which are particularly useful "means" to enable groups of people working together to achieve a wide range of purposes. Corporations serve several useful functions. Above all, they reduce transaction costs. For example, it would be difficult for a student of a college to sign contracts with all the individuals responsible for providing him or her with an education, particularly since those individuals may not remain at the school while the student is there. Thus, it is far easier for the student to enter into a binding, legally enforceable contract with the college itself, not with its ever-changing component parts.

As with creditors' rights, the Court had difficulty determining the precise legal sources of corporate rights, powers, and obligations. In *Osborn v. Bank of the United States*, the Court utilized the word "faculty," which Enlightenment philosophers like Hume often used to describe human capacities and skills, to describe the governmental creation of corporations. A corporation, like a human being, is "a bundle of faculties."[134] Through its charter, the government defines this creature: "This being can acquire no right, make no contract, bring no suit, which is not authorized by a law of the United States. It is not only itself the mere creature of a law, but all its actions and all its rights are dependent on the same law."[135] Thus, even the right to bring lawsuits must be found or inferred from the original legislative charter.[136] Consequently, corporations do not automatically have the natural law and constitutional rights of citizens, even of those American

---

127 6 U.S. (2 Cranch) 127, 167 (1804).

128 Gregory A. Mark, 'The Court and the Corporation: Jurisprudence, Localism, and Federalism', 1997 *Supreme Court Review* 403, 421.

129 *McCulloch*, 17 U.S. at 422.

130 *Cohens*, 19 U.S. at 442.

131 *McCulloch*, 17 U.S. at 410.

132 *Osborn v. Bank of the United States*, 22 U.S. (9 Wheat.) 738, 859 (1824).

133 *McCulloch*, 17 U.S. at 409.

134 *Osborn*, 22 U.S. at 898.

135 Ibid., at 823.

136 Ibid.

citizens who had to go through a formal process to be naturalized: "A naturalized citizen is indeed made a citizen under an act of Congress, but the act does not proceed to give, to regulate, or to prescribe his capacities. He becomes a member of society, possessing all the rights of a native citizen, and standing, in the view of the constitution, on the footing of a native. The constitution does not authorize Congress to enlarge or abridge those rights."[137]

This conceptual constraint did not prove important, because the Court found that the legislatures had imbued, explicitly or implicitly, corporations with many important faculties: They can make binding promises,[138] sue in federal court, and have immortal existences.[139] As the value of the private corporation became more evident to the Justices over the course of the early Nineteenth Century, the Justices became more willing to use their common law power to "imply" additional important corporate rights. Hemmed in by the facts surrounding a particular charter in *Bank of United States v. Dandridge*, the Court turned to the ever flexible doctrine of "implication": "To corporations, however erected, there are said to be certain incidents attached, without any express words or authority for this purpose; such as the power to plead and be impleaded, to purchase and alien, to make a common seal, and to pass by-laws."[140] Furthermore, once a corporation is in litigation, it assumes all the collateral rights and obligations of that process: "In short, we think, that the acts of artificial persons afford the same presumptions as the acts of natural persons."[141] Thus corporations can be bound by implications, including implied promises, as much as individuals. Marshall created the most valuable corporate asset, limited liability, in *Bank of United States v. Planter's Bank of Georgia*: "This suit is against a corporation, and the judgment is to be satisfied by the property of the corporation, not by that of the individual corporators."[142] Because these implied powers were based upon federal common law, not upon "general principles," Congress or the States theoretically retained the capacity to alter them through legislation.

This semi-positivist approach did not preclude corporations from also obtaining a limited mix of natural law and constitutional rights. In one of Marshall's earliest cases, he held that corporations could be considered "citizens" for the limited purpose of establishing jurisdiction in federal

---

137 Ibid., at 827.
138 *Bank of United States v. Dandridge*, 25 U.S. (12 Wheat.) 64, 74 (1827).
139 *Dartmouth College*, 17 U.S. at 635.
140 Ibid., at 67.
141 Ibid., at 70.
142 22 U.S. (9 Wheat.) 904, 907 (1824).

court to represent the rights of their corporate membership.[143] The individuals who benefit from the corporation will "use the name of the corporation, for the purpose of asserting their corporate rights."[144] To support this definition, which extended the notion of citizenship to any aliens[145] who participated in the corporate form, Marshall stated that it was easy to infer from the registering acts that the legislature intended the corporations to be citizens for this limited purpose.[146] One problem with this approach is that a larger corporation might have citizens from a variety of States, which would make it harder for it to gain diversity jurisdiction whenever one of those citizens resided in the same State as an opposing party. A few years later in *Osborn*, the Court solved this problem by turning corporations into "persons," much to the frustration of Justice Johnson:

> Making a person, makes a case, and thus a government which cannot exercise jurisdiction unless an alien or citizens of another State be a party, makes a party which is neither alien nor citizen, and then claims jurisdiction because it has made a case. If this be true, why not make every citizen a corporation sole, and thus bring them all into the Courts of the United States.[147]

Once the corporations gained jurisdiction in federal courts to assert the their members' rights, they quickly and easily obtained separate constitutional protections of property. The trustees of the Episcopal Church of Virginia gained a "vested" right in the land their corporate church purchased pursuant to their colonial charter which gave them authority to purchase, hold, alienate, repair, and regulate their own property.[148] The State had given all churches this power "to enable all sects to accomplish the great objects of religion by giving them corporate rights for the management of their property, and the regulation of their temporal as well as spiritual concerns."[149] Consequently, this Church had the same rights to use its land as any individual; the State could not deprive them of that discretion by forcing them to divest the lands to benefit the poor.

This string of cases (along with several others not discussed) created such a rich source of background law that the famous *Dartmouth College* case is as much a summation as the foundation of corporate law. The college successfully argued that the State of New Hampshire

143 *The Bank of the United States v. Deveaux*, 9 U.S. (5 Cranch) 61, (1809).
144 Ibid., at 90.
145 Ibid., at 87.
146 Ibid., at 91.
147 *Osborn*, 22 U.S. at 898.
148 *Terrett v. Taylor*, 13 U.S. (9 Cranch) 43, 46-47 (1815).
149 Ibid., at 49.

unconstitutionally impaired their original charter with the King by passing a new law that effectively placed the college under the control of New Hampshire politicians. Marshall first created a state limitation which was all but equivalent to the Fifth Amendment's prohibition against the Federal government's taking property without just compensation/due process of law: "[The Contracts Clause] must be understood ... to restrain the legislature in the future from violating the right of property."[150] Thus Marshall revealed, as every Justice must, his hierarchy of constitutional norms. He was unwilling to apply all of the Bill of Rights against the States in *Barron v. Baltimore*, but he interpreted the Contract Clause, which did apply to the States, to make it a close relative of the Fifth Amendment's clause protecting private property from federal deprivation without due process of law. The core of his corporate law doctrine was quite simple. Although the State had vast discretion in creating and limiting the faculties of corporations, it had very little power over those corporations after they had been formed. Thus, states helped determine basic corporate structures and rights, but could rarely interfere in subsequent corporate operations.

Justice Story's concurrence extended Marshall's analysis from eleemosynary corporations to such private corporations as banks. But Story also provided the State with a loophole: it could alter corporate charters if it put a clause in the original charter expressly giving it powers of revision.[151] In the absence of such a clause, the State could only intervene if it showed that the trustees of the College acted in bad faith. Even more strongly than Marshall, Story equated the Contracts Clause with the Due Process Clause: the trustees had the perpetual right to run the college "unless its corporate franchises should be taken away by due process of law."[152]

Marshall's eagerness to create a national law for corporations, which can be traced from his very first corporate law case in 1804, could be seen as either premature or exceptionally prescient. In the new Republic's early years, relatively few States had created private corporations for profit: between 1781 and 1790, only thirty-three charters for private businesses were granted.[153] In addition, these early private corporations were small, local affairs.[154] In this regard, the Hamiltonian system differed from its English inspiration, which had relied upon huge trading entities like the East India Company.[155] For instance, Hamilton did not even mention

---

150 *Trustees of Dartmouth College v. Woodward*, 17 U.S. (4 Wheat.) 518, 628 (1819).
151 Ibid., at 675 (Story, J., concurring).
152 Ibid., at 689.
153 Mark, op. cit., *supra* ch. 6, n.128, at 410.
154 Ibid., at 410.
155 Ibid., at 417.

corporations in his Report on Manufacturers.[156] But there was one exception to this corporate localism, an exception that made all the difference: the perpetually controversial National Bank. Hamilton designed this corporation, which combined assets from both the Federal Government and private shareholders, to serve several national purposes. It would stabilize and strengthen the national government by controlling the currency, attracting capital, facilitating tax collection and federal distribution of dollars, and creating an even stronger partnership between the government and the wealthy. In the course of upholding the constitutionality of the bank in *McCulloch v. Maryland*, Marshall explicitly included the bank within his imperial vision that extended far beyond the country's existing boundaries at the Mississippi River: "Throughout this vast republic, from the St. Croix to the Gulf of Mexico, *from the Atlantic to the Pacific*, revenue is to be collected and expended, armies are to be marched and supported."[157] By validating the right of the federal government to create corporations, immunizing federal corporations from state harassment, fleshing out the "universal law" of corporations in a variety of State "contract" cases, and implying numerous important rights, Marshall created a blueprint for a powerful institution that governments could use in any way they saw fit. By the time Justice Taney replaced Marshall as Chief Justice, corporations had firmly established their economic value; Taney explicitly noted their growing importance in the national economy in *Bank of Augusta v. Earle*.[158]

Story's *Dartmouth* concurrence revealed legal limits to private power, just as to public power. States need not grant corporate charters, could limit the faculties within those charters, and could put reserve clauses in any new charters. They also could rescind charters if they could prove that the corporate leadership abused their trust or created a "public mischief."[159] State sovereignty precluded generous protection of corporate rights outside their immediate jurisdiction; a District of Columbia corporation authorized to sell lottery tickets did not create immunity for those who sold those tickets in a State that outlawed them.[160] But most importantly, both the Federal and State governments retained the implied power of taxation. Corporations had no implied immunity from taxation.[161] Thus, through the

---

156 Ibid., at 415.
157 *McCulloch*, 17 U.S. at 408 (italics added).
158 38 U.S. (13 Pet.) 519 (1839).
159 *Gibbons*, 22 U.S. at 209.
160 *Cohens*, 19 U.S. 264.
161 *Providence Bank v. Pittman*, 29 U.S. (4 Pet.) 514, 560-64 (1830).

taxing power, the people retained ultimate control of private power. Pure politics, not law, would determine levels of taxation.[162]

Like Hamilton before them, neither Marshall nor Story fully appreciated the new dynamic economy growing around them. Just as they had doggedly tried to constitutionalize creditors' rights, they also remained strongly committed to rights granted under corporate charters. But those grants, which gave special favors and monopolies to well-connected groups, were inconsistent with the ever more egalitarian political culture and the exploding economy which looked more to future profits than to the protection of past interests. Thus, *Charles River Bridge* justly remains one of the most important constitutional law cases because it represents a shift from the Marshall-Story perspective to the Taney-Jackson view that markets should remain open and flexible. In that case, Taney held Harvard College had no constitutional right to prevent the State of Massachusetts from authorizing another corporation to build a rival toll bridge across the Cambridge River, even though that bridge, which eventually would become toll free, would quickly destroy Harvard's extremely valuable asset. While Marshall and Story wanted to imply conditions into the original charter that would protect the status quo monopoly, Taney simply changed the burden of proof, arguing that Harvard had not obtained an explicit ban in its charter.

C. The Marshall Court's "Train of Reasoning"

One reason why courts write opinions instead of simply issuing conclusions is that they seek to persuade the rest of the country of the validity of their decision. The Court is no different than in any other governmental institution relying on force and persuasion; it must convince the citizenry that it properly threatened and/or used force to resolve domestic disputes. Most opinions, of course, are aimed at lawyers, the segment of the elite delegated to handle such responsibilities. But some opinions, including several by the Marshall Court, needed to reach and convince much larger audiences. Marshall was helping design the republic's structure in a way that angered many. We have already seen how he used threats of impending civil war and the metaphors of social contracts and "natural law" to reinforce a wide range of judgments.

All these crucial concepts, from vague natural law precepts to technical "implications" of corporate law, constituted the Marshall Court's frequently self-described "train of reasoning,"[163] a concept now popularly known

---

[162] Ibid., at 563.

[163] *Gibbons v. Ogden*, 22 U.S. (9 Wheat.) 1, 221 (1824).

among legal academics as "legal interpretation." In many ways, "train of reasoning" is a more illuminating conception of what judges do. The philosopher Wittgenstein once defined "interpretation" as "substitution."[164] In other words, the interpreter supplants the existing set of words with a new collection of words, which may or may not include some or all of the original words. To the degree that Wittgenstein is correct, the word "interpretation" does not get us very far. "Train of reasoning," on the other hand, suggests a self-consciously chosen cluster of argumentative concepts and facts, coupled together in a particular order to create an overall impression of legality. Each judge or person designs his or her own train. In *Ogden v. Saunders*, Marshall highlighted his main components of constitutional interpretation, which he saw as a search for the document's intentions:

> To say that the intention of the instrument must prevail; that this intention must be collected from its words; that its words are to be understood in the sense in which they are generally used by those for whom the instrument was intended; that its provisions are neither to be restricted into insignificance, nor extended to objects not comprehended in them, nor contemplated by its framers; – is to repeat what has already said more at large, and is all that can be necessary.[165]

Although the "train of reasoning" contains numerous steps that probably can never be fully catalogued, it is worth sketching Marshall's approach. Marshall's constitutional engine was "the people." The popular sovereign could do whatever it liked. In the United States, the people had chosen to make a particular written Constitution the supreme law of the land and the Supreme Court the primary interpreter of that text. The Marshall Court took a "common sense" approach to interpreting that text, an approach that the average person could follow. Knowing that words have multiple meanings[166] and that meanings vary with context,[167] the Court would choose the most "natural and obvious sense."[168] It would not get entangled in legalistic jargon, or strict construction. It would consider both the text's breadth[169] and its purposes.[170] For example, the Court broadly construed the word "contract" in *Fletcher v. Peck* to cover Georgia's corrupt land grants, because the word "contract" is a very general phrase

---

164 Wittgenstein, op. cit., *supra* ch. 1, n.7, at 81.

165 *Ogden*, 25 U.S. at 332.

166 *Fletcher*, 10 U.S. at 137 (extending the "general term contract" to legislative land grants).

167 *Cherokee Nation*, 30 U.S. at 19.

168 *Martin*, 14 U.S. at 326.

169 *Ogden v. Saunders*, 15 U.S. (12 Wheat.) 213, 356 (1827).

170 *Gibbons*, 22 U.S. at 189.

that easily extends to gifts and grants where there is little or no consideration. The Court would consult history to determine what mischief the text and its framers were trying to prevent; the goal was to regulate "things," real behavior, not "names."[171] Because the people only acted when they ratified the entire document, the Court relied upon the "Framers" to determine what particular clauses meant.[172] Out of all the available sources, Marshall elevated Hamilton, Madison, and Jay's *The Federalist* as the best source of purposes.[173] The determination of purposes and problems permitted the Court to then assess the costs and benefits of alternative solutions; Justices frequently considered the "bad effects" of choosing the losing alternative. For example, Justice Story warned in Dartmouth College that permitting the State to alter corporate charters would "extinguish all future eleemosynary endowments; and we should find as little of public policy, as now find of law to sustain it." The Court would also consider earlier relevant decisions; it need not extend those decisions beyond their facts.[174] Out of this mix of history, text, rules of construction, purposes, and precedents, the Court created a "general legal principle." From this high-level doctrine, the Court would generate particular legal standards. But all of these principles and modes of reasoning are still not the equivalent of a final decision. At some point the Court needed to choose between the plaintiff and defendant's competing "trains of reasoning," an intuitive choice that invariably transcends any particular legal argument.

Marshall's theory and methodology all served the same goal: to convince the American people of the continuing need for a strong Union, for a powerful empire. From his initial premise of "the People," his opening references to civil war, his construing constitutional text in ways the average person would understand, to his particular outcomes, Marshall consistently elevated the people and their national Constitution above the States. The States, after all, barely appeared in Marshall's "train of reasoning," except as losers. They were primarily the vehicles that set up the independent State Conventions through which the People expressed their will. The Civil War is a grim reminder that persuasion's "train of reasoning" can only travel so far. At certain moments in history, armed conflict becomes the primary tool of constitutional evolution.

It has become a bit of a commonplace for legal scholars to emphasize the limits of Marshall's opinions. *Marbury* is now almost as famous for

---

171 *Craig*, 29 U.S. at 433.

172 *See McCulloch*, 17 U.S. at 420; *Marbury*, 5 U.S. at 179; *Fletcher*, 10 U.S. at 137-38; *Cohens*, 19 U.S. at 416.

173 *See McCulloch*, 17 U.S. at 433 and 434; *Cohens*, 19 U.S. at 418.

174 *Ogden*, 25 U.S. at 333.

what it did not do by refusing to take jurisdiction to protect Marbury's "vested right" as for what it did do – striking down a Congressional statute and finding a particular executive action to be illegal. Particularly when it comes to teaching law students, it is important to discuss a case's limits and hesitations as well as its actions, i.e., some of the alternatives not taken by a Justice. Law professors want students to look behind arguments, not to absorb them at face value. Although there is truth to the claim of Marshall's caution – he wrote *Marbury* soon after the Republican Congress had eliminated the lower federal courts and had tried to impeach Justice Chase – there is also truth in the proposition that Marshall consistently and aggressively used the federal courts to increase national power, to constitutionalize as much as he could Hamilton's imperial vision.

Marshall's creative use of natural law and constitutional text to facilitate the growth of the American empire adds another perspective to the historiographic debate over the validity of the basically Marxist thesis of Professor Morton Horwitz's classic, *The Transformation of American Law 1780-1860*. In that book, Horwitz used a vast number of State Court decisions and legal treatises to demonstrate how the court system protected the ruling class.[175] Many critics complained that he overstated his case. They supplied many cases in which courts favored the poorer party over the more powerful one, such as Judge Shaw's dismissal of a conspiracy charge against organizing bootmakers in *Commonwealth v. Hunt*.[176] Reductionism is always a risk, but there remains much to be said for continuing to use the concepts of wealth and power to analyze the actions and motives of the wealthy and powerful. After the Marshall Court combined a property-based theory of natural law and rights with the text of a conservative, pro-property Constitution to establish and protect the basic relationships between public and private power, the game was largely over. At the margin, the wealth of a particular party would be (and generally should be) irrelevant. But at the core, money and power continued to work their gray magic.

---

[175] Morton J. Horwtiz, *The Transformation of American Law 1780-1860* (Cambridge, 1977). *See also* Jay M. Feinman, 'The Development of the Employment at Will Rule', 20 *American Journal of Legal History* 118 (1976).

[176] 45 Mass. (4 Metc.) 111 (1842). *See* Stephen Presser, 'Revising the Conservative Tradition: Towards A New American Legal History', 52 *New York Univeristy Law Review* 700 (1977), and A.W.B. Simpson, The Horwitz Thesis and the History of Contracts, 46 *University of Chicago Law Review* 533 (1979).

7 Imperial Competition During the Ante-Belleum Era

Another way to test an historical hypothesis is to determine its ability to coexist with prior historians' related claims, i.e., does it support their propositions with additional insights and evidence? Vernon Parrington organized his second volume of *Main Currents in American Thought*[1] around the Nineteenth Century "imperialist" visions of the East (hereinafter referred to as the "North"), West, and South. Like other Progressive historians, Parrington drenched those visions in economics. Each section had its "economic romance" of a uniquely different political/economic utopia designed to fulfill its citizens' quest for redemption through wealth. Based upon Alexander Hamilton's Anglican model, the North was constructing the world's second "industrial capital order."[2] The South founded its Utopia on cotton, creating "an imperialistic dream of expanding fields of white bolls and black slaves, reaching into Mexico and embracing the West Indies."[3] The West preferred a more decentralized, individualistic future, "[seeking] its Utopia in county-seat towns where land holdings mounted in value with every new wave (of immigrants)."[4] Although these empires often benefited from each other's successes, they were destined to clash.[5] America's continued imperial success was a perpetually destabilizing force; sectional differences flared up whenever the United States expanded their geographical empire and/or formally turned existing Territories into equal States. Parrington developed his case with a scintillating analysis of a spectrum of literary and political figures, ranging from Nathaniel Hawthorne and Herman Melville to John Taylor of Caroline, William Leggett, Andrew Jackson, and Abraham Lincoln.

---

1 Vernon Louis Parrington, *2 Main Currents in American Thought* (Norman, 1987).
2 Ibid., at xiii.
3 Ibid.
4 Ibid., at xiv.
5 Ibid., at xvii.

As he worked through the details, Parrington's imperial thesis became more nuanced. The East consisted of two subcultures: Puritan New England and the Quaker Middle Atlantic region. In addition, ideological influences flowed between the three regions. Parrington analogized John C. Calhoun, the South's intellectual and political leader until his death in 1850, to the Federalist President John Adams. Both men sought to solve the problem of protecting aristocratic property and culture – political systems they believed to be both inevitable and desirable – by creating elaborate constitutional structures that would maintain political and cultural equilibrium.[6] Adams, for example, supported a bicameral legislature; an aristocratic Senate would check the inevitable excesses of the more democratic House of Representatives. Calhoun sought to guarantee the slave culture by giving both his State and his region ultimate veto power over the Federal government. Such intersectional influences extended beyond analogy. Early in the century, Calhoun studied at Yale University and Litchfield Law School, where he met and was taught by Yankee Federalists who had developed "small-town, localist, antinational sentiment, combined with skepticism of numerical majorities" in response to Jefferson's presidency.[7]

This chapter reconfirms Parrington's conception of three rival empires by comparing and contrasting the three regions' competing theories of the formal structure of the American Republican Empire. The Jefferson-Madisonian commitment to equality among the States throughout the empire could not provide a stable solution. First, the concept of "state equality" hovered at too high a level of abstraction; it could not determine the particular equal rights and powers of each state. At the same time, it operated at too low a level of abstraction because it could not resolve the debate over which entities were the original, legitimating Constitutional contractors: the States, the people of each State, individual citizens, We the People of the States, or We the People? Nor could it determine what rights and powers, if any, those entities retained after entering into their Constitutional contract. The concept of "equality of citizenship" was also too general; it begged the central question of whether the right to take one's slaves into a new Territory was a constitutionally protected right of national citizenship.

Each section tried to expand its own empire through expansion and/or economic force, often facing vigorous opposition from a rival part of the country. As the struggle became ever more self-consciously sectional, the issue of states' rights was subsumed into the issue of sectional rights. Quite

---

6 Ibid., at 81-82.

7 Ross M. Lence, 'Foreword,' Calhoun, op. cit, *supra* ch. 1, n.185, at xiii.

simply, there was no definition of formal equality among the States that could ameliorate political tensions caused by one sectional empire's gaining ascendancy over another.

As is usually the case, dissent contained a mixture of self-interest, rivalry, jealousy, and decency. Whether we are looking at individuals, sections, or nations, we invariably find a unique mix of avarice, ambition, aggression, and decency. But when it comes to ranking different motivations' contributions to any particular mode of constitutional consciousness, Lincoln's description of the devolution of constitutional morality from the Declaration of Independence to *Dred Scott v. Sandford* is a reminder that Mammon remains as good a place to start as any: "Mammon is after [the black slave], ambition follows, and philosophy follows, and the Theology of the day is fast joining the cry."[8] One starts with the lusts for wealth and dominion; turns to political ambition; studies how political theory reconceptualizes these two forces into reputable arguments; and observes how organized religion all too frequently reinforces the glorification of power.

Whatever their political persuasions, the country's leading politicians all agreed that the United States' continual successes in expanding its formal boundaries exacerbated sectional differences. In his eulogy of Henry Clay, Abraham Lincoln praised Clay's crucial role "[i]n all the great questions which have agitated the country, and particularly in those great and fearsome crises, the Missouri question, the Nullification question, and the later slavery questions, as connected with the newly acquired territory, involving and endangering the stability of the United States."[9] In other words, it is likely that the Civil War would not have taken place, at least when it did, if the Americans had encountered serious geographical or political/military constraints on their expansionism. This chapter will briefly review the major events from the Van Buren administration to the outbreak of civil war to confirm once again the United States' relentless commitment to growth, to support Parrington's thesis of three rival empires, to provide background for a better understanding of the constitutional theories of sectional leaders like Calhoun, Webster, Lincoln, and Douglas, and to more fully appreciate the legal arguments that would appear in *Dred Scott v. Sandford.*

Andrew Jackson maintained his political influence after he stepped down upon completion of his two terms as President. His chosen successor, Martin Van Buren, continued Jackson's populist tradition of

---

[8] Abraham Lincoln, 'Speech on the Dred Scott Decision at Springfield, Illinois', (June 26, 1857), Abraham Lincoln, *1 Lincoln: Speeches and Writings 1832-1858* (Don E. Fehrenbacher, ed., 1989), 396.

[9] Lincoln, 'Eulogy on Henry Clay', ibid., at 261.

fighting the banking interests during the Panic of 1837. But Jackson was enraged when Van Buren did not aggressively pursue the opportunity to gain control of the newly formed Republic of Texas.

The Whig victory in the 1840 election must have turned Jackson's anger into despair. Deliberately avoiding controversy by nominating the popular war hero William Henry Harrison instead of Webster or Clay, the Whigs ran the first of many Presidential elections premised upon imagery, not content. The Whig leader Nicholas Biddle had described the strategy five years earlier: "If General Harrison is taken up as the candidate, it will be on account of the past. Let him say not one single word about his principles, or his creed – let him say nothing – promise nothing."[10] While blaming the Jacksonians for the Depression, the Whigs managed to muddle the issue of expansion, which many of them opposed, by making conflicting arguments in different regions: "In the North, they charged that the Seminole War proved the administration to be proslavery; in the South they made the refusal to annex Texas the basis of the charge that the administration was anti-slavery."[11] Although Harrison successfully adopted Clay's position that slavery should remain protected, he offered himself as a non-partisan alternative committed to a less corrupt, more nationalistic economic system. He wanted the country to consolidate its gains by better developing the West and the economy in general. Harrison adopted Clay's western strategy of hedging on the slave issue so the three empires could bind more closely. As the ambivalent West gained power, it often used that power not to divide and conquer the other two regions, but to develop a more unified political culture. The West resembled a vigorous young adult trying to keep his or her parents from destroying the family.

Beyond these vague possibilities, the country never learned more about Harrison's principles – he died of pneumonia one month after his inauguration. Harrison's death proved to be a major twist of historical fate because his running mate, Vice President John Tyler, suddenly became President. After much flailing about, the Northern Whigs had agreed to put this Southern States Rights advocate on the Presidential ticket with Harrison to appease the Southern Whigs who were outraged by the party's rejection of their beloved Clay. The first Vice President to assume the nation's highest office, Tyler consulted with Daniel Webster to create an important constitutional convention that the Vice President would claim the title of President and all the powers of the Presidency whenever the elected President could no longer serve. Tyler quickly asserted those powers to interfere with Clay's attempt to pass legislation fully implementing his

---

10 Malone and Rauch, op. cit., *supra* ch. 2, n.28, at 474.

11 Ibid.

cherished American System of high tariffs, a national bank, and distribution to the States of proceeds from the sales of public lands. Although the two men initially reached some compromises, they broke after Tyler vetoed the Third National Bank on the ground of unconstitutionality.[12]

Tyler's apostasy did not drive his first Secretary of State, Daniel Webster, from office. Continuing the New England elite's tradition of maintaining close connections with the English, Webster negotiated a Treaty in 1842 that quashed border tensions between expansionist Americans and their Canadian neighbors. These conflicts included American support for an abortive insurrection in 1837, the Canadians' burning an American steamship, thousands of Americans joining secret Hunters' Lodges that had expansionist ambitions, several pathetic incursions into Canada by American citizens in 1838, and the tense but relatively bloodless "Aroostook War" between Maine and Canadian lumberjacks.[13] Somewhat "apologizing" for the burning of the American ship, the British agreed to settle the Maine border and defer resolution of the Oregon question. This treaty may well have prevented war, for Americans correctly saw systemic English opposition in Texas, Mexico, Oregon, and the northern borders, as well as in the refusal to return slaves who had successfully seized the slave ship *Creole*.[14] The English used their opposition to slavery as moral authority for their foreign policy of containment.

Early in his term, Tyler had a singular capacity to alienate each section. His signing the Tariff Bill enraged the Democrats, particularly the ever-rabid South Carolinians, who once again contemplated secession. Caught in a crossfire, Tyler opted for the South and expansion, making Calhoun his Secretary of State and Texas his quest. Clay shifted to a more Northern perspective, no longer spearheading the country's drive for growth and thereby dooming his Whig Party to eventual extinction. American history might have turned out much differently if the Whigs had nominated Clay as President or not nominated Tyler as Vice President in 1840. When Clay finally received the Presidential nomination in 1844, there was too much momentum to include Texas within the Union. He lost the election to James Polk.[15] This book's thesis that American imperial ambition was a constant motivator should not be reconstructed into the argument that American imperial ambition was inevitably bound to prevail at a continental or hemispheric scale. Many dreams of empire falter and even

---

12 Ibid., at 537.

13 Ibid., at 539-40.

14 Ibid., at 540.

15 William W. Freehling, *The Road to Disunion* 426-39 (New York, 1990), 426-39.

crash because of bad luck, poor leadership, an insufficiently aggressive populace, domestic dissent, civil war, and foreign counter-measures.

The South desperately wanted to add the Texas Republic, which was almost as large as the six Lower Southern States, to the Union. The slave economy would no longer be threatened by encirclement; it could stretch to the Pacific and further south into Mexico. The Lower South, which had too many slaves to exploit profitably, would have a new market that would bolster prices. Texas could also shift the balance of power at the national level. The annexation agreement of 1845 permitted Texas to be divided into five separate States,[16] potentially providing more Southern representation, already swollen by the three-fifths rule for slaves, in both elected branches of the Federal Government. Finally, Texas was actively engaged in negotiations with English diplomats, who saw a way to expand English power at the expense of the existing Union while preventing the extension of slavery. Such an alliance could contain slavery as much as a statutory extension of the Northwest Ordinance to Texas. Only Missouri would provide a relatively small avenue to the remainder of the West.

Although it probably did not matter very much to Southern expansionists, the United States would not violate any international norms by annexing Texas like it did when Madison invaded the Floridas and Canada. The United States government did not need to pretend, as it had in East Florida, that it was protecting local citizens who had successfully revolted. Led by their wily President of Texas, Sam Houston, Texans had already triumphantly rebelled against Mexico in 1836. Nor was the country worried about local revolutionaries who wanted the public lands for themselves. There would be no violence, no spontaneous aggression by enthusiastic, ambitious generals, because Texas President Sam Houston wanted his country to join the Union. Although Houston was not enthusiastically pro-slavery and Texas had relatively few slaves at the time, he and most of his fellow Texans were willing to accept the introduction of slave agriculture from the bordering Deep South States when that policy turned out to be a necessary condition for admission into the Union.

But the North, which effectively controlled Congress, was equally aware of these reasons. Each region's desire to protect itself from rival regions overcame any national commitment to Manifest Destiny. Tyler eagerly pursued annexation despite widespread opposition from Congress and the North. Jefferson, Madison, and Monroe's aggressive expansion of Executive Power gave Tyler ample precedents for action.

Given such widespread opposition, President Tyler did not have unlimited discretion. At some point the Constitution's text required the

---

16 Ibid., at 353-439.

Senate to ratify any treaty with Texas. Congress also needed to pass related annexation laws and ultimately decide to admit any Texan State(s) into the Union. Fortunately for Tyler and the South, they emphasized the English threat, real and imagined. While many historians subsequently concluded that Tyler outlandishly exaggerated the role of England for political purposes, Professor Freehling believed that the risk of an English-Texas alliance was far more advanced than any American knew at the time.[17] Two leading anti-slavery advocates, one from the North and other from Texas, convinced John Quincy Adams of the need for English action: " I believe the freedom of this country and all mankind depends upon the direct, formal, open and avowed interference of Great Britain to accomplish the abolition of slavery in Texas."[18] Adams' willingness to look to his country's old rival is another indication of the divisiveness of the slavery issue; it could prevail over the general presumption in favor of growth. In 1843, Santa Anna proposed that Texas pretend to end its revolution and theoretically rejoin Mexico while retaining actual independence. The English enthusiastically supported this plan so long as Texas gave up slavery, offering "the tender of British mediation based upon the abolition of slavery in Texas and declaring that Abolition would be a *great moral triumph for Mexico*."[19] Soon, both political parties in Parliament were supporting some sort of Texas-Mexico-English alliance and Lord Aberdeen was sending secret signals to the Texas Republic.[20] Whatever his motivations, President Houston not only agreed to talk to Mexico, but also stopped his Washington agents from pushing for annexation.[21]

Fortunately for Houston, Abel P. Upshur became Secretary of State. Like his close ally Calhoun, Upshur was dedicated to protecting the South through expansion of the slave empire and the creation of a sectional political party. For Upshur, Texas was "a Southern question, and not one of Whiggism and Democracy." The administration must "rouse" the slaveholders to see Texas as "indispensable to their security. In my opinion, we have no alternative."[22] Andrew Jackson wrote a letter to his old friend Sam Houston to convince him to opt for the United States instead of Mexico/England.[23] When Upshur suddenly died in March 1844, Tyler replaced him with the equally zealous John C. Calhoun, who also saw the English as part of a worldwide anti-slavery movement. After all, four

17 Ibid., at 381.
18 Ibid., at 383.
19 Ibid., at 396 (italics in original).
20 Ibid., at 398.
21 Ibid., at 370.
22 Ibid., at 401.
23 Ibid., at 404.

months earlier, John Quincy Adams had presented a proposed Constitutional Amendment to eliminate the three-fifths rule.[24] Should Texas not adopt slavery, its free labor system would "expose the weakest and most vulnerable...frontiers..." of the slave empire.[25] Calhoun effectively employed the diffusion argument – spreading slavery throughout the West would lead to its gradual demise – to gain the support of Southerners who were lukewarm about slavery and even more ambivalent Northern allies. The diffusion argument, like so many major political arguments, may not have really been all that convincing but it provided a way for many people to live with injustice while claiming to oppose it. As Northern opposition mounted, Southern rhetoric became more extreme. Having promised annexation to Sam Houston, Andrew Jackson wrote many public letters in support of annexation. He broke with Martin Van Buren over the issue because "the safety of the republic" requires "annexation regardless of the consequences."[26]

Some Southern empire builders were more cautious than their more western counterparts, who looked to the Pacific while keeping a restless eye on Canada. Many South Carolinians sought above all to maintain their existing elevated station at the local level. According to William Freehling, neither Calhoun nor Jackson had immediate continental ambitions; they preferred to take a step at a time. Excessively rapid expansion would threaten slavery in the Old South by transferring too many slaves to the new region. The South Carolinian Waddy Thompson worried that the new demand for slaves would make them "an encumbrance we shall be glad to get rid of; and I confess for myself that it will afford me very little consolation in riding over my fields, grown up in broom-sedge and washed into gullies, that... slavery still exists and is prosperous."[27] On the other hand, men like Calhoun did not want the white man's republic to become encircled by Indians and Englishmen.[28] New Orleans was the center of a more aggressive Southern vision, seeking to rapidly expand slavery throughout the Caribbean. Such regional nuances could be multiplied in many directions, turning this book's generalities into lengthy explorations.

Faced with the probable annexation of Texas, the voters turned the 1844 Presidential election into a mandate for continued expansion. In another example of the fluid history of American imperial ambition, the Whig nominee Henry Clay, who once had so enthusiastically proposed the invasion of Canada, clearly stated that he would not annex Texas without

---

[24] Ibid., at 410.
[25] Ibid., at 409.
[26] Ibid., at 417.
[27] Ibid., at 421.
[28] Ibid., at 416.

Mexico's consent.[29] For Northerners like John Quincy Adams and the increasingly influential abolitionists, Texas annexation would destroy the Union. The leading Democratic contender for Presidency, Martin Van Buren, infuriated his mentor Andrew Jackson by expressing reservations about annexation. The Democratic Southerners, supported by a few Northern allies, solved the problem by nominating James Polk to be President. They defeated Van Buren by changing the nominating convention's rules; a candidate had to receive two-thirds of the votes, not the majority that Van Buren received on the first ballot.

Polk did not suffer from Clay's diminishing commitment to expansion, Calhoun's sectionalism placing slavery above growth, or Webster's satisfied nationalism; he wanted to quickly expand the country to the Pacific, both for the land and the opportunity to trade with Asia.[30] He gained Andrew Jackson's enthusiastic public support. Although the election was close, reflecting strong sectional divisions, Polk prevailed by convincing enough voters in the Old Northwest that they too could benefit from expansionism. Polk won New York by a few thousand votes, even though a majority had voted against expansionism because the Liberty Party's James K. Birney siphoned off almost 16,000 votes that probably would have gone for Clay. Overall, the anti-annexationists Clay and Birney had received 47,462 more Northern votes than Polk.[31] Polk's Democratic Party platform speciously called for the "reannexation" of Texas and the "reoccupation" of Oregon. But it contained a far grimmer domestic message: for the first time, it did not include Jefferson's phrase from the Declaration of Independence that "All men are created equal."[32] This extremely close election is another reminder of history's contingency. During certain moments of American history, many citizens, well represented by powerful leaders, have opposed a particular expansion, formal or informal, of the empire. But one of the interesting patterns in American history is how often the anti-imperial advocates lost.

At the end of his term, Tyler and the Southerners cleared the way for Polk's ambitions by ramming annexation through Congress. When they could not get two thirds of the Senators to approve a treaty, they convinced a majority in each House to pass a law authorizing annexation. Thus the Democratic Southerners, who always claimed to be concerned about the rights of minority regions and interests, relied on majoritarianism in Congress to obtain Federal protection of their interests while insisting upon supermajoritarianism in terms of slavery and during the Presidential

29 Ibid., at 427.

30 Ibid., at 430.

31 Ibid., at 439.

32 Malone and Rauch, op. cit., *supra* ch. 2, n.28, at 548.

selection process at the Democratic convention.[33] Constitutional text, theory, and tradition were sacrificed to immediate sectional interests. But such constitutional aggression had its costs. Missouri's influential Senator Thomas Hart Benton attacked this flagrant violation of the constitutional system. Reflecting the West's steady drift away from the Deep South, Benton believed Missouri's future lay with free labor, not slavery.[34] Proposing that half of Texas be made free, he wanted the country to continue to grow (but not solely to benefit slavery). The Southerners countered by including in the annexation bill the possibility of subdividing Texas into five new slave States to "check the infernal spirit of abolition."[35] After all, the varying size of the original Thirteen States demonstrated that there was no pre-existing constitutional standard determining the appropriate size of a new State. Seeking a compromise, Senator Benton dropped his original proposal to make Texas half-free. With both sides hoping that President Polk would support them once in office, Congress delegated its constitutional responsibilities and covered over its blatant violation of the Constitution by letting the new President determine how Texas should be annexed. President Tyler, however, was still in office after the bill passed. With Polk's concurrence, Tyler admitted Texas with the possibility that it later could be divided into five States.[36] The Southern elitists had won the battle, making it clear to their nervous Western allies that they valued slavery above everything else, including the rights of free whites. William Freehling summarized the differences between both the means and ends of the Southern and Western republican empires, cultural traits that extended far beyond constitutional maneuvering at the national level:

> [D]ictatorial control over blacks also led sometimes to quasi-dictatorial ways of controlling whites. Lynching [of white dissidents], censorship, and cries about loyalty, although neither constantly present south nor always absent north, were a much more valued means of controlling heresy in the South. Southern slaveholders could also be more imperious than northern leaders amongst white folks in neighborhood gatherings. Ultimatums to Van Buren Democrats and gag rules on white discussion were national manifestations of a southern republican atmosphere which allowed uncensored, uninhibited egalitarian discussion to proceed only so far.[37]

---

33 Freehling, op. cit., *supra* ch. 7, n.15, at 431.
34 Ibid., at 432.
35 Ibid., at 441.
36 Ibid., at 448-49.
37 Ibid., at 452.

Happily for the American empire, its new President was far more interested in extending the country's boundaries than in slavery or sectionalism. In his first Annual Message to Congress, Polk proudly traced the lineage of his policies back to the previously moribund Monroe Doctrine, which "will apply with greatly increased force should any European power attempt to establish any new colony in North America."[38] Attacked by leaders throughout the nation, Polk nevertheless expanded the continental empire to its present-day size (except for Alaska and a strip of land purchased from Mexico in 1854) before the country turned against itself.

Although Polk had successfully run on the campaign slogan "Fifty-four forty or fight," a claim extending American boundaries to the edge of Russia's Alaska, he chose not to go to war with England over the contested Northwestern lands. After all, England was a far more formidable foe than the Indians, Spain, or Mexico. Furthermore, Polk had already begun his war with Mexico. On June 15, 1846, Polk entered into a treaty settling for Oregon and Washington, relinquishing the claims that helped win him the Presidency.[39] Always fearful of new Free States, John Calhoun opposed this growth.[40]

Polk initially tried to negotiate a settlement with Mexico. But Santa Anna regained power on a wave of anti-Americanism. When Polk signed the Congressional agreement formally annexing Texas, Mexico terminated diplomatic relations on the ground that the United States had gone to war. Polk next sent John Slidell to assert the Americans' claim to Texas and to offer to purchase New Mexico for five million dollars and California for twenty-five million dollars.[41] After the Mexicans refused to meet Slidell, apparently thinking that the proposed terms were completely inadequate, Polk ordered Zachary Taylor to lead the United States Army into a contested part of the region between the Neuces and Rio Grande Rivers that Texas had never formally controlled.[42] When the Mexicans crossed the Rio Grande, captured a cavalry patrol, and killed a few American soldiers, the Americans struck back immediately. Like his predecessor Jackson, General Taylor did not wait for Congress to formally declare war or even for Presidential authorization to begin invading Mexico. Congress quickly ratified Polk and Taylor's aggression, accepting Polk's question-begging assertion that Mexico "had invaded *our territory* and shed American blood

---

38 Perkins, op. cit., *supra* ch. 1, n.109, at 65.

39 Freehling, op. cit., *supra* ch. 7, n.15, at 458-59.

40 Peterson, op. cit., *supra* ch. 5, n.33, at 414.

41 Malone and Rauch, op. cit., *supra* ch. 2, n.28, at 553.

42 Ibid.

on American soil."[43] The American armed forces overwhelmed the Mexicans in every major battle, soon conquering Mexico City. During the conflict, American forces seized New Mexico and California. Already under secret orders to grab San Francisco should war break out, Commodore Sloat annexed California on July 7, 1846, soon after Captain John Fremont led the American settlers' "Bear Flag Revolution" against Mexico. At the same time, Colonel Stephen Kearney's forces took Santa Fe without a battle and then marched to California to aid their fellow Americans in suppressing residual Mexican resistance.[44]

Sectional animosity increased with every victory. From the very beginning, the South had indicated its enthusiasm for more slave territory by sending many volunteers and militia regiments to assist the federal army.[45] Many of them advocated an "all Mexico" solution, taking over the entire country.[46]

On the other side, Abraham Lincoln first gained national recognition by helping lead Whig opposition against the war through the threat of cutting off military appropriations. This political resistance, combined with the oddity that Whig generals were leading the forces to victory and personal political prominence, forced Polk's hand. One of the generals, Zachary Taylor, would follow in the tradition of Jackson and Harrison by reaching the White House, another reminder that a majority of the American public consistently endorsed aggressive military leaders during this era. Polk sent Nicholas Trist to negotiate with Mexican leaders. Like so many American generals and diplomats before him, Trist ignored subsequent Presidential orders and made a settlement with a rapacious group claiming to represent Mexico. The United States would pay Mexico fifteen million dollars for all the land west of Mexico to the Pacific, including New Mexico and California. In return, Mexico would acknowledge American sovereignty over Texas.[47] Although Trist's disobedience enraged Polk, who agreed with several of his Southern Cabinet members that the United States should have gained more territory, Polk endorsed the treaty. He had to act quickly because the Wilmot Proviso, which would have banned slavery in any lands acquired from Mexico, passed the House of Representatives, only to fail in the Senate.[48] From a nationalist's point of view, that legislation, which would eventually be pressed on Congress more than forty times, was

---

43 Ibid., at 554 (italics added).
44 Ibid., at 556.
45 Ibid., at 554.
46 David M. Potter, *The Impending crisis 1848-1861* (New York, 1976), 2n.3.
47 Malone and Rauch, op. cit., *supra* ch. 2, n.28, at 459-64.
48 Ibid., at 558.

particularly threatening because Wilmot was a Pennsylvania Democrat, not a Whig.[49]

Nor was there complete consensus in the South; Calhoun and his fellow South Carolinian Waddy Thompson opposed taking all of Mexico, the goal of the "All Mexico" movement, because they thought it would be difficult to establish slavery amidst so many "mongrelized" Mexicans.[50] There were so many reasons to dissent, ranging from fear of slavery and partisan politics to moral indignation. On an individual level, Henry David Thoreau set a worldwide precedent for civic virtue by going to jail rather than paying taxes to support the conflict. How can widespread opposition by many of the United States' leading politicians – Clay, Webster, and Lincoln – to President Polk's war with Mexico be reconciled with this book's thesis of pervasive American imperial ambition? Most importantly, the dissenters lost. The war consisted of one military triumph after another, leading to the culmination of the United States' long march to the Pacific Ocean. Second, the invasion of Mexico was a triumph of nationalistic imperial ambition over regional ambivalence. Polk did not care about the North's caution and humanitarianism; nor was he worried about pacing the expansion of the empire to protect slavery. He simply wanted to get as much land as possible (after the war ended, he contemplated intervening in a nasty little civil war in Yucatan and offered Spain one hundred million dollars for Cuba).[51] Third, dissent was often qualified, particularly as the military victories multiplied. Many of the Whig dissenters were more motivated by partisan politics and fear of slave power than by any principled opposition to aggression.

Although the Senate never ratified the Wilmot proviso's general principle opposing the expansion of slavery, the nation was fated to fierce debate over the entry of every new State into the Union. The North's relentless support of the Wilmot Proviso led Calhoun to claim in that Congress did not have the constitutional power to exclude citizens from bringing their property into the territories because the territories belonged to all the States.[52] Calhoun's blend of equal sovereignty among the States with every citizen's equal right to take his/her property anywhere in the Territories laid the foundation for Chief Justice Taney's *Dred Scott* decision. One year after Calhoun published his arguments, the State Democratic convention in Alabama[53] repudiated the Missouri Compromise,

---

49 Ibid., at 561.
50 Freehling, op. cit., *supra* ch. 7, n.15, at 457.
51 Malone and Rauch, op. cit., *supra* ch. 2, n.28, at 558.
52 Ibid., at 561.
53 Ibid.

threatened secession should the Wilmot Proviso ever pass, and asserted the obligation of Congress to protect slavery in all the territories.[54]

Polk tried to smooth the debate over by extending the Missouri Compromise to the Pacific, which would have given each region half the republic. But Michigan Senator Lewis Cass created a constitutional convention that temporarily solved the problem: the majority in each territory could determine whether it wanted slavery or not when it applied to join the Union.[55] This solution proved to be particularly popular with Northern Democrats, who sympathized with the South, despised the abolitionists as a threat to the Union, could not afford to be completely pro-slavery in the North, and sought to maintain principles of popular sovereignty, as well as with those Western settlers who desired complete discretion over their newly gained land. But each side's abstract commitment to popular sovereignty fluctuated with each particular outcome. When Oregon's new territorial constitution in 1847 virtually incorporated the Wilmot Proviso by banning the importation of slaves, the South felt insult had been added to injury.[56] The newly formed Oregon territorial legislature demonstrated how racially unenlightened its citizens' antislavery position was by forbidding all free blacks to enter the territory, thereby confirming the free States' limited, racist conception of equal citizenship. The South pointed to such legislation as examples of Northern hypocrisy approaching incoherence. If the North were unwilling to admit free blacks, what would happen to black slaves once they became free? From that perspective, the racial debate was about the proper means of regulating or even eliminating blacks, not ends. It was easy for the Southerners to conclude free state moralizing was destabilizing, condescending, and likely to be a pretext for more nefarious goals, such as the destruction of the Southern culture and economy. For example, the free States acted hypocritically by complaining about the "three fifths" rule that gave the South additional representation for black slaves while still taking full representational credit for free blacks who did not have equal citizenship rights under their laws. Nevertheless, the North's relentless attack, led by John Quincy Adams, on the "three fifths" rule[57] damaged the Southern position by exposing its antimajoritarian roots during a period of ever-increasing white male majoritarianism. The South's system permitted a minority of whites to check a majority. The robust West, committed to white egalitarianism, was bound to bristle at this ancient compromise. In other words, the only way the South could continue to maintain the strong

---

54 Ibid.

55 Ibid., at 563.

56 Ibid.

57 Freehling, op. cit., *supra* ch. 7, n.15, at 410.

link between the widespread racism in free States and Southern slavery would have been to concede white majoritarianism, a concession that was far too risky because the South would no longer have the House and Senate votes to protect slavery once a majority of States became free.

The South's hope that California, or at least Southern California, would become another slave State was shattered by the Gold Rush of 1848, which attracted thousands of free white prospectors. Without Congressional authorization, President Taylor took advantage of this population growth to endorse Californians' plan to skip the Territorial stage and immediately apply for Statehood as a free state. These disappointments did not completely enrage the South, because it was more concerned about extending slavery to areas nearer its own borders: Missouri, Texas, Kansas, and Cuba.[58] In addition, Southerners were upset by several other slavery issues, particularly the ever-increasing flow of fugitive slaves, aided by the Underground Railroad, northern public opinion, and Northern States' refusal to pursue the slaves (an option the Supreme Court gave the Northern States in *Prigg v. Pennsylvania*).

Congress was also wrestling with the propriety of slave trading in the District of Columbia.[59] Once again, Senator Henry Clay somehow cobbled together a compromise on these issues that prevented the Union from falling apart. In exchange for a vigorous federal fugitive slave law, the South agreed to stop slave trading in the District and admit California immediately into the Union.[60] Although the Compromise of 1850 sufficiently appeased most Americans to prevent war for another decade, the South Carolinian response to the permanent free State majorities in the House and Senate was predictable. At a Southern convention in Nashville, South Carolinian Langdon Cheves thundered that the South "can form one of the most splendid empires on which the sun has ever shown... But submit! Submit! The very sound curdles the blood in my veins."[61]

While the Compromise of 1850 did not preclude slavery in any of the other Mexican Territories, Southerners could foresee that the arid Southwest would not be a welcoming land for the slave-crops of cotton and rice. Nevertheless, President Zachary Taylor veered the country close to war when he encouraged the New Mexicans to follow California's example of bypassing the Territorial stage, even though New Mexico had not resolved its border dispute with Texas. Once again, death altered the course of history. Taylor suddenly died before he could implement his plan of sending federal troops into the disputed territories, an act that would

---

58 Ibid., at 528.
59 Malone and Rauch, op.cit., *supra* ch. 2, n.28, at 566.
60 Ibid., at 569.
61 Freehling, op. cit., *supra* ch. 7, n.15, at 519.

probably have polarized the nation. The new President, Millar Fillmore, quickly worked out a territorial settlement that divided New Mexico into the territories of Utah and New Mexico. Congress dodged the slavery issue by relying on the doctrine of popular sovereignty; each territory could choose to ban or include slavery in its Constitution when it applied to become a State. But any geopolitical Southerner could see that Utah, settled by Mormons, would soon be another free State. As South Carolina Governor Francis Pickens explained, the South's very existence was at stake: "You are obliged to go forward. You must increase, and the moment you stand still, it will be the law of your destiny to decay and die."[62]

Hemmed in to the West, much of the South looked beyond the continental land mass. In 1859, a Virginia editor named Edward Pollard frankly described the region's ambitions:

> Regarding the magnificent country of tropical America, which lies in the path of our destiny on this continent, we may see an empire as powerful and gorgeous as ever was pictured in our dreams of history... It is an empire founded on military ideas; representing the noble peculiarities of Southern civilization; including within its limits the isthmus of America and the regenerated West Indies; having control of the two dominant staples of the world's commerce – cotton and sugar, possessing the highways of the world's commerce, surpassing all empires of the age in the strength of its geographical position; and in short, combining the elements of strength, prosperity, and glory, such as never before in the modern ages have been placed within reach of a single government.
>
> What a splendid vision of empire! How noble and inspiriting the idea, that the destiny of Southern civilization is to be consummated in a glory brighter than that of old.[63]

I would like to pause the narrative for a moment, to ask the reader, particularly the one who has remained skeptical about this book's prior interpretations of the word "empire," how he or she reacted to Pollard's frequent assertions of "empire." Was it a fairly humble or narrow word, the equivalent of "nation" or "jurisdiction?" Or was it a confident, aggressive word, intimating the lusts for dominion and glory? My hunch is that most of us, unsympathetic to Southern empire-building, effortlessly applied more assertive, disturbing definitions of "empire." So why shouldn't similar associations apply to some of the Founders' use of the word? Those of you who are reluctant to utilize similar definitions to understand the motives of American political and legal leadership throughout this period may be

---

62 Ibid., at 461.

63 Malone and Rauch, op. cit., *supra* ch. 2, n.28, at 643-44.

anachronistically applying your conceptions of "empire" depending upon your underlying political preferences (the very charge that will be made against this book). As stated earlier, one can err by failing to apply contemporary meanings of words to prior usages, just as one is almost certain to blunder by crudely imposing all current meanings upon past usages.

Because there was no consensus at the national level, the South turned to a mixture of public and private power to pursue its imperial dreams. Although these initial efforts to use private power abroad as a tool of empire were sporadic, chaotic, and even counterproductive, their very failures established illuminating precedents for those who would design future collaborations between public and private power. Supported by many Southern political leaders, General Narcisco Lopez twice led abortive invasions into Cuba. The second invasion cost him his life.[64] Three times William Walker led military forces into the Caribbean. His first effort was his most successful. After conquering Nicaragua, he made himself dictator and immediately abolished that country's law proscribing slavery. Ironically, another private American, Cornelius Vanderbilt, defeated Walker by blockading his fledgling government because it threatened Vanderbilt's profitable trade route across the isthmus. One problem with delegating foreign policy to private power is that there are many private actors who have radically different agendas. Walker caused additional turmoil when he marched into Lower California in 1853 to claim it as another slave State. Recognizing that he had made the situation very volatile, both the Mexicans and the Americans rushed to finalize the Gadsden Purchase, which obtained the Mesilla valley from Mexico. Neither the Mexicans nor the Americans were happy with that outcome. The Mexicans felt oppressed by American aggression, while American diplomats thought they could have obtained more land if Walker had not interfered.

The South also needed the federal government to check the power of rival Britain, which still had its powerful navy dominating regional trade. Seeing the military and economic need for an easy passage through the Caribbean isthmus, the United States signed a treaty with Nicaragua giving it effective control over the country.[65] The United States also entered into a treaty in 1850 with Britain pledging not to control "any part of Central America." When neither side showed any interest in abiding by that agreement, the Democrats successfully turned the dispute into a Presidential election issue in 1852. Seeking control of both continents,

---

64 Ibid., at 640.
65 Ibid., at 637.

Stephen A. Douglas encouraged his "Young America" followers to support Franklin Pierce.[66] Pierce proudly stated that he would not "be controlled by any timid forebodings of evil from expansion"; America needed additional lands for self-defense, commercial growth, and world peace.[67] Pierce pursued world peace by authorizing a ship to shell Greytown in 1854 after an American official was slightly injured during a riot.

Pierce could not act in such a direct way against Cuba. The New Orleans slave owners' desire to seize Cuba to expand Congressional representation and to have access to Cuba's cheaper slaves conflicted with the Upper South's wishes to keep slave prices high and the North's opposition to admitting even more black slaves into the republic.[68] Pierce supported General Quitman's plans to organize a large private military force to invade Cuba. But the Democrats were pounded at the 1854 Congressional elections because of the controversial Kansas-Nebraska Act, which extended the possibility of slavery north of the Mason-Dixon line that Clay had established as the appropriate boundary during the 1820 Compromise, and the publication of the Ostend Manifesto, in which English, French, and American diplomats agreed that America could seize Cuba from Spain if Spain would not sell it. Consequently, Pierce withdrew his support for Quitman. Quitman's expedition collapsed completely when his private donors learned that he could not account for one half million dollars out of the money they gave him.[69] In the future, private investors would find it less expensive and more reliable to turn to the United States' government for the use of massive force against recalcitrant forces further south.

During this same period, a portion of America's political leadership developed a different form of partnership between public and private power that would radically change its "military constitution": the United States would encourage and defend private investments abroad. In other words, the United States would no longer limit its use of sovereign power to protect trade on the high seas, but would extend that power into other countries' lands to protect American capital projects. The debate did not follow existing political patterns. In 1851, Secretary of State Daniel Webster, who had been consistently wary of external expansion, strongly advocated the use of force to reinstate an American corporation that the Mexicans had booted out of the Isthmus. Webster's position reflected a major theme of Northern imperialism; the United States did not need to expand its formal borders but could dominate the rest of the hemisphere

---

66 Ibid.
67 Ibid., at 641-42.
68 Ibid., at 639.
69 Ibid., at 643.

through a combination of capital and force.[70] On the other hand, President Fillmore and William H. Seward resisted committing American forces to protect private American interests. As we shall see, Seward was a Northern Whig who much preferred the traditional technique of geographical expansion (so long as slavery did not benefit). Partially because the United States never took formal control of the hemisphere, Webster's position eventually prevailed. Not surprisingly, slavery was a major factor. The Gadsden Purchase had aggravated border tensions between Mexico and the United States. The Mexican leadereship believed the United States, aided by Walker's filibuster, had bullied it into selling the land. Mexico tried to impose trade restrictions against American speculators. Southerners were particularly angry about Mexico's sheltering fugitive slaves. At a particularly intense moment, President Pierce's Secretary of State William Marcy threatened to use force if the Mexicans did not respect American rights. Perhaps Marcy had learned a lesson from the fate of Gadsden, who was removed from his position as Minister to Mexico after he angered American speculators by trying to constrain their activities there.[71]

With the deaths of Calhoun, Clay, and Webster, Illinois Senator Stephen Douglas became the leading politician of the early 1850s. Defiantly indifferent to slavery, Douglas sought to maintain the Union by encouraging Southern expansion into Cuba while resolving the country's internal dispute by letting each Territory determine the slavery issue via the constitutional convention of "popular sovereignty." With the assistance of President Pierce, Douglas pushed the Kansas-Nebraska Act through Congress in 1854. The Act enraged anti-slavery sentiment by repealing the Missouri Compromise's ban on slavery in northern territories. In theory, the settlers of the Territory of Nebraska, which reached up to the Canadian border, could vote for slavery. While Douglas saw this compromise as more symbolic than real, Northern Whigs characterized it as a profound deviation of the principles in the Declaration of Independence, the Northwest Ordinance, and the Missouri Compromise. Several Northern "Independent Democrats" accused their opponents of developing "an atrocious plot" to exclude "immigrants from the Old World and free laborers from our own States, and convert [the land] into a dreary despotism, inhabited by masters and slaves."[72] Needless to say, the South bristled at such brutal characterizations of their culture.

Southern aggression destroyed Douglas' conciliatory legislation. Heavily armed Missouri slave owners flooded into Kansas, took control of the legislative process (which led to an ill-conceived boycott by the anti-

---

[70] Ibid., at 645.
[71] Ibid., at 646.
[72] Ibid., at 650.

slavery majority), and implemented the LeCompton Constitution, which would permit slavery in the new State. Accompanied by violence from both sides, this maneuver demonstrated one problem with the doctrine of popular sovereignty: how should Congress determine who appropriately spoke for the majority? Douglas was caught in crossfire. The South demanded that Kansas be admitted as a slave State, but many Northerners and Westerners claimed the Southerners had violated the doctrine of popular sovereignty. In his book *1857*, Kenneth Stampp concluded that the Kansas dispute (not *Dred Scott*) effectively destroyed Douglas and the Democratic Party, thereby making civil war nearly inevitable.[73]

---

[73] Kenneth Stampp, *America in 1857: A Nation on the Brink* (New York, 1990), 109.

8 John C. Calhoun, *Dred Scott v. Sandford*, and the Lincoln-Douglas Debates: Turning Constitutional Theories and Conventions into Constitutional Law

A. John C. Calhoun's Reconceptualization of the American Constitution

John C. Calhoun's constitutional vision is worth studying for several reasons. He was the most creative and influential American constitutional thinker since James Madison and Chief Justice John Marshall. And, he proposed a radically different structure for the United States' republican empire, one that was sufficiently powerful and coherent that it helped inspire white Southerners, including most of those who did not own slaves, to fight the North in America's most gruesome war. Just as Hamilton provided through theory and practice the basic contours of the constitutional system that Justice Marshall eventually converted into constitutional law, so Calhoun developed through words and deeds a conception of empire that Justice Taney would temporarily imbed into the legal constitution in *Dred Scott v. Sandford*.[1]

[1] 60 U.S. (19 How.) 393 (1857). *See* Donald E. Fehrenbacher, *The Dred Scott Case, Its Significance in American Law and Politics* (New York 1978) and Donald E. Fehrenbacher, *The Slaveholding Republic: An Account of the United States Government's Relation to Slavery* (completed and edited by Ward M. McAfee) (Oxford 2001).

On a more theoretical level, Calhoun's creative solutions demonstrate the inability of "formal equality" to resolve many constitutional problems, and thus the inherent incapacity of the judiciary, which tends to be instinctively attracted to formal equality to avoid the appearance of bias, to handle many crucial constitutional controversies. Calhoun provided a brilliantly articulated interpretation of the Constitution for those who perceive themselves to be gradual losers in the enduring struggles for wealth and power. Constitutional losers cannot afford the fancy rhetoric, feigned neutrality, and smug sentimentality of winners. They tend to look at real effects as well as abstract principles. They must discuss candidly how wealth and power are actually distributed and employed in any particular constitutional system. They need to invent various constitutional doctrines to protect their vulnerable interests from rival, more dominant powers. Each society must contend with its version of the recurring problems of continuing economic and political subordination, whether it be the actual rights of putatively equal blacks during Reconstruction or the current existence of worker exploitation at home and actual slavery and child labor abroad. Thus, on a variety of levels, we can learn a great deal by temporarily suspending our moral outrage at the antebellum Southerners' repressive,[2] racist politics.

Such suspension will take much effort, because racial genocide often lurked behind race slavery. Jeffersonian Republicans' ambivalence about slavery partially resulted from their fear of race war. While noting that slavery helped produce admirable citizens in both Greece and the South, John Taylor of Caroline prayed: "I shall pass over the enlistment of the Deity in the question with an humble hope, that his justice and mercy do not require the whites and blacks to be placed in such a relative situation, as that one colour must extinguish the other..."[3] Three decades later, Calhoun had little time for Taylor's anxieties, which typified Enlightenment thought from border States like Virginia. Calhoun foresaw race war more optimistically. In 1842, he explained to social reformer Albert Brisbane:

> I care nothing about slavery, it is entirely a secondary question with me. In three hundred years' time there will not be negro on the face of the globe. As the Indian is now retreating before our civilization, so the negro will gradually be eliminated and his place taken by a higher and more intelligent race; it is

---

2 Michael Kent Curtis, 'The 1837 Killing of Elijah Lovejoy by an Anti-Abolition Mob: Free Speech, Mobs, Republican Government, and the Privileges of American Citizens', 44 *UCLA Law Review* 1109 (1997).

3 John Taylor, op. cit., *supra* ch. 4, n.68, at 122.

> only a question of time. I advocate slavery in the South because it is a guarantee of stability.[4]

Calhoun then explained that the Southern slave system of exploitation was more stable than the Northern capitalists' approach of brutalizing large numbers of laborers, who lived and worked in close proximity, thereby guaranteeing class conflict that might lead to victory for the lower orders.

It may be a bit easier to study dispassionately Calhoun's constitutional vision knowing that he first used it to attack the Federal Government's protective tariffs, which he believed were gouging the South to advantage Northern industry and Western expansion. Even though the tariffs did not facially discriminate against the South, they had a discriminatory impact because Southern farmers had to pay tariffs on goods produced in Europe but Northerners did not have to support the Southern agricultural interests who could only charge market rates to compete at home and abroad. The West, in the meantime, benefited because much of the tariff tax revenues were transferred to that region via internal improvements. Calhoun had initially supported internal improvements because he thought they would also benefit the South, but the Southern Appalachians proved to be such a formidable geographical barrier to creating transportation lines between the South and the West that Calhoun soon became a strict constructionist of federal powers. Calhoun explained that white Southerners made up one third of the populace, paid one third of the tariff duties while producing two thirds of the exports, but did not receive back even one third of the benefits: "The effect on us is, to compel us to purchase at a higher price, both what we obtain from [the North] and from others, without receiving a correspondent increase in the price of what we sell."[5] He estimated the transfer at many million dollars per year.[6] He concluded: "We are the serfs of the system."[7]

Calhoun's early political concessions and practices were predicated upon the hope that the North would not take advantage of its ever-increasing superiority and the fearful knowledge that he and his fellow South Carolinian radicals could not leave the Union alone. In addition, Calhoun hoped that the South would prevail in the long run, largely through its alliance with the West and expansion into the Caribbean. There were also personal motives: premature radicalism would destroy his presidential aspirations. For many years he played a double game, designing a theory of State and sectional power that helped make him the leader of the South

---

4 Quoted in Peterson, op. cit, *supra* ch. 5, n.33, at 221-22).

5 Calhoun, "Exposition', Calhoun, op. cit., *supra* ch. 1, n.185, at 321.

6 Ibid., at 317-22.

7 Ibid., at 320.

Carolinian dissidents, but also opposing, on tactical grounds, many of their more aggressive actions in his quest to build a coalition that would make him President. But as the country became more divided over slavery, his theory and his tactics became increasingly rigid and bitter.

Although Calhoun could creatively parse Constitutional text with the very best, he based his constitutional analysis upon perceptions of economic reality. Calhoun identified northern banks[8] as the "dominant interest"[9] that had sufficient power to impose its will through majoritarian politics.[10] The banks and the manufacturing interests they financed were destroying America's constitutional equilibrium by passing tariff laws that transferred massive amounts of capital from the Southern States, which produced agricultural staples, to Northeast industries and to Western expansionists. Calhoun conceded that the tariffs were neutral on their face; all Americans had to pay the same premium on rival foreign goods if they did not buy protected American products, which would have artificially high prices. Consequently, the courts could not play a major role in rectifying this constitutional injustice because it is very hard for them to determine what improper, unconstitutional motives might lie behind a facially neutral act.[11] It would be very difficult, perhaps even inappropriate, for the Supreme Court to agree with Calhoun that the Northern capitalists implemented this law to reduce the South to something resembling a colony. In other words, one cannot determine if a particular government action is constitutional merely by looking at its text and the Court's imprimatur; one has to determine if the law is "unconstitutionally applied"[12] to oppress one economic/regional interest. It was all too easy for plunder to flourish under the "forms of law."[13]

Calhoun also made a series of textual arguments to demonstrate that "the people of the United States," represented in their collective capacity by those States, were the original contracting parties that formed the Constitution. The States called the original convention; the delegates at the Convention voted as States; and each State did not have to join the new system if it did not ratify the Constitution. This argument was supported by tradition. Madison and Jefferson drafted the Kentucky and Virginia Resolutions of 1798, which asserted the right of States to question the

---

8 Calhoun, 'Public Letter to J[ohn] Bauskett and Others, Edgefield District, S.C.', (Nov. 3, 1837), ibid., at 483.

9 Calhoun, 'Speech on the Veto Power' (Feb. 18, 1842), ibid., at 500.

10 Ibid., at 510.

11 Calhoun, 'Exposition and Protest' (Dec. 19, 1828), ibid., at 314.

12 Calhoun, 'Speech on the Revenue Collection [Force] Bill' (Feb, 15, 1833), ibid., at 404.

13 Calhoun, 'Speech on the Veto Power', ibid., at 501.

constitutionality of the Federalists' oppressive Alien and Sedition Act. The New England Federalists made similar arguments during the War of 1812.

Although his analysis began with state sovereignty, it developed a strain of "sectional sovereignty," an approach that he hoped would create a Southern Party, a Southern convention, and eventually a Southern nation. Calhoun needed to develop a Southern consciousness because the South, just like the North, was not a monolithic political culture. Having exhausted their farmlands through excessive tobacco farming, Border States like Virginia and Maryland no longer needed vast numbers of slaves. In the early 1800s, white Virginians dreamed of the eventual elimination of slavery. Even when the Virginians revived their support for the institution at the Constitutional Convention of 1829,[14] much of their motivation came from their desire to sell their slaves to States and Territories where slavery was still more economically viable. Aristocratic South Carolina also suffered from depleted lands, but hoped to lead the South to cultural supremacy while somehow maintaining their elevated station.[15] The cotton States, centered on the port of New Orleans, represented the New South, ever eager to expand. William Freehling summed up the differences: "Virginia's elite, with few exceptions, loathed South Carolina disunionism no less than New Orleans imperialism."[16]

Thus Calhoun had to formulate doctrine that straddled the line between immediate disobedience and perpetual sectional subservience. Under his doctrine of "concurrent majorities," the Federal Government could not act until it had received support from regional as well as national majorities. If the dominant economic interest exclusively enforces and interprets the Constitution and Congressional laws, the country will lose its "balance,"[17] tumbling into dangerous sectionalism.

Calhoun explicitly rejected Madison's argument in *Federalist Number Ten* that large size prevented factionalism. Instead, large size guaranteed that there would be warring factions representing different parts of the nation. As the country expanded, it would become increasingly difficult to stabilize the system by maintaining equality among the rival economic and cultural systems; systemic plunder could occur under laws that "on their face, appear fair and equal."[18] The only solution was to have "moderate"

[14] That convention also had to wrestle with malapportionment between the Eastern and Western part of the State, as well as the continuing disenfranchisement of approximately half the white males, Freehling, op. cit., *supra* ch. 7, n.15, at 169-77.

[15] Ibid., at 221.

[16] Ibid., at 31.

[17] Calhoun, 'Speech on the Admission of California – And the General State of the Union' (March 4, 1850), Calhoun, op. cit., *supra* ch. 1, n.185, at 575.

[18] Calhoun, 'Disquisition on Government', ibid., at 15. Calhoun warned that the vast size of the nation contains such a variety of economic forces that all involved must be

national politics, guaranteed by two constitutional structures that were not explicitly within the text. First, any State could prevent any Federal officials (including members of the federal judiciary) from enforcing any Federal laws if the State legislature believed the central government had acted unconstitutionally. For example, South Carolina legislature could pass a law to prevent the tariff from being collected in that State. Since every powerful political interest would by definition be able to control at least one state, the federal government could not even begin to exploit such an interest once the State invoked its power of nullification. The Federal government must get all the major interests to concur on any legislation; it would have to gain "concurrent majorities" from every State or else face constitutional conflict.

Calhoun, however, knew that the Constitution could not endure if it could be completely disrupted by a single state. He thus implied another constitutional structure from the Constitution's text concerning constitutional amendments; the country could override any single state's veto by passing a Constitutional amendment granting the federal government the challenged authority. For instance, should three fourths of the States pass an amendment authorizing Congress to pass import taxes for purposes of protecting industry from foreign competition, South Carolina would need to comply. Thus, any region containing more than a quarter of the States could perpetually protect itself from the dominant interest, the political majority, or a coalition of other regions. There would have to be a concurrence of the majorities within each section before any major constitutional changes could take place.

Nevertheless, the single State retained the last word because it was the original party that endorsed the Constitution. A State like South Carolina could always secede from the Union after its nullification had been reversed by constitutional amendment. South Carolina need not walk out alone; the current Constitution was created and ratified under an extralegal process that any group of States could imitate to form their new, smaller confederacy that could be just as effective and would be more internally cohesive. Just as Madison and Hamilton led a spontaneous extralegal constitutional revolution to overturn the Articles of Confederation, so Calhoun could lead his beloved South to leave the Union. In response to the argument that these doctrines were not explicitly in the text, Calhoun retorted that the basic doctrine of judicial review was also not in the Constitution, yet few argued that such power could not be implied from the structure and purposes of the Constitution. Consequently, one could

---

cautious not to upset such a fragile structure: "[W]hat extreme caution any system of policy ought to be adopted, and with what a spirit of moderation pursued, in a country of such great extent and diversity as ours." Calhoun, 'The Fort Hill Address', ibid., at 387.

reasonably infer additional protections for the States once their basic interests became threatened. Every other part of the Constitution – The people, the Courts, Congress, and the Presidency – had powerful means to defend themselves. Shouldn't the States also have tools of self-defense? These additional structural powers would guarantee "moderate politics," for the country would have to take every region seriously. In short, the constitutional culture would be committed to substantive equality and stability through reasonable distribution of power, not to a facial neutrality that can mask unjust distributions of power.

Having protected the South as a section by reinterpreting the Amendment process and by giving each State the powers of nullification and secession, Calhoun also championed the "equal rights" of States and individual citizens. Each State (and Territory) could determine for itself whether it wanted slavery or not, and every citizen from every State had an equal right to settle with all their property (including slaves) in the Territories, which were jointly held by the States[19] for the benefit of all the citizens.[20] The "Necessary and Proper Clause" of the Constitution[21] had an implicit substantive "equality" requirement preventing Congress from discriminating between States, citizens, and the common forms of property[22] in the Territories. Otherwise, the Territories would not be equally "open to all."[23] Quite simply, it was "improper" for Congress to invidiously discriminate against particular States or citizens.[24] If opponents had complained that Calhoun implied this equality standard[25] from the

[19] Calhoun, 'Speech on the Oregon Bill' (June 27, 1848), op. cit., ibid., at 566.

[20] Sheldon Gelman pointed out that this notion of "equal citizenship" may best explain the "right to travel" cases such as *Shapiro v. Thompson*, 394 U.S. 618 (1969) and *Saenz v. Roe*, 526 U.S. 489 (1999).

[21] Calhoun, 'California', Calhoun, ibid., at 594.

[22] Calhoun, 'Speech on the Introduction of His Resolutions on the Slave Question', ibid., at 518-19.

[23] Calhoun, 'California', ibid., at 599.

[24] Calhoun, 'Oregon', ibid., at 557.

[25] Calhoun's egalitarianism had several components. First, there must be regional equality: "The relation of equality between the parts of the community, established by the Constitution, would be destroyed (by one region exploiting another through such means as tariffs), and in its place would be the relation of sovereign and subject, between the stronger and weaker interests, in its most odious and oppressive form." Calhoun, '*Rough* Draft of What is Called the South Carolina Exposition', ibid., at 338. Second, each part of the constitution must have equal power; the States must have the power to check the federal government, Calhoun, 'Speech on the Revolution Collection [Force] Bill' (Feb. 15-16, 1833) ibid., at 406. Third, there must be equality among the states, Calhoun, 'Speech on the Veto Power' (Feb. 28, 1842), ibid., at 493. Finally, and most importantly for the *Dred Scott* case, there must be equality among the citizens who compose each of the states, *id.* In particular, each citizen must have the equal right to move with all of their property (slaves) into the Territories, which are "common property" of the "States of this Union." Calhoun,

Necessary and Proper Clause, he could have responded that they also relied on doctrines of constitutional implication to support their claim that Congress had additional powers over the Territories, powers which immunized Congress from basic constitutional principle of "equality of liberty."[26] The Constitution does not explicitly authorize Congress to ban slavery in the Territories. Nor does it authorize Congress to establish a national bank. Embittered by the Wilmot Proviso's attempts to ban slavery from recently gained Mexican lands, Calhoun gloomily concluded "The North is making the most strenuous efforts to appropriate the whole to herself, by excluding the South from every foot of it."[27] The sectional imperial struggle was not just over slavery and culture, but also land, wealth, and political power.

B. Chief Justice Taney's Effort to Extend Slave Power

Calhoun's constitutional vision permeated Chief Justice Taney's labors in *Dred Scott v. Sandford*[28] to protect slavery wherever it already existed and to facilitate its future expansion within and outside the United States' existing boundaries. Given such a vile lineage, it is both customary and appropriate to condemn the opinion as one of the worst the United States Supreme Court has ever made – an overreaching decision immediately challenged by Lincoln and millions of others, fought over during the Civil War, and ultimately reversed in part by the Fourteenth Amendment. But that comforting reaction overlooks several progressive aspects of *Dred Scott*, constitutional doctrines that should be (but often are not) basic components of the American constitutional structure. This somewhat jarring conclusion is another demonstration of the "empire thesis's" potential for generating interesting insights about American constitutional law and theory.

'Speech on the Introduction of His Resolutions on the Slave Question' (Feb. 19, 1847), ibid., at 517-18. Calhoun completed the circle by arguing that refusing to permit the migration of slave owners is also "a violation of the constitution and the rights of the States from which such citizens emigrated, and in derogation of that perfect equality which belongs to them as members of this Union – and would tend directly to subvert the Union itself," *id.* at 521. Congress thus has no power to give preference to one set of state citizens over another by outlawing slavery in the Territories, Calhoun, 'Speech on the Oregon Bill' (June 27, 1848), ibid., at 557.

26 Calhoun, 'Disquisition', ibid., at 42.

27 Calhoun, 'Speech on the Admission of California – And the General State of the Union' (March 4, 1850), ibid., at 579.

28 60 U.S. (19 How.) 393 (1857).

The African-American Dred Scott filed a lawsuit in a Missouri federal court seeking his family's freedom on the ground that they had become free when their master had taken them with him to reside in the free State of Illinois and in territories that the 1820 Missouri Compromise had designated as free. By residing in a free State and territory, Scott's family had become as free as any the other residents, a freedom they retained when they returned to the slave state of Missouri. Quite simply, Scott's master had permanently waived his state-based property rights over them by taking them to regions outlawing slavery. Tragically, the family had returned with their master to the slave State of Missouri. Chief Justice Taney could have easily written an opinion like Justice Nelson's concurrence, holding that the law of Missouri determines Scott's status and that the Missouri Supreme Court had already decided that Scott was once again a slave under Missouri law, whatever his status elsewhere.[29] In other words, Scott waived any rights to freedom by returning to the slave State with his master. The case would have been a simple conflicts of law issue – local State law exclusively determined a person's slave status. There was ample precedent for such a state-focused conclusion. But Taney did not rush to the merits; he designed an elaborate structure of constitutional doctrine to resolve most of the pressing slavery issues dividing the country.

Taney first held that Scott could not bring his case in federal court under "diversity jurisdiction" because all blacks, whether free or not, were not United States "citizens." This broader holding resolved the ambiguous status of free African Americans, who created practical and theoretical constitutional problems in the South. After *Dred Scott*, free blacks could no longer argue that they had any equal rights under the Privileges and Immunities Clause of Article IV, section 2. For example, a free black from New York who visited South Carolina could not sue to have the same "fundamental rights" as white South Carolinians. Freed blacks were inherently unsettling examples for remaining slaves. To permit them to come from other States, entitled to the constitutional rights of free speech, juries in criminal cases, carry arms, and equal treatment under local law would threaten slavery's existence.[30] Taney asserted that the Framers and Ratifiers – particularly those from the South[31] – never intended for any African-Americans, whether free or not, to be United States citizens. Blacks could have whatever State citizenship rights a State was willing to offer them so long as they resided in that State, but States could never convert them into United States citizens. Only Congress had the power to naturalize United State citizens, a limited power extending only to those

---

29 Ibid., at 457-69 (Nelson, J., concurring).
30 Ibid., at 417.
31 Ibid., at 416.

voluntarily entering the country from abroad. Thus all African-Americans were left in perpetual legal limbo – they could never gain American citizenship from either the States or Congress.

Taney needed to eliminate free blacks' national citizenship rights because the next part of his opinion proclaimed the general principle that all American citizens have equal rights, protected from federal and State interference, to move with their property throughout the Territories. Consequently, Congress' banning slavery in the Missouri Compromise was not only an action outside the scope of its limited, delegated authority, but also a taking of property from innocent people in violation of due process. Like Justice Marshall in *McCulloch v. Maryland*, who converted Hamilton's constitutional system into constitutional law, Justice Taney plunged into a raging political debate over how the elected branches should interpret the Constitution by turning Senator Douglas' convention of "popular sovereignty" into constitutional law. Slave owners could now move into any Territory with their slaves and attempt to make that Territory a slave State. Calhoun's argument of equal white citizenship prevailed over the rival theme of Congressional control of newly acquired lands. Once again, the Court determined which constitutional issues should remain "political," regulated by evolving constitutional conventions, and which should become "legal." As always, the Constitution did not provide any method for determining which should be which. The Justices needed to rely upon their own ideological conceptions about the complex relationships between citizens, States, the federal government, and the unelected Court.

Chief Justice Taney was so confident that *Dred Scott* would solve the slavery issue that he slipped a reassuring message to President Buchanan during Buchanan's inauguration. The case certainly compensated for an initial miscalculation by Southern politicians at the original Constitutional Convention. They had erroneously believed that population would increase the most in the South and West; the Northeast would only have a temporary majority. But massive immigration into the Mid-West refuted that prediction, creating a seemingly perpetual majority in the increasingly anti-slavery North. By striking down the Missouri Compromise, Taney enabled slavery to move further North into Territories that previously had been designated as "free." Thus the Southern slave empire could possibly flank the Northern industrial empire by reaching into the Northwest as well as the Southwest.

But Taney must have known that permitting slavery throughout the Western Territories would probably not, by itself, guarantee slavery's future. The massive migration of freemen from the Northeast to the West would soon create more free majorities, whatever the abstract constitutional rights of slave owners. Anti-slavery Mormons already controlled Utah, while California had been swamped with gold diggers. Wary of competition from either slaves or free blacks and imbued in their own racist ideologies, most of these whites wanted to create free, whites-only States. *Dred Scott* helped resolve that problem by laying the legal foundation for Southern slavery to expand more easily into the Caribbean and South America. We have seen how the South had long envisioned the Southern continent and Caribbean islands as avenues for growth. In 1855, Colonel Walker invaded Nicaragua during a civil war to turn it into a bastion for slavery. Although he briefly succeeded, declaring himself President, he and his mercenary forces were soon driven out. When the Federal Government indicted and tried him for interfering with American foreign policy, a Southern jury set him free, much to the delight of the local population (another example of constitution-interpreting by the populace). The Southerners foresaw that few Northern freemen or immigrants would want to move to steamy Latin America to compete against slave plantations.

Imagine that a new Walker triumphed after *Dred Scott*. The South would not have wanted Nicaragua to remain a slave colony; it needed additional representation in the House, Senate, and Presidential Electoral College. To guarantee equality throughout the empire, *Dred Scott* maintained that Congress had no constitutional authority to maintain perpetual colonies.[32] By requiring that all lands eventually had to be admitted as equal States,[33] Taney fully constitutionalized Franklin and Jefferson's belief in a geographically equal republic. Not only must all States be equal, but all American lands must also be States. But this approach created a major legal problem for the slave interests. Admitting Nicaragua into the Union might provide every adult male in that jurisdiction with full United States citizenship, with the right to vote and other important constitutional privileges.[34] Local residents, mostly of color, would constitute a voting majority within the new State. By themselves, the few white slave owners' slaves might never gain control. This threat to white supremacy was similar to Jefferson's concerns about the influence of mulattos, Creoles, and French after the Louisiana Purchase.

Whether he had Southern Slave Power expansion in mind or not, Chief Justice Taney wrote *Dred Scott* in such a way that it could be easily

[32] Ibid., at 446. See also Chief Justice Marshall opinion and 8 How. 312 (1845).

[33] Ibid.

[34] Bertrand Russell helped inspire this entire book by observing: "But annexation of territory has difficulties under the American Constitution: it involves the admission of new voters, who may be thought undesirable," Bertrand Russell, *Power* (Kirk Willis, intro., 1995), 111.

reinterpreted, particularly by someone as creative and determined as himself, to solve such problems. In the first part of *Dred Scott*, Taney held that African-Americans could never be United States citizens because the white people, at the time of the Founding, considered them inferior. So even those blacks who were free at the time of the Founding, including those who fought in the Revolutionary War (as well as all their progeny), were doomed to perpetual subordination solely because of their race. Only whites were presumptively members of "the citizen race."[35] Taney thereby not only confirmed that the Constitution had imbedded slavery, for which there was much textual and historical support, but also held that the document had permanently incorporated race slavery, premised on racism.[36] In this regard, the American empire now regressed far behind the ancient Greeks, who freed many slaves and made them full citizens. *Dred Scott's* constitutionalization of racism could enable subsequent pro-slavery Justices to conclude that whites only could automatically be United States citizens. Most of the State and Federal statutes that Taney relied upon provided rights exclusively to whites and/or denied rights to Africans, mulattoes, and Indians.[37] A subsequent Supreme Court need only conclude that the Framers and Ratifiers considered whites to be superior to all other races. Only whites would have an automatic right to State and Federal citizenship; they alone would determine the racial political structure of any new Territory. After all, the conquered natives had not voluntarily entered the United States; nor had Congress given them any citizenship rights. A future court might even proceed further in limiting Congressional power adopting Justice Daniel's concurring argument that Congress could only naturalize "free white aliens."[38] Taney observed that the Territories gained through the Louisiana Purchase had no right to enter the Union as equals until they were "settled and inhabited by a civilized community capable of self-government,"[39] an elegant euphemism for white supremacy. Thus Congress could not keep slavery out of any new Territory but probably could block

---

[35] *Dred Scott*, 60 U.S. at 420.

[36] Taney's treatment of Native Americans somewhat complicates the equation. He held that their situation was unique; they had always been considered a free people, with whom the United States had made numerous treaties. But they had no innate rights to American citizenship; Congress could decide to admit them, "like the subjects of any other foreign Government." Ibid., at 404. But should the United States, led by the South, conquered Caribbean lands, a future Court could easily have left the choice of citizenship up to Congress, which in turn would probably have deferred to the white settlers' limited definitions of citizenship since only whites had a "presumption of citizenship." Indeed, a future Court might have held that Congress had to accept the whites' version of the proposed Constitution because only settling (invading) white Americans already were citizens.

[37] Ibid., at 408-16.

[38] Ibid., at 481 (Daniel, J., concurring).

[39] Ibid., at 448.

any Territory from entering the Union until it had created an acceptable racial hierarchy. After a sufficient number of new slave States from the Southwest, Northwest, and South America had joined the Union, the South would be able to control future congressional discretion.

In addition, Congress and the Court might permit the Southerners to turn the conquered natives into slaves. Or the Court and/or Congress might label the local inhabitants Indians, having no vested right in citizenship. Under such approaches, the United States could extend its empire over both continents while maintaining racial, cultural, and political control. The North would control most of the Western Territories, but the South would seize the Caribbean basin, which had a climate more hospitable to slavery crops because it was tropical and because few free men would choose to compete against slavery under such hard conditions favoring forced plantation-style farming.

Taney spent several pages distinguishing Marshall's opinion in *American Insurance Co. v. Canter*. Taney agreed with Marshall that Congress had constitutional power to regulate new Territories. Thus, Taney's tortured interpretation of the Territories Clause, restricting it to the preexisting Northwest Territories, ultimately made little difference, because he cited in italics Marshall's non-textually based conclusion that Congress' power resided in "*the inevitable consequence of the right to acquire territory*."[40] But Taney strictly limited this generous implied power. In *Canter*, both the United States' treaty with Spain and the Congressional law establishing the Florida Territory had prohibited any laws contrary to the United States Constitution.[41] Thus, equality of citizenship had been imbedded both into an international treaty and the Congressional power to regulate newly acquired lands. But even if there had been no positive law mandating compliance with the Constitution, it still would and should have applied. Otherwise, Congress could create regions where it could reign imperiously. Taney pointed out that the alternative interpretation would mean that Congress could ban free speech in the Territories.

The least controversial part of the opinion was Taney's conclusion that Congress had exclusive power over naturalization.[42] There are only two avenues to becoming an American citizen: The Constitution vests national citizenship rights to everyone born in this country and Congress can extend citizenship to anyone else. Thus, the Constitution guarantees a large number of citizens no matter what Congress does, thereby perpetuating the country's republican system. Because the rights of national citizenship extend beyond state boundaries, the states should not participate in the

---

40 Ibid., at 443.
41 Ibid., at 444.
42 Ibid., at 405.

creation of national citizens. The extent of naturalization is a national issue best resolved by the national legislature.

Dred Scott's grisly consequences, both real and imagined, make it easy for anyone to overlook its numerous humane contributions to constitutional law, to more progressive conception of the republican empire. The trick is to forget temporarily that the case is about race and slavery, just as the key to appreciating Calhoun's brilliance is to suspend moral judgment about his racism.

The Taney-Calhoun principle of equal citizenship can be easily traced back to Franklin and Jefferson's revolutionary ideology and Madison's views at the Constitutional Convention. Admittedly, "equal citizenship" need not imply complete equality of rights among all citizens; minors by definition have less citizenship rights than their elders. They are "minor" citizens. Nevertheless, there should be a strong presumption in favor of equal citizenship. Nor should the Taney-Calhoun principle of equality among the States be completely discarded as a dangerous States rights doctrine that invariably protects racism and suppression. Madison's victories over Gouverneur Morris, who wanted to favor preexisting States at the expense of new entrants, was another example of the virtues and strengths of equality throughout the republican empire. All national resources were held "for the common benefit of the United States" and were thus "common property" of the States.[43]

To prevent future inequalities, Taney also held that Congress could not maintain perpetual colonies. All parts of the republic had to become full participating, State members.[44] This principle ensures that the republic could never degenerate into a more odious form of empire, the typical type of empire that formally subordinates other regions for its long-term gain. The doctrine also guarantees that all people born under the American flag are immediately American citizens who have full access to all constitutional rights and privileges, including the right to elect national representatives – thereby preserving a broad based republican structure (unlike those that had existed in Athens or England). Nor should we have any reservations about equal property rights, once the Thirteenth Amendment eliminated the property right to own slaves. Formal economic equality is a basic component of citizenship. The right to vote is insufficient without the right to own property and to enter into contracts. In addition, Taney effectively created "the national right to travel" out of these doctrines, a right the Court would soon protect in *Crandall v. Nevada*[45] and

---

[43] Ibid., at 433.
[44] Ibid., at 446.
[45] 73 U.S. (6 Wall.) 35 (1868).

later extend in *Shapiro v. Thompson*.[46] One should be able to move anywhere in the Republic without forfeiting any personal, economic, or constitutional rights.

In the course of writing his opinion, Taney also articulated a standard for interpreting the scope of federal powers: "[T]his government was to be carefully limited in its powers, and to exercise no authority beyond those expressly granted by the Constitution, or necessarily to be implied from the language of the instrument, and the objects it was intended to accomplish..."[47] Although I find this construction too rigid, Justice Thomas recently presented an even narrower version in *Term Limits v. Thornton*: "The Federal Government and the States thus face different default rules: where the Constitution is silent about the exercise of a particular power – that is, where the Constitution does not speak either expressly or by necessary implication – the Federal Government lacks that power and the States enjoy it."[48] For those who find this is a coincidence beyond irony, Thomas could easily reply that he, like this book's author, is merely preserving the good parts of *Dred Scott*. The main problem with that response is that Civil War was in part fought over the scope of federal power. The Jefferson-Calhoun-Taney version of limited federal power was defeated at Gettysburg and elsewhere. I am reluctant to revive such a divisive and vague doctrine, so easy for Justices to manipulate for partisan reasons.

Finally, Taney created the perpetually controversial doctrine of "substantive due process," which the Court subsequently employed to protect everything from slavery, deregulation, parochial schooling, contraceptives, and abortion. People can reasonably disagree over whether the Court should have such a constitutional "catch-all" to combat unforeseeable legislative actions that seem outrageous and "irrational" to the Justices. So long as Congress can pack the Court with additional Justices if the Court abuses the doctrine, I find a final constitutional screen to be an acceptable check on legislative injustices. Indeed, if one omits the slavery issue, Taney properly relied upon the doctrine in *Dred Scott* to protect the "fundamental right" to equality of citizenship:

> Thus the rights of property and united with the rights of person, and placed on the same ground by the fifth amendment of the Constitution, which provides that no person shall be deprived of life, liberty, and property, without due process of law. And an act of Congress which deprives a citizen of the United States of his liberty or property, merely because he came himself or brought his property into a particular Territory of the United States, and who

---

46 394 U.S. 618 (1969). I wish to thank Sheldon Gelman for this observation.

47 *Dred Scott*, 60 U.S. at 435.

48 514 U.S. 779, 848 (Thomas, J., dissenting).

> committed no offence against the laws, could hardly be dignified with the name of due process of law.[49]

Although people will disagree about the constitutional meaning of the word "innocence," seizing property from a person when they have not violated any laws is a paradigm of unjust confiscation. Any citizen should be able to move anywhere in the empire without losing basic property/ constitutional rights. As Justice Catron explained in his concurrence: "Dr. Emerson was a citizen of Missouri, and he had an equal right to go to the Territory with every citizen of the other States."[50] One can even make a "law and economics" argument that the doctrine guarantees the free flow of capital and labor throughout the nation. Thus Taney correctly distinguished *Canter*, at least at the highest level of abstraction. Whatever their source, Congress' powers over Territories do not include the authority to treat entering citizens unconstitutionally by putting "unconstitutional conditions" on their right to travel.

That high level principle somewhat begs the question about slavery, which even then was perceived as a unique, suspect form of property that could only find legitimacy through local positive law. The legal presumption should be in favor of freedom. Slavery could not be able to expand unless Congress or the Territories had explicitly authorized it. At the very least, either Congress or the Territories should be able to create local property laws, just as they had in *Canter* formulated property rights to salvage, to ban slavery. For example, one cannot legally enter a state outlawing marijuana with a pound of the substance to use or sell even if such possession were legal in one's prior home state. There should be constitutional differences among slaves, drugs, and the usual collection of chattel and capital. Under such situations, the slave owner and the pot-owner are no longer "innocent," having entered the Territory or State in violation of local laws that have more than a "rational purpose." Justice McLean dissent explained how Congress did not violate the equality of citizenship requirement: "It is said that the Territories are common property of the States, and that every man has a right to go there with his property. This is not controverted. But the court say a slave is not property beyond the operation of the local law which makes him such."[51]

In a concurrence, Justice Campbell from Georgia construed Congressional powers even more narrowly than Taney. Echoing Montesquieu and some Anti-Federalists, he argued that the goal of "empire" had been unconstitutionally superimposed upon the constitution

---

49 *Dred Scott*, 60 U.S. at 450.
50 Ibid., at 527 (Catron, J., concurring).
51 Ibid., at 549 (McLean, dissenting).

after its ratification: "[A] consolidated power had been inaugurated, whose subject comprehended an empire, and which had no restriction by the discretion of Congress."[52] Jefferson acted illegally when he purchased Louisiana. Campbell savagely alluded to Jefferson's ambivalence, noting that the Court had a duty to enforce the constitution instead of imitating Jefferson and Congress, who had made "it blank paper by construction."[53] But limiting the republic's formal size did not mean constraining the growth of the empire. For authority, Campbell extensively quoted the ever-blunt Gouverneur Morris's reflections on the constitutionality of the Louisiana Purchase. Because Campbell and Morris's views would partially prevail in *The Insular Cases*, it is worth quoting those passages again:

> I knew then, as well as I do now, that all North America must at length be annexed to us. Happy indeed, if the lust of dominion stops here. It would therefore have been perfectly utopian to oppose a paper restriction to the violence of popular sentiment, in a popular Government." A few days later, Morris developed his views to the same correspondent: "I perceive I mistook the drift of your inquiry, which substantially is, whether Congress can admit, as a new State, territory which did not belong to the United States when the Constitution was made. In my opinion, they cannot. I always thought, when we should acquire Canada and Louisiana, it would be proper to GOVERN THEM AS PROVINCES, AND ALLOW THEM NO VOICE in our councils."[54]

Justice Campbell's views are another reminder that historical generalities are just that – generalities. Even at the eve of the Civil War, Southern leaders were not in complete agreement about the basic structure and future design of the country.

Like all other important governmental actions, major Supreme Court decisions need to be accepted (or at least tolerated) by the court of public opinion.[55] Taney's attempt to resolve the slavery issue through constitutional law helped drive the West, the crucial swing section, toward the North. The further the distance from the epicenters of Southern imperialism, Charleston and New Orleans, the less rabid the defense of slavery. Despite Andrew Jackson's gory pursuit of a white man's republic, Westerners remained profoundly ambivalent. They knew slavery conflicted with their belief in individual economic freedom, yet they did not want to share that freedom with other races. Henry Clay expressed his ambivalence by owning slaves while helping to found and then presiding

---

52 Ibid., at 447 (Campbell, J., concurring).

53 Ibid., at 512.

54 Ibid., at 507 (quoting 8 Mor. Writ., 185 and 8 Mor. Writ., 192).

55 James G. Wilson, The Role of Public Opinion in Constitutional Interpretation, 1993 *Brigham Young University Law Review* 1037.

over the American Colonization Society. While many Westerners, already hardened by their continuing conquest of Native-Americans, owned or wanted to own slaves, other immigrants, who had little to offer but their labor, sought lands in which they did not have to compete against the slave system, in a culture where hard physical work was not considered degrading. *Dred Scott* interacted with Western racist, expansionist ideology in two divergent ways. If one believed blacks were inferior, the case prevented whites from keeping them out of new Territories. On the other hand, *Dred Scott* had turned the controversial constitutional convention of popular sovereignty into constitutional law, thereby satisfying Western settlers' demand to control their own destiny.

C. Disagreement in the West: The Lincoln-Douglas Debates

Although Lincoln's complex views of slavery and race have often been analyzed, there has been relatively little consideration of how his racial politics intermingled with his views of empire. In both cases, Lincoln relied upon many of more universal, humane norms contained in the best of Jeffersonian Enlightenment, while making compromises, both theoretical and practical, whenever he felt it politically expedient. Lincoln's commitment to containment – allowing slavery's continuation wherever it already was legal but keeping it from spreading to newly acquired lands until it would eventually collapse within from its own failings – can be traced back to his youth. As a child, he easily accepted his Separate Baptist parents' belief that slavery was immoral.[56] He learned firsthand slavery's adverse effects on freemen. His father moved from slaveholding Kentucky to Indiana, a Free State under the Northwest Ordinance, "partly on account of slavery; but chiefly on account of the difficulty in land titles in Ky."[57] It was difficult to compete against the wealthy plantation slave owners, who could purchase the best land and profitably farm them with what Calhoun called that "great and peculiar agricultural capital."[58] All surplus labor and profits went to the owner. If the slave-owner faced a poor crop or weak prices, he could sell off a few slaves until conditions improved. In addition, the wealthy could hire lawyers to exploit Kentucky's sloppy system of land titles.[59] The Lincoln family's preference for living apart from slavery was not unique. One may obtain a better understanding of the

56 David Herbert Donald, *Lincoln* (New York, 1995), 24.

57 Ibid., at 23-24.

58 Calhoun, 'The Fort Hill Address: On The Relations of the States and Federal Government', Calhoun, op. cit., *supra* ch. 1, n.185, at 388.

59 Donald, op. cit., ibid., at 24.

opposition to slavery among small, free farmers if one makes the admittedly anachronistic comparison between slavery and modern agribusiness, which is currently driving the small family farm out of existence.

Once he became an elected politician, Lincoln quickly turned these beliefs into action. He was only one of two members of the Illinois General Assembly to vote against a plan to move the State capitol to Springfield and provide massive internal improvements – proposals he enthusiastically endorsed – because those proposals were combined with a set of resolutions attacking abolitionists and declaring that the Constitution protected slavery.[60] But even at this early stage of his political career, Lincoln's timing was crafty. The two dissenters did not act until the legislature had passed the two desirable parts of the bill. Lincoln's qualifications were so cautious that they did not anger his electorate. The two men sought to replace the General Assembly's resolution that "the right of property to slaves, is sacred to the slave-holding States by the Federal Constitution" with "The Congress of the United States has no power, under the Constitution, to interfere with the institution of slavery in the different States,"[61] a States Rights position that failed to imply anything about Congressional power over newly acquired Territories.[62] Not that Lincoln always supported humane treatment of minorities. A few years later, he attacked Martin Van Buren for letting blacks vote in New York elections.[63] In 1847, he unsuccessfully represented a slave owner who was trying to recapture slaves that had left while doing seasonal farming in free Illinois.[64] This sort of waffling on both the empire and race issues would characterize Lincoln's career.

Lincoln had fully developed his theory of encirclement by 1845. In a letter to a sympathetic Whig abolitionist, he first criticized the abolitionists for their purity: "If the whig abolitionists of New York had voted with us last fall, Mr. Clay would be president, whig principles on the ascendant, and Texas not annexed; whereas by the division, all that either had at stake in the contest, was lost."[65] Lincoln then applied his theory to Texas, revealing much less imperial ambition than many other Americans. He

---

60 Ibid., at 63.

61 Ibid., at 63-64.

62 The two dissenters rejected the Assembly's claim that "we highly disapprove of the formation of abolition societies, and of the doctrines promulgated by them." They offered as a substitute: "that the institution of slavery is founded on both injustice and bad policy; but that the promulgation of abolition doctrines tends rather to increase than to abate its evil." Ibid., at 64.

63 Ibid., at 80.

64 'Chronology' in Lincoln, op. cit., *supra* ch. 7, n.8, at 841.

65 Letter from Abraham Lincoln to Willaimson Durley (Oct. 3, 1835), ibid., at 111.

reverted back to the old Jeffersonian notion that the continent could have several different nations so long as they all were republics. The letter is worth quoting in some length because it demonstrates how the questions of empire and slavery were so deeply entangled at that moment in history:

> I perhaps ought to say individually I was never much interested in the Texas question. I never could see much good to come of annexation; inasmuch, they were already a free republican people on our own model; on the other hand, I never could very clearly see how annexation would augment the evil of slavery. It always seemed to me that slaves would be taken there in about equal numbers, with or without annexation. And if more were taken because of annexation, still there would be just so many the fewer left, where they were taken from. It is possibly true, to some extent, that with annexation, some slaves may be sent to Texas and continued in slavery, that otherwise might have been liberated. To whatever extent this is true, I think annexation is an evil. I hold it a paramount duty of us in the free states, due to the Union of the states, and perhaps to liberty itself (paradox though it may seem) to let the slavery of the other states alone; while, on the other hand, I hold it to be equally clear, that we should never knowingly lend ourselves directly or indirectly, to prevent that slavery from dying a natural death – to find new places for it to live in, when it can no longer exist in the old. Of course, I am not now considering what would be our duty, in cases of insurrection among the slaves.[66]

With the slavery issue perpetually lurking in the background, Lincoln's public opposition to President Polk's war with Mexico partially relied upon the Old Republicans' moral distinction between defensive and offensive wars. In 1847, the year after Polk and Congress had declared, Lincoln wasted no time as a freshman member of Congress thrusting himself into the controversy. He drafted a series of "Spot" resolutions that asked pointed questions about the grounds for starting the war. His eighth and final question summed up his belief that the Polk administration had neither constitutional nor moral grounds for invading Mexico: "Whether the military force of the United States, including those *citizens* [who were armed], was, or was not, so sent into that [Mexican] settlement, after Genl. Taylor had, more than once, intimated to the War Department that, in his opinion, no such movement was necessary to the defence or protection of Texas."[67] He continued to criticize Polk's conduct of the war, particularly Polk's use of patriotic gore to justify his imperial aggression:

---

[66] Ibid., at 112.

[67] Lincoln, "Spot" Resolutions in the U.S. House of Representatives, ibid., at 159. *See also*, Letter to John M. Peck (May 21, 1848), ibid., at 183-85.

> [T]o involve the two countries in a war, and trusting to escape scrutiny, by fixing the public gaze upon the exceeding brightness of military glory – that attractive rainbow, that rises in showers of blood – that serpent's eye, that charms to destroy – he plunged into it, and has swept, *on* and *on*, till, disappointed in his calculation of the ease with which Mexico might be subdued, he now finds himself, he knows not where. How like the half insane mumbling of a fever-dream, is the whole war part of his late message![68]

Despite such rhetoric, Lincoln and the other Whigs hedged their opposition. His letter to his law partner, William H. Herndon, explained that the Whigs voted against the preamble declaring that Mexico started the war, but voted for supplies for the troops (which, of course, permitted the war to continue). Furthermore, at least after the victories continued to accumulate, the Whigs focused their criticism on with the way Polk began the war, not its subsequent developments and outcome.[69] According to Lincoln, the Whigs did not even want to make that initial opposition public:

> [The opposition] here will not let the Whigs be *silent*. Their very first act in congress was to present a preamble declaring that war existed by the act of Mexico, and the Whigs were obligated to vote on it... I protest against your calling the condemnation of Polk 'opposing the war.' In thus assuming that all must be opposed to the war, even though they vote supplies, who do not endorse Polk, with due deference I say I think you fall into one of the artfully set traps of Locofocoism.[70]

After the war ended, Lincoln joined his fellow Whigs in running General Zachary Taylor for President, even though Taylor was "the hero of the Mexican war." Lincoln argued that the Whigs were neither inconsistent about the War nor their choice of Taylor. They had proved their loyalty and support through their actions.[71] No matter how the war started, all citizens had the duty to end the war as quickly and honorably as possible.[72] Thus, Lincoln did not fully commit himself to Old Republican anti-militarism. Nevertheless, his anti-aggression position was sufficiently unpopular that it may well have caused the defeat of his former law partner, Stephen T. Logan, when Logan ran for the seat after Lincoln vacated it

---

[68] Lincoln, 'Speech in the U.S. House of Representatives on the War with Mexico' (Jan. 12, 1848), ibid., at 198.

[69] Letter from Abraham Lincoln to William H. Herndon (Feb. 1, 1848), ibid., at 173.

[70] Letter from Abraham Lincoln to Usher F. Linder (March 22, 1848), ibid., at 178-79.

[71] Lincoln, 'Speech in the U.S. House of Representatives on the Presidential Question: Gen: Taylor and the Veto' (July 27, 1841), ibid., at 219.

[72] Ibid., at 220.

under the prevailing Whig theory that the office should be rotated among local leaders.

Frederick Douglas forced Lincoln to revisit this issue during their famous debates. In the course of defending a political ally, General Shields, Lincoln offered a more inspiring interpretation of the Mexican War: "[Shields] had covered the State and the Union with immortal glory on the bloody fields of Mexico in defence of the honor of our flag..."[73] When Douglas called Lincoln's patriotism into question because of Lincoln's "course on the Mexican War,"[74] Lincoln pointed out that he never voted against supplies. Douglas provoked "tremendous shouts of laughter" by responding: "I never charged him with voting against the supplies in my life, because I knew that he was not in Congress when they were voted. * * * [B]y the time Mr. Lincoln entered Congress we had enough men and enough money to carry on the war, and had no occasion to vote any more."[75]

Although Lincoln was willing to pander to racism, he never was as ambivalent about slavery as he was about the Mexican War. In his speech opposing Douglas' Kansas-Nebraska Act, Lincoln asserted that the economically powerful slave interests would overwhelm "local and unorganized opposition" in furtherance of "planting of slavery wherever in the wide world."[76] Two years later, he told an audience at Kalamazoo that slavery threatened the nation by undermining individual rights that apply to everyone: "We are a great empire. * * * [W]e must enquire what it is that has given us so much prosperity, and we shall understand that to give up that one thing, would be to give up all future prosperity. This cause is that every man can make himself."[77] Lincoln seized upon *Dred Scott* as proof of a Southern conspiracy to extend slavery throughout the Union: "Every measure of the Democratic party of late years, bearing directly or indirectly on the slavery question, has corresponded with this notion of utter indifference whether slavery or freedom shall outrun in the race of empire across the Pacific – every measure, I say, up to the Dred Scott decision, where, it seems to me, the idea is boldly suggested that slavery is *better* than freedom."[78]

The Lincoln-Douglas debates captured the Western dispute over the structure of the growing republic: does every Territory have an equal right

---

[73] Lincoln, 'Third Lincoln-Douglas Debate' (Sept. 15, 1858), ibid., at 592.

[74] Stephen A. Douglas, 'Fourth Lincoln-Douglas Debate' (Sept. 18, 1858), ibid., at 662.

[75] Douglas, 'Seventh Lincoln-Douglas Debate', (October 15, 1858), ibid., at 815.

[76] Lincoln, 'Speech on Kansas-Nebraska Act' (October 16, 1854), ibid., at 336.

[77] Lincoln, 'Speech at Kalamazoo, Michigan' (August 27, 1856), ibid., at 379.

[78] Lincoln, 'Speech at Edwardsville, Illinois' (September 11, 1858), ibid., at 581.

to be admitted into the Union so long as it has a Republican form of government, a form that all agreed could include the institution of slavery? Douglas defended *Dred Scott* as a validation of the unifying, neutral doctrine of popular sovereignty – a constitutional doctrine that appealed to Midwestern love of local government.[79] He also could rely upon the Madison/Jefferson constitutional doctrine that "all States are created equal" just as Lincoln could invoke Jefferson's famous statement in the Declaration of Independence, so hated by Calhoun, that "All men are created equal." Douglas and Calhoun would substitute for that universal norm that racial rule that "All white citizens are created equal," an equality that guaranteed their rights to migrate to any Territory with their lawfully acquired property and choose the form of government they would live under once that Territory applied for Statehood. Unwilling to dismiss Jefferson's popular text as dangerous sentimentality, Douglas argued that Jefferson could have only meant white people, otherwise "you charge the signers of it with hypocrisy."[80] As Lincoln had explained in a speech two years earlier, this constitutional battle over the appropriate conceptions of constitutional equality – "the equality of men" versus "State equality" – would be one of the "central ideas" that would animate public opinion, the true foundation of the United States government.[81]

But the debate extended far beyond constitutional questions of equality. Unlike Lincoln, Douglas embraced an ever-expanding nation:

> We have enough for the present, but this is a young and growing nation. * * * In less than fifteen years, if the same progress that has distinguished this country for the last fifteen years continues, every foot of vacant land between this and the Pacific ocean, owned by the United States, will be occupied. Will you not continue to increase at the end of fifteen years as well as now? I tell you, increase, and multiply, and expand, is the law of this nation's existence.[82]

In the third debate, he generated "Terrific applause" for recommending the immediate seizure of Cuba. Immediately after that applause, he eyed "any portion of Mexico, or Canada, or of this continent or the adjoining islands."[83] In the sixth debate, he foresaw that the country's growing population would "require more room, until we make this continent one

---

79 Turner, 'The Middle West', Turner, op. cit., *supra* ch. 1, n.19, at 140.

80 Douglas, 'Fifth Lincoln-Douglas Debate' (October 7, 1858), Lincoln, op. cit., *supra* ch. 7, n.8, at 698. Lincoln had earlier accused both Taney and Douglas of misreading the Declaration of Independence in a speech, 'Speech on Dred Scott Decision' (June 26, 1857), ibid., at 398-400.

81 Lincoln, 'Portion of Speech at Republican Banquet in Chicago, Illinois' (Dec. 10, 1856), ibid., at 379.

82 Douglas, 'Second Lincoln-Douglas Debate' (August 27, 1858), ibid., at 555.

83 Douglas, 'Third Lincoln-Douglas Debate' (September 15, 1858), ibid., at 601.

ocean-bound republic."[84] All subsequently obtained lands would be regulated by the egalitarian doctrine of popular sovereignty, which he had incorporated into the Kansas-Nebraska Act[85] and which the Supreme Court had made mandatory law: "I hold it to be a fundamental principle in our republican form of government that all States of this Union, old and new, free and slave, stand on exact equality. Equality among the different States is a cardinal principle on which all our institutions rest."[86] But like Jackson before him, Douglas limited his egalitarianism: "I say to you, frankly, that in my opinion this government was made by our fathers on the white basis."[87] He drew cheers when he exclaimed "I care more for the great principle of self-government, the right of the people to rule, than I do for all the negroes in Christendom."[88]

The Framers understood that the only way a large nation could accommodate so many different interests was to let each State create appropriate local laws "adapted to its condition and wants."[89] Turning to the particular issue of slavery, Douglas concluded that Lincoln's solution to "smother slavery out" could only be accomplished by extinguishing slavery through starving them to death.[90] Douglas analogized Lincoln's position to George III's theory of empire: a central authority would tell outlying regions (and the individual citizens who lived there with their legally obtained property) how to act without first obtaining their consent.[91] In a variant of Madison's argument that size would protect the republic, Douglas argued that large size required diversity: "(The Framers) did not believe at that day that in a republic so broad and expanded as this, containing such a variety of climate, soil, and interest, that uniformity in the local laws and domestic institutions were either desirable or possible."[92] During this period of so-called division, the country has "increased with a rapidity never before equaled in wealth, the extension of territory, and all the elements of power and greatness, until we have become the first nation on the face of the globe."[93] This glorious history was being threatened by Republicans who want to turn the North into an aggressor: "The leaders of that party hope they will be able to unite the northern States in one great

---

84 Douglas, 'Sixth Lincoln-Douglas Debate' (October 13, 1858), ibid., at 763.
85 Douglas, 'Second Lincoln-Douglas Debate' ibid., at 556.
86 Douglas, 'Fifth Lincoln-Douglas Debate' (October 7, 1858), ibid., at 689.
87 Ibid., at 698.
88 Douglas, 'Seventh Lincoln-Douglas Debate' (October 15, 1858), ibid., at 819.
89 Douglas, 'Sixth Lincoln-Douglas Debate', ibid., at 777.
90 Douglas, ibid., at 753.
91 Douglas, 'Seventh Lincoln-Douglas Debate', ibid., at 821.
92 Douglas, 'Third Lincoln-Douglas Debate' (September 15, 1858), ibid., at 597.
93 Douglas, 'Fourth Lincoln-Douglas Debate' (September 18, 1858), ibid., at 674.

sectional party, and inasmuch as the North is the strongest section, that they will thus be enabled to out vote, conquer, govern, and control the South."[94]

Lincoln agreed with Douglas that this vast republic needed diversity: "The great variety of the local institutions in the States, springing from differences in the soil, differences in the face of the country, and in the climate, are bonds of Union."[95] Variety per se will not create "a house divided against itself." The question is whether slavery is such an adhesive institution or is instead "an apple of discord and an element of division in the house."[96] Northern opposition was not a politicians' plot, but a widespread reaction to the South's continual efforts to "spread this institution."[97] During the debates, Lincoln continued[98] his relentless attacks on *Dred Scott*. In his 'House Divided' Speech,[99] he predicted that a clever Supreme Court would extend the reasoning in Dred Scott to prevent all States from banning slavery: "Welcome or unwelcome, such decision is probably coming, and will soon be upon us, unless the power of the present political dynasty shall be met and overthrown."[100]

Because Lincoln thought the decision was so dangerously immoral, he concluded that it should be limited to its facts. In the final minutes of the Seventh and final debate, he concluded: "I do not believe it is a constitutional right to hold slaves in a Territory of the United States. I believe the decision was improperly made and I go for reversing it."[101] Lincoln thus solidified President Andrew Jackson's precedent that the Supreme Court does not have the final word in determining constitutional structures and rights. While Douglas demanded complete, silent deference to the judicial decision, Lincoln argued for continued nonviolent dissent. Whatever the "rule of law" meant before, it now included the general public's authority to reconsider any of the Court's "central ideas." Thus, the "rule of law" is just one of many competing social norms.

Competing interests were the foundation of these rival constitutional, moral, and legal visions. Frederick Jackson Turner explained why Lincoln received such a strong reception among his fellow Midwesterners, one that would not only lead him to the White House, but far more importantly,

---

94 Douglas, 'Fifth Lincoln-Douglas Debate' (October 7, 1858), ibid., at 693.

95 Lincoln, 'First Lincoln-Douglas Debate' (August 21, 1858), ibid., at 513.

96 Ibid., at 513-14.

97 Lincoln, 'Seventh Lincoln-Douglas Debate' (October 15, 1858), ibid., at 805.

98 Lincoln, "House Divided" Speech at Springfield, Illinois (June 16, 1858), ibid., at 426; Speech on the Dred Scott Decision at Springfield, Illinois (June 26, 1857), ibid., at 390-403.

99 Lincoln, "House Divided" Speech, ibid., at 432.

100 Ibid.

101 Lincoln, 'Seventh Lincoln-Douglas Debate' (October 15, 1858), ibid., at 812.

would presage the Midwest's willingness to ally with the North in the upcoming war:

> These Free Soil forces and the nationalistic tendencies of the Middle West proved too strong for the opposing doctrines when the real struggle came. Calhoun and Taney shaped the issue so logically that the Middle West saw that the contest was not only a war for the preservation of the Union, but also a war for the possession of the unoccupied West, a struggle between the Middle West and the States of the Gulf Plains.[102]

Lincoln also opposed Douglas's argument that the American empire should continue to expand indefinitely, spreading slavery in the process, by cleverly playing on his audience's own racial biases while still mocking his opponent's far more flagrant racism. Should the United States follow Douglas's advice and conquer Mexico, "the rich lands of South America," and adjoining islands, then Douglas should abide by the votes of those who already live there, voters that Douglas presumably despised: "When we shall get Mexico, I don't know whether the Judge [Douglas] will be in favor of the Mexican people that we get with it settling that question for themselves and all others; because we know the Judge has a great horror for mongrels, [laughter,] and I understand that the people of Mexico are most decidedly a race of mongrels. [Renewed laughter.]"[103] Rather than face such awkward racial constitutional questions, Lincoln generated "loud and long continued applause" by proposing a different variant of a race-conscious nation: "I am not in favor of this [growth] merely… for our own people who are born among us, but as an outlet for *free white people everywhere…*"[104]

Time and again, Lincoln distinguished between slavery, which he opposed, and racism, which he accepted. Like Douglas, he had his own conception of state equality: each state should be able to establish the citizenship of its residents:

> Now my opinion is that the different States have the power to make a negro a citizen under the Constitution of the United States if they choose. The Dred Scott decision decides that they do not have that power. If the State of Illinois had that power I should be opposed to the exercise of it. [Cries of "good," "good," and applause.] That is all I have to say about it.[105]

---

[102] Turner, 'The Middle West', Turner, op. cit., *supra* ch. 1, n.19, at 141.

[103] Lincoln, 'Fifth Lincoln-Douglas Debate' (October 7, 1858), op. cit., *supra* ch. 7, n.8, at 719.

[104] Lincoln, 'Seventh Lincoln-Douglas Debate' (October 15, 1858), ibid., at 807 (italics in original).

[105] Lincoln, 'Fourth Lincoln-Douglas Debate' (September 18, 1858), ibid., at 675.

Lincoln probably did not want to say anything more because his position was neither completely clear nor sufficiently coherent. He did not explicitly say that the States have the power to make a black person a United States citizen, with all the national rights and privileges (most notably equal rights under the Privileges and Immunities Clause, Article IV, section 2) that come with that status. *Dred Scott* was an admittedly cruel, aggressive, and broad opinion, but it did emerge out of a Constitution profoundly committed to slavery. If Lincoln meant that the State of Illinois could turn any Negro resident into a United States citizen, then that Negro could move South and claim all rights and privileges under the Privileges and Immunities Clause or at least could move to a "free" state like Oregon in contravention of its racist constitution prohibiting the entry of free blacks. But many Westerners eagerly embraced the distinction between the natural right to the fruits of one's efforts and political rights of citizenship. Lincoln solved the constitutional problem by incorporating, with the notable exception of continuing tolerance of slavery in the existing slave states,[106] the Declaration of Independence into the Constitution: "I have no purpose to introduce political and social equality between the white and black races. * * * [B]ut I hold that, notwithstanding all this, there is no reason in the world why the negro is not entitled to all the rights enumerated in the Declaration of Independence – the rights of life, liberty, and the pursuit of happiness."[107] Perhaps the reason Lincoln's constitutional positions could not create a stable system is that he did not expect any easy resolution. As early as 1855, he wrote that the American experience has demonstrated "that there is no peaceful extinction of slavery in prospect for us."[108]

In addition to employing Jefferson's famous phrase from the Declaration of Independence, Lincoln also assumed the mantle of Henry Clay, the recently deceased political idol of the West. In a classic example of his extraordinary constitutional rhetoric, Lincoln's first paragraph of his eulogy on Henry Clay had effortlessly combined July the Fourth, 1776, the birth of Henry Clay one year later, and four references to "nation." Although he was a slave owner, Clay stood for liberty and union: "As on a question of liberty, he knew no North, no South, no East, no West, but only the Union, which held them all in a sacred circle..."[109] During the debates, Lincoln frequently accused Douglas of violating Clay's principle,

---

106 Lincoln, 'Sixth Lincoln-Douglas Debate' (October 13, 1858), ibid., at 734.

107 Lincoln, 'Sixth Lincoln-Douglas Debate' (October 13, 1858), ibid., at 734.

108 Letter from Abraham Lincoln to George Robertson (Aug. 15, 1858), ibid., at 359.

109 Lincoln, 'Eulogy on Henry Clay at Springfield, Illinois' (July 6, 1852), ibid., at 260.

established by the Missouri Compromise, of keeping slavery south of Mason-Dixon line when Douglas pushed through the Kansas-Nebraska Act.

Lincoln also needed to rebut the powerful argument that his party's policies interfered with every national citizen's equal right to migrate into the Territories. Slavery was not the same as other property like horses and cattle.[110] Slavery was based upon the "same tyrannical principle" as the divine right of kings: "It is the same principle in whatever shape it develops itself. It is the same spirit that says, 'You work and toil and earn bread, and I'll eat it.'"[111] It was a "moral, social, and political evil"[112] that violated the fundamental natural law principle of liberty and could only exist under positive law. The Constitution was silent about slavery in the Territories, giving all reasonable power to Congress and Territorial governments. The Southerners' conceptions of equality would permit slave owners not just to settle in the new lands at the expense of white migrants, but would also enable those owners to return with their slaves to the free states. Lincoln reduced the Calhoun-Douglas argument to a syllogism, one that he found logically coherent but factually flawed in its second premise:

> Nothing in the Constitution or *laws of any State* can destroy a right distinctly and expressly affirmed in the Constitution of the United States.
>
> The right of property in a slave is distinctly and expressly affirmed in the Constitution of the United States.
>
> Therefore, nothing in the Constitution or laws of any State can destroy the right of property in a slave.[113]

Quite simply, Northern antislavery laws interfered with the equal right to travel and migrate in exactly the same way the Missouri Compromise had limited slavery's growth. Thus Lincoln could quite plausibly assert that the animating principles behind *Dred Scott* could eventually lead to the expansion of Slave Power throughout the nation.

Although Lincoln lost the Senatorial election to Douglas, he had eloquently launched his successful ascension to the Presidency. Calhoun may have designed the theory; Chief Justice Taney may have written the final legal word; but Lincoln, the electorate, and eventually the Northern Army would have the very last word.

---

110 Lincoln, 'Fourth Lincoln-Douglas Debate' (September 18, 1858), ibid., at 677.

111 Lincoln, 'Seventh Lincoln-Douglas Debate' (Oct. 15, 1858), ibid., at 811.

112 Lincoln, 'Fifth Lincoln-Douglas Debate' (October 7, 1858), ibid., at 709.

113 Lincoln, 'Fifth Lincoln-Douglas Debate' (October 7, 1858), ibid., at 714 (italics added).

9 The Formation of the Modern American Empire

A. Cascading Imperial Triumphs: The Civil War, Alaska, the Final Conquest of the Native-Americans, Hawaii, South America, and the Spanish-American War

This book's somewhat sympathetic readings of John Calhoun's works and *Dred Scott* is rather perverse. Nevertheless, this approach helps answer one of the more difficult questions concerning the Civil War: Why did so many decent Southerners, including many non-slave owners, fight so hard and so long against the North? Although slavery was clearly the central, triggering issue, it was not the only source of contention.[1] Intelligent Southerners correctly foresaw that their region would soon be economically politically subordinated to Northern capitalism. The Abolitionists' constitutional arguments undermined not only fundamental property rights, but also conceptions of equality throughout the republic that can be traced back to the American Revolution. Although it is tempting to characterize Southern constitutional propositions as window-dressing that obfuscated the underlying venal motives of Slave Power, such a harsh view of Southern beliefs is akin to the equally fallacious argument that Northerners and Americans in general have never believed in the more inspiring aspects of their constitutional faiths, but have merely used them as pretexts for exploitation and glory.

It is far closer to the truth to acknowledge the mixed motives that invariably surround republican wars. When republics go to war, they prefer

[1] Of course, there were many other motivating factors aside from slavery and different constitutional ideologies. Up to the current day, the two regions reflected different cultures. The average person tends to support his or her community whenever it goes to war, whatever the original reasons. That person senses, quite reasonably, that they and their family will probably be better off if their country prevails. There also appears to be an atavistic "tribal spirit" that binds people together during times of conflict.

to demonize their opposition while emphasizing their own virtuousness. Should they win, they tend to write histories emphasizing their opponents' sins. After all, it is hard to see the Civil War as simply a struggle between freedom-loving Northerners and grasping Southerners when it took two years of conflict until Lincoln freed most slaves for a mixture of moral, military, and foreign policy benefits. Even then, he did not liberate the slaves in Union-controlled areas because that would have undermined the war effort. The Civil War was a struggle between two imperial republics with radically different economic systems, interests, and constitutional ideologies. It was both a "War Between the States" and a "Civil War," a war of Northern as well as Southern aggression. At some point violence replaces argument and the rule of law as the arbiters of constitutional disputes. That war is another grim reminder of the capacity of all humans to commingle their lust for dominion with sincerely held beliefs in their moral superiority, beliefs that often temper that lust and provide the possibility for a more humane society in the future.

When the war ended, the opportunity for a vast empire had never been brighter. The North had created a military-industrial complex, combining the brute force of military power with the flexible, aggressive productive capacities of the modern corporation, a system which would help lead to American eventual worldwide supremacy. This express (and latent) power made effective control of the rest of the Hemisphere much easier. The mighty British Empire could prevent any thoughts of invading Canada, but it had to accommodate American interests throughout the hemisphere. No longer could the British think of hemming in the Americans through alliances with Mexico or Texas. The divisive slavery issue had been eliminated, leaving the workers and ex-slaves to the tender mercies of the capitalists and Southern landowners. Whether the North had originally fought the war to end slavery or extend its imperial vision and power at the expense of the South, the outcome was clear: The South itself became a semi-colony, a source of raw materials and extorted profits that undermined rival industrial development.

Lincoln described the new technological innovations that made it far easier to maintain a continental empire geographically required because there was "no line straight or crooked, suitable for a national boundary upon which to divide".[2]

That portion of the earth's surface which is owned and inhabited by the people of the United States is well adapted to be the home of one national family, and it is not well adapted for two or more. Its vast extent and its

---

[2] Lincoln, 'Second Annual Message to Congress' (Dec. 1, 1862), Lincoln, op. cit., *supra* ch. 7, n.8, at 404.

variety of climate and productions are of advantage in this age for one people, whatever they might have been in former ages. Steam, telegraphs, and intelligence have brought these to be an advantageous combination for one united people.[3]

For Madison, diversity of interests and large size diffused faction. For Lincoln, those factors provided needed power and flexibility. Some of the old Anti-Federalist arguments against vast empires – areas distant from the center would be hard to defend, regulate, and integrate – were undermined not so much by theory, as by technology and the brutal art of modern warfare.

The South did not completely capitulate after losing the Civil War; white southerners quickly developed practices and institutions (such as the Ku Klux Klan) to suppress the freed African-Americans. In response to this combination of public and private terror, Radical Republicans passed the Reconstruction Amendments, which repealed much of *Dred Scott*. The first sentence of the Fourteenth Amendment states: "All persons born or naturalized in the United States, and subject to the jurisdiction thereof, are citizens of the United States and of the State wherein they reside." In other words, all adult males, whatever their color, were full citizens of both the United States and the State they reside in. Taney's effort to create a racial constitution was explicitly rejected. The country had taken a major step toward creating a republic truly grounded on "compact and equality."

For those Americans with additional imperial ambitions, the Fourteenth Amendment created a serious legal obstacle. Conquering and absorbing as equals a country like Mexico would give all Mexican males the full rights of United States citizens.[4] They would be able to vote, speak freely, have the right to a jury trial by their peers, and could move anywhere within the country. This sort of political/racial dilution was unacceptable. Recall Lincoln's sardonic warning that Douglas' imperial ambitions would lead to the admission of many "mongrels" into the country. Even before the civil War, Lincoln had pointed out that were no "uninhabited lands" for Americans to acquire aside from "some extreme northern regions."[5] No longer would Republicans support a blatantly racist system. For many years after the Civil War, there was a "growing sense that blacks were entitled to some measure of civil equality."[6]

---

3 Ibid.

4 Stannard, op. cit., *supra* ch. 1, n.7, at 31.

5 Lincoln, 'Fifth Lincoln-Douglas Debate' (Oct. 7, 1858), Lincoln, op. cit., *supra* ch. 7, n.8, at 719.

6 Eric Foner, *Reconstruction: America's Unfinished Revolution 1863-1877* (New York, 1988), 34.

Consequently, the Fourteenth Amendment was a significant force in determining the ultimate shape of the United States' geographic empire. Its influence provides a partial answer to Bernard DeVoto's two major questions about the shape of the American empire: (1) Why was the American political regime the same size as its empire and (2) Why was the country of continental size? First, republican egalitarianism required that the political regime be basically the same size as the empire. Second, the country stopped expanding its official boundaries because of the nature of the people it would have to conquer or purchase land from. Racial homogeneity prevailed over relentless formal expansion.[7] The Americans only had to contend with a few Indians and Mexicans in the land they had gained before the Civil War. Only Canada, protected by England, and Alaska remained as desirable entrants into the Republic. But President Polk's earlier unwillingness to reinvade Canada to gain the Northwest demonstrates that other factors, including the fear of defeat, are also important explanations for the shape of the American empire.

By purchasing Alaska from the Russians in 1867, William Henry Seward, Lincoln's Secretary of State, self-consciously continued the Jeffersonian vision of an empire.[8] Despite his opposition to the invasion of Mexico, Seward had his own imperial approach. In 1860, he had smugly informed the Canadians "you are building excellent states to be hereafter admitted into the American Union."[9] That same year he told an audience in Wisconsin that they were at the epicenter of future power: "The empire established at Washington is of less than a hundred years' formation. It was the empire of thirteen Atlantic states. Still, practically, the mission that empire is finished. * * * [Y]ou are the heirs to it. When the next census shall reveal your power, you will be found to be the masters of the United States of America, and through them the dominating political power of the world."[10] Although he did not want colonies in Latin America, he sought military bases on Caribbean Islands and foresaw Mexico City as the future capital of the American empire, which could grow rapidly in this new technological era.[11] When Seward looked west, he looked beyond California to Asia. In the same year he purchased Alaska, Seward gained control of the Midway Islands, over a thousand miles west of Hawaii. In

---

7 America's unwillingness to reinvade Canada demonstrates that there are other factors at work than racial constitutional politics.

8 LaFeber, *New Empire*, op. cit., *supra* ch. 1, n.76, at 24-32. *See also* Walter LaFeber, *The American Search for Opportunity, 1865-1913* (Cambridge, 1993).

9 LaFeber, *New Empire*, ibid., at 24.

10 Quoted in Turner, 'Mississippi Valley', Turner, op. cit., *supra* ch. 1, n.19, at 200.

11 LaFeber, New Empire, op. cit., *supra* ch. 9, n.8, at 28.

some way, Seward's geopolitics were more encompassing than Jefferson's views:

> [A] political law – and when I say political law, I mean a higher law, a law of Providence – that empire has, for the last three thousand years... made its way constantly westward, and it must continue to move westward until the tides of the renewed and of the decaying civilizations of the world meet on the shores of the Pacific Ocean.[12]

Many Americans opposed Seward's aggressive expansionism, claiming America already had more than enough land. As every schoolchild once knew, critics called his purchase of Alaska "Seward's folly." The opponents also did not want to spend any money on additional colonies.

Expansionist white Americans like Seward could continue to look beyond their borders because they had finally completely defeated the Native American enemies that they had so relentlessly fought for centuries. The technique had not changed since the Spanish first invaded the "New World." The Unionists betrayed those Native Americans who fought with them during the Civil War. As soon as the War ended, all Native Americans were once again labeled savages that had to be swept aside in favor of relentless white expansionism.[13] Consider the following eyewitness account of the 1864 Sand Creek Massacre, a genocidal event that Nobel Peace Prize winner Theodore Roosevelt would later laud "as righteous and beneficial a deed as ever took place on the frontier":[14]

> After the firing the warriors put the squaws and children together, and surrounded them to protect them. I saw five squaws under a bank for shelter. When the troops came up to them they ran out and showed their persons, to let the soldiers know they were squaws and begged for mercy, but the soldiers shot them all... There were some thirty or forty squaws collected in a hole for protection; they sent out a little girl about six years old with a white flag on a stick; she had not proceeded but a few steps when she was shot and killed. All the squaws in that hole were afterwards killed, and four or five bucks outside. The squaws offered no resistance. Every one I saw was scalped. I saw one squaw cut open with an unborn child, as I thought, lying by her side... I saw quite a number of infants in arms killed with their mothers.[15]

President Grant solved the Fourteenth Amendment problems by reviving and toughening the Monroe Doctrine: "[H]ereafter no territory on this continent shall be regarded as subject to transfer to a European

---

12 Ibid., at 26.
13 Phillips, op. cit., *supra* ch. 1, n.94, at 489.
14 Stannard, op. cit., *supra* ch. 1, n.7, at 135.
15 Stannard, ibid., at 132.

power."[16] When Cubans revolted against Spain in 1868, Grant's Secretary of State, Hamilton Fish, supported their quest for independence. Yet Fish successfully resisted Grant's and Congress' desire to intervene because he feared war with Spain would result in annexation of Cuba, which he opposed on racial grounds and his belief that American institutions could not work there.[17] After the Cuban revolution ended in 1878, American citizens increased their influence by buying up depressed sugar plantations. Many Cubans also became American citizens to immunize them from Spanish oppression or future revolutionary threats. They knew that America had the right, power, and duty to protect any of its citizens when they were abroad. In 1888, the *North American Review* concluded that this new, informal "species of ownership" provided profits without incurring political obligations.[18]

The most important imperial development following the war was the reintegration of the South as a compliant, subservient region. Once again, racially motivated geopolitics prevailed over any moral obligations to subordinated peoples. Although slavery was obviously a major cause of the Civil War, Kevin Phillips explained how protection of black rights after the war turned out to be ruthlessly temporary:

> In the minds of hard-boiled power brokers, Reconstruction may have been less a long-term commitment to blacks – the Lower North itself was rejecting racial equality in legislature after legislature – than a six- to eight-year partisan necessity. Federal troops kept ex-slaves enfranchised, and ex-Confederates disenfranchised, across the South long enough for the Republican Party to consolidate much of its economic, commercial, and industrial revolution and a necessary minimum of its political revolution.
>
> The economic downturn of 1873 had cost the Republicans control of Congress in 1874. Grant's leverage in occupying the White House through March 1877 was what enabled the great North-South bargain to be struck over the Hayes-Tilden election: Northern troops would be withdrawn and the cause of black voting rights substantially abandoned. What *would* be upheld were the interest of manufacturers, bankers, and capitalists.[19]

The enthusiastic reception of Frederick Jackson Turner's frontier thesis by intellectuals and politicians alike illuminates the mindset of the ruling class in the 1890s almost as much as Turner's theory clarifies American

---

16 Ibid., at 38.

17 Ibid., at 37-38.

18 Ibid., at 38.

19 Phillips, op. cit., *supra* ch. 1, n.94, at 474. The classic work documenting the quasi-colonization of the South remains C. Vann Woodward, *Origins of the New South 1877-1913* (1951).

history. Like Henry Adams, Turner did not mince his words. The first paragraph of his famous article states: "Up to our own day American history has been in a large degree the history of the colonization of the Great West."[20] Turner argued that historians' emphasis on slavery obscured the even greater importance of expansionism on the American mind[21] (just as the contemporary obsession with racial and sexual injustices underemphasizes the country's relentless quest for power): "But what constitutional historian has made any adequate attempt to interpret political facts by the light of these social areas and changes?"[22] Although Turner used his thesis to make many valuable insights, his basic claim was hardly original. To a large degree, he was simply verifying Madison and Jefferson's Malthusian fear that their agrarian, republican empire would eventually disappear under the pressures of population growth. Like Madison and Jefferson, Turner and his generation looked upon this development with alarm. No longer would there be an inexpensive agrarian system to absorb excess or oppressed labor.[23] Somehow the country had to contend with the concentration of labor in urban cities. Finally, the country needed outlets for its surplus agricultural goods, capital, and manufacturing products.

But where the Virginians foresaw urban decadence and corruption, Turner and his admiring compatriots (which included Theodore Roosevelt) foresaw new opportunities. The demise of the first American empire, premised upon the availability of land to all whites who were willing to work it, required the country to adapt. But there was no need to change the United States' basic character: "He would be a rash prophet who should assert that the expansive character of American life has now entirely ceased. Movement has been its dominant fact, and, unless this training has no effect upon a people, the American energy will continually demand a wider field for its exercise."[24] Like Madison, Turner recommended greater growth as the corrective. In an *Atlantic Monthly* article written three years after his dramatic presentation as the American Historical Association, Turner explained: "For really three centuries the dominant fact of American life has been expansion... The demands for a vigorous foreign policy, for an interoceanic canal, for a revival of our power upon the seas, and for the extension of American influence to outlying islands and

[20] Turner, 'The Significance of the Frontier in American History', Turner, op. cit., *supra* ch. 1, n.19, at 1.
[21] Ibid., at 24.
[22] Ibid., at 12.
[23] Turner, 'Pioneer Ideals and the State University', ibid., at 275.
[24] Turner, 'Significance', ibid., at 37.

adjoining countries, are indications that the movement will continue."[25] Turner accurately prophesized Theodore Roosevelt's future when he concluded that the unification of the old West with the new South "might mean a drastic assertion of national government and imperial expansion under a popular hero."[26] At that moment in American history, imperialism was not a dirty word but a fundamental part of American history and character: "And yet in important historical ideals – in the process of expansion, in the persistence of agricultural interests, in imperialistic ways of looking at the American destiny, in hero-worship, in the newness of its present social structure – the Old Northwest has much in common with the South and the Far West."[27]

This same conflicting blend of capitalism and racism reemerged when the Senate decided not to annex Hawaii in 1898. Antiexpansionists argued that America did not need the additional responsibility. Some of them were opposed to expanding American territorial sovereignty beyond the continent. For instance, William Graham Sumner explained why Cuba had to be kept out of the Union:

> Our system is unfit for the government of subject provinces. They have no place in it. They would become seats of corruption, which would react on our own body politic. If we admitted the island as a state or a group of states, we should have to let it help govern us. The prospect of adding to the present Senate a number of Cuban senators, either native or carpet-bag, is one whose terrors it is not necessary to unfold.[28]

Sumner's solution was worldwide economic growth, not territorial extension:

> What private individuals want is free access, under order and security, to any part of the earth's surface, in order they may avail themselves of its natural resources for their use, either by investment or commerce. If, therefore, we have free trade with Hawaii while somebody else has the jurisdiction, we should gain all the advantages and escape all the burdens.

He correctly feared that the proposed imperial structure would undermine the basic constitutional principle that all men are created equal.[29] Because

---

[25] Turner, 'The Problem of the West', ibid., at 219.

[26] Ibid., at 220.

[27] Turner, 'Dominant Forces in Western Life', ibid., at 242.

[28] William Graham Sumner, 'The Fallacy of Territorial Extension', William Graham Sumner, *On Liberty, Society, and Politics: The Essential Essays of William Graham Sumner* (Robert C. Bannister, ed., 1992), 269.

[29] Sumner, 'The Conquest of the United States by Spain', ibid., at 280.

of their racial biases, Americans would establish the fundamentally inegalitarian colonial system that they had rebelled against in 1775.[30]

The next year, President Cleveland followed President Tyler's dubious constitutional precedent of bypassing the Senate, which must confirm all Treaties by a two-thirds majority, when he annexed Hawaii by using a joint resolution requiring a majority from both Houses.

The victorious Spanish-American War forced the country to choose between humane constitutional principles and the further growth of its empire. Because the Americans wanted to retain their strategically placed spoils of war, they had to jettison the Republican standards of equal citizenship throughout the empire and to narrow the text and spirit of the Fourteenth Amendment. America would have perpetual colonies. Native populations in Puerto Rico and the Philippines would not be brought into the Republic via "compact and equality." Particularly in the Philippines, they would be subjugated through relentless violence and permanent inequality. Among other things, they could be taxed without representation. The United States had returned to the Athenian/English model, maintaining formal equality in North America while establishing unequal, but important outposts throughout the World.

In a series of popular books, Josiah Strong intimated more frightening ways to resolve the racial problem inhibiting imperial growth. With the closing of the Western Frontier, the West was about to "enter on a new stage of its history – the final competition of the races."[31] Although Strong preferred to use peaceful means to resolve this conflict, he did not oppose force.[32]

The American empire also slowed its geographical growth because it devised other means for broadening its influence, creating what William Appleman Williams called an "informal empire."[33] America facilitated its naval/commercial presence throughout the world by gaining control of many strategic locations: Alaska, Hawaii, Puerto Rico, Samoa, the Panama Canal, the Virgin Islands, Cuba, and the Philippines. The brutal subjugation of the Philippines demonstrated that force and conquest remained integral parts of American foreign policy. In addition to developing a formal colonial system, American Presidents would engage in "gunboat

---

30 *Id.* at 283-5

31 LaFeber, *New Empire*, op. cit., *supra* ch. 9, n.8, at 79.

32 Ibid., at 80. LaFeber concluded that Strong passionately combined his muscular Christianity with the major intellectual imperial messages of the era: "the frontier thesis of Turner, the themes of the westward movement of empire and the increasing concentration of society stressed by Brook Adams, and the Anglo-Saxon commerical and military mission outlined by Alfred Thayer Mahan."

33 William Appleman Williams, *The Tragedy of American Diplomacy* (New York, 1972), 47.

diplomacy." Periodic invasions of South American countries to maintain "stability" occurred throughout the coming century.

The United States had developed another institution after the Civil War that would effectively extend imperial power without needing to expand territorial sovereignty: the modern multi-national corporation. Protected by government subsidies, internal free trade, and military force abroad, American corporations helped formulate foreign policy in Washington and domestic policy throughout the Americas. In *Santa Clara County v. Southern Pacific Railroad Co.*,[34] The United States Supreme Court entrenched these organs of private power into the Constitution by characterizing them as constitutional "persons" under the Fourteenth Amendment deserving constitutional rights, even though that Amendment was primarily designed to protect Southern blacks from racist oppression. These increasingly powerful corporations worked closely with the government to further both military and economic expansion. As early as the mid-1880s, John Hay, who worked in the State Department, lamented: "This is a government of the people, by the people, and for the people no longer. It is a government of corporations, by corporations, and for corporations..."[35] The historian Walter LaFeber has described in great detail how the alliance between government, the military, military contractors, and private power became ever tighter by the end on the Nineteenth Century, culminating in the Spanish-American War.

The Monroe Doctrine truly had defined the aspirations of the early American empire; it only needed to be made tougher and more exclusive. When the Americans confronted the British over a boundary dispute in Venezuela, they expanded the Monroe Doctrine yet again. Henry Cabot Lodge explained that the American people would not "give up their rightful supremacy to the Western Hemisphere."[36] According to Lodge, the Monroe Doctrine contained an explicit double standard: "The Monroe Doctrine has no bearing on the extension of the United States, but simply holds that no European power shall establish itself in the Americas or interfere with American governments."[37] Congressman Leonidas F. Livingston was even more blunt: "This related to a matter on our continent. Our trade and other relations with those people are involved in this settlement."[38] Secretary of State Olney explained why the United States eventually worked out a peaceful settlement with England:

---

34 118 U.S. 394 (1886).

35 LaFeber, '*New Empire*', op. cit., *supra* ch. 9, n.8, at 17.

36 Ibid., at 249.

37 Ibid.

38 Ibid.

> Today the United States is practically sovereign on this continent, and its fiat is law upon the subjects to which it confines its interpretation. Why? It is not because of the pure friendship or good will felt for it... It is because, in addition to all other grounds, its infinite resources combined with its isolated position render it master of the situation and practically invulnerable as against any or all other powers.[39]

Having solidified control of South America, post-Civil War leaders joined Seward in looking to Asia, a tradition that reaches as far back to Franklin's effort to discover the Northwest Passage. As usual, they combined republican virtues with imperial growth. Americans would liberate Japan, China, and even India first by expanding American commercial power, with republicanism soon to follow. The United States would once again be the "redeemer nation," commingling self-interest and humanity into a relentless political/economic force.[40] Overall, the new American Empire consisted of "freedom and compact," brute force, mercantile-style economics within its Hemispheric domain, and distant colonies – a potent mix of Athenian, British, and American norms and techniques.

The Supreme Court contributed to the structure of the new empire in the *Slaughter-House Cases*, which are generally known for an excessively crabbed reading of the Fourteenth Amendment. Notable among the few national citizenship rights listed by Justice Miller was the "privilege of a citizen of the United States ...to demand the care and protection of the Federal government over his life, liberty, and property when on the high seas or within the jurisdiction of a foreign government."[41] At long last, Daniel Webster's preference of expanding American power through private investment instead of territorial growth received its constitutional imprimatur. In the same case, dissenting Justice Field temporarily revived *Dred Scott's* theme of equality throughout the republic: "[The] equality of right, with exemption from all disparaging and partial enactments, in the lawful pursuits of life, throughout the whole country, is the distinguishing privilege of citizens of the United States."[42]

Turner's thesis had empirically confirmed Madison and Jefferson's Malthusian fear that the new nation would soon become overpopulated. Both Madison and Turner saw the need for continued expansion lest the

---

39 Ibid., at 262.

40 Pocock, *Moment*, op. cit., *supra* ch. 1, n.140, at 542.

41 The *Slaughter-House Cases*, 83 U.S. (16 Wall.) 36, 79 (1873). The Supreme Court subordinated property rights to foreign policy considerations when it upheld President Carter's Iranian hostage placing all private claims against Iran in a special tribunal, *Dames & Moore v. Regan*, 453 U.S. 654 (1981).

42 *Slaughter-House*, 83 U.S. at 109-110 (Field, J., dissenting).

populace turn upon itself.[43] Both times, relatively minor figures provided practical solutions containing important elements of "informal empire." President Monroe's Doctrine asserted American supervision of both North and South America (Canada reluctantly excepted). Nearly a century later, John Hay's Open Door Policy in China established similar principles in the Far East; the United States would protect its markets and increase its military/political power by preventing any other country from formally seizing China. Under both approaches, lofty anti-imperialist principles did not apply to the United States. The United States could and would seize whatever territory it needed to protect its interests anywhere in the world, most notably the Philippines. Senator Beveridge's defense of the new empire enthusiastically captured the enduring racial component of American expansionism:

> We will not repudiate our duty... We will not abandon our opportunity in the Orient. We will not renounce our part in the mission of our race, trustee under God, of the civilization of the world... We will move forward with our work.. with gratitude... and thanksgiving to Almighty God that He has marked us as His chosen people, henceforth to lead the regeneration of the world.
>
> Our largest trade henceforth must be with Asia. The Pacific is our ocean. More and more Europe will manufacture the most it needs...Where shall we turn for consumers of our surplus? Geography answers the question. China is our natural customer... The Philippines give us a based at the door of all the East...
>
> The power that rules the Pacific... is the power that rules the world. And, with the Philippines, that power is and will forever be the American Republic.[44]

B. The Supreme Court's Ratification of America's Racist Republican Empire

Never before had the United States gained control of land containing large majorities of nonwhite people for the foreseeable future. No major American politician wanted these people to be equal participants in either American political or labor markets. Williams Jennings Bryan concluded

---

[43] Williams, *Tragedy*, op. cit., *supra* ch. 9, n.33, at 22-23.

[44] Quoted in Van Alystyne, Rising American Empire, op. cit., *supra* Intro., n.8, at 187. For analysis of the conquest of the Philippines, *see* Stanley Karnow, *In Our Image: America's Empire in the Philippines* (New York, 1989) and Vicente L. Rafael, 'White Love', in *Cultures of United States Imperialism* (Amy Kaplan and Donald E. Pease, eds., Durham, 1993).

with characteristic bluntness: "[T]he Filipinos cannot be citizens without endangering our civilization."[45] The new empire consisted of small islands (and Panama), many thousands of miles from North America, seized to serve commercial and military interests. There no longer existed a section of the country, like the Antebellum South, that desperately needed to expand formal jurisdiction further south to preserve its political economy. Yet America's revolutionary Republicanism, a tradition reaching from Franklin and Jefferson to Chief Justice Taney, required that all parts of the Union be equal. Parts of *Dred Scott* still stood in the way; Taney had held that the Constitution gave Congress no power to maintain perpetual colonies. Congress could set up administrative structures to maintain the new territories until they could become States, but it could not interfere with any individual constitutional rights.

In *Reynolds v. United States*, the post-Civil War Court reconfirmed that principle in the course of upholding Congressional power to prohibit polygamy in the Territory of Utah: "Congress cannot pass a law for the government of the Territories which shall prohibit the free exercise of religion. The first amendment of the Constitution expressly prohibits such legislation. Religious freedom is guaranteed everywhere throughout the United States, as far as congressional interference is concerned."[46] Conversely, the pre-Spanish American War Supreme Court upheld Congressional exclusions of Chinese aliens who were attempting to return to the United States. The Court deferred to Congress because the aliens were not citizens and the power to exclude foreigners was "an incident of sovereignty."[47] In addition, the Court held that a Native American had no right to vote unless Congress had granted him citizenship rights through a statute or treaty.[48] Thus Congress retained the power to use racial categories at least in certain situations.

The United States Supreme Court solved these imperial difficulties in a group of decisions known as the *Insular Cases*. The first two major cases created a presumption in favor of free trade between the new colonies and the mainland.[49] The presumption arose once the colony had "official notice" that the Senate had ratified a treaty transferring sovereignty to the

---

[45] Quoted in Williams, *Tragedy*, op. cit., *supra* ch. 9, n.33, at 46.

[46] 98 U.S. 145, 162 (1878).

[47] *Chae Chan Ping v. United States*, 130 U.S. 581, 609 (1889).

[48] *Elk v. Wilkins*, 112 U.S. 94 (1884). As late as 1923, the Court still considered it to be an "open question" whether Pueblo Indians were American citizens, *United States v. Sandoval*, 231 U.S. 28, 39 (1913).

[49] *DeLima v. Bidwell*, 182 U.S. 1 (1900) (Tariffs could not be imposed as "imports" on shipments from Porto Rico to United States ports) and *Dooley v. United States*, 182 U.S. 222 (1900) (Tariffs could not be imposed upon shipments from United States ports to Porto Rico).

United States.[50] The Court then modified that presumption to permit military occupying forces to collect pre-existing import duties to provide for military expenses until Congressional treaty ratification and formal exchange of sovereignty.[51] These cases' scope and authority remained uncertain because Congress had not established any tariffs. The United States government was trying to collect additional revenue under pre-existing duty laws. Nevertheless, the cases demonstrate the Court's eagerness to protect and promote private power's expansion inside and outside America's formal boundaries.

Downes v. Bidwell's answers to this question places it among the most despicable Supreme Court opinions of all time. In terms of its constitutional premises, it rivals *Plessy v. Ferguson*, which held that States could segregate blacks and whites under the "separate but equal" doctrine, and is arguably worse than *Dred Scott*, which at least had supporting constitutional text and a commitment to a form of republican egalitarian empire. *Downes* deserves to be pulled out of the collectivity known as the *Insular Cases* and considered on its own merits. After all, unlike *Plessy* and *Dred Scott*, it has never been repudiated by Constitutional Amendment or judicial decision. In a sharply divided opinion, containing yet another stirring dissent by Justice Harlan, the Supreme Court held that Congress had the power to set tariffs on goods shipped from Puerto Rico to the United States even though Congress would have violated the text of the Constitution if it had set similar tariffs within the mainland. The Constitution proscribes "all duties, imposts, and excises shall be uniform throughout the United States."[52] Thus the United States could have it both ways with its new colonies: it could create free trade zones whenever desirable, yet tax those any of those colonies' imports that threaten domestic interests. Although the Fourteenth Amendment said nothing about colonies, the Court rejected that progressive aspect of *Dred Scott* holding that the Constitution must be applicable throughout the land. In fact, the *Downes* Court quoted the Fourteenth Amendment as another authority for imperialism: it only applies to "all persons born or naturalized in the United States, and subject to the jurisdiction thereof, are citizens of the United States, and of the State wherein they reside."[53] Because the colonies were neither in the United States nor States, their inhabitants had no constitutional rights. The Court cobbled together some dubious "precedents." For example, it discussed Jefferson's efforts after the Louisiana Purchase to limit citizenship to whites, a rather questionable

---

50 *DeLima v. Bidwell*, 182 U.S. at 186-87 (1900).

51 *Dooley v. United States*, 182 U.S. 222 (1900).

52 United States Constitution, Art. I. Section 8, cl. [1].

53 *DeLima*, 182 U.S. at 251.

precedent since race slavery was flourishing at the time. The precedent was also weak because Jefferson promised to turn the new Territories into States as soon as it was appropriate. The District of Columbia provided some textual authority that not every part of the country had to be completely equal.

This convenient outcome did not come easily for the Court; it still wanted to protect some of constitutional rights of American citizens who would enter the colonies. Otherwise, there might be few immigrants or entrepreneurs. Like all Supreme Courts before and since, it resolved this problem by creating a hierarchy of constitutional rights precisely limiting Congressional power.[54] Although American citizens did not have a constitutional right to have free trade with these colonies, they retained their Constitutional right to property.[55] Nor could Congress pass ex post facto laws, bills of attainder, or grant titles of nobility. Although the First Amendment protected entering American citizens, the Court explicitly did not speculate about the rest of the Bill of Rights,[56] with one notable exception. American citizens had no right to a jury in criminal cases; Congress could establish consular courts to regulate local affairs.[57] Local inhabitants fared worse. They had no constitutional rights, particularly the dreaded right to be treated as an equal human being throughout the United States under the Privileges and Immunities Clause of Article IV, section two.[58]

The Court explicitly relied upon imperial necessity and racial difference to justify its peculiar doctrine that facilitated lucrative trade but little else. Whatever the Framers may have thought about republican empires, Congress needed to have the same powers all other countries have when they conquer a new land.[59] Rigid constructions of the Constitution constraining Congress could lead to disaster: "A false step at this time might be fatal to the development of what Chief Justice Marshall called the American Empire."[60] Although it had rejected Chief Justice Marshall's

---

[54] Ibid., at 268.
[55] Ibid.,at 270.
[56] Ibid., at 277.
[57] Ibid., at 271.
[58] The Court also made a curious statement about natural rights. It suggested that these rights, which include the freedom of speech, immunities from unreasonable searches and seizures, and equal protection of the laws, are applicable to immigrants and inhabitants. It explicitly excluded the right to franchise, the core right of republicanism, from this list. But there was no indication that the Court would enforce any of these rights. Its next paragraph seemingly delegated the allocation of these rights to the "American people." Ibid., at 282-83.
[59] Ibid., At 285.
[60] Ibid., At 286.

reasoning that the Constitution fully extended throughout the States and Territories, it endorsed his description of the system as the "American empire:[61]

> We are also of opinion that the power to acquire territory by treaty implies not only the power to govern such territory, but to prescribe upon what terms the United States will receive its inhabitants, and what their status shall be in what Chief Justice Marshall termed the "American Empire." There seems to be no middle ground between this position and the doctrine that if their inhabitants do not become, immediately upon annexation, citizens of the United States, their children thereafter born, whether savages or civilized, are such, and entitled to all the rights, privileges and immunities of citizens. If such be their status, the consequences will be extremely serious. Indeed, it is doubtful if Congress would ever assent to the annexation of territory upon the condition that its inhabitants, however foreign they may be to our habits, traditions and modes of life, shall become at once citizens of the United States.[62]

Congress could establish any racial hierarchy it wanted within the colonies, such as granting white Alaskans, but not "uncivilized native tribes," rights to citizenship. It did not violate the Constitution by giving itself exclusive power to determine "the civil rights and political status of the native inhabitants" in Puerto Rico and the Philippines.[63] The *Insular Cases* also echoed Marshall's jurisprudence by elevating property rights to the highest level of constitutional protection. Marshall had construed the Contracts Clause to protect a wide range of property rights from state interference, but had refused to extend the Bill of Rights to the States. The *Insular Cases* protected the constitutional right to free trade, but none of the more personal individual rights.

While the *Plessy* Court maintained that it was not being racist in permitting "separate but equal" facilities for blacks and whites, the *Downes* case explicitly relied upon the racial superiority. It first reassured those who worried about Congressional oppression that both American immigrants and native inhabitants would be protected by "certain principles of natural justice inherent in the Anglo-Saxon character..."[64] The majority next imbedded racism into the American empire after the Fourteenth Amendment as much as Taney imbedded race slavery into the original Constitution: "It is obvious that in the annexation of outlying and distant possessions grave questions will arise from differences of race, habits, laws and customs of the people... which may require action on the part of

---

61 Ibid., At 259, quoting from *Loughborough v. Blake*, 18 U.S. (5* Wheat. 317) 317 (1820).

62 Ibid., at 279-80.

63 Ibid., at 280.

64 Ibid.

Congress that would be quite unnecessary in the annexation of contiguous territory inhabited only by people of the same race, or by scattered bodies of native Indians."[65] Even as strong an advocate of democracy as Frederick Jackson Turner accepted such compromises:

> This extension of power, this undertaking of grave responsibilities in new fields, this entry into the sisterhood of world-states, was no isolated event. It was, indeed, in some respects the logical outcome of the nation's march to the Pacific, the sequence to the era in which it was engaged in occupying the free lands and exploiting the resources of the West. When it had achieved this position among the nations of the earth, the United States found it confronted, also, with the need for constitutional readjustment, arising from the relations of federal government and territorial acquisitions. It was obliged to reconsider questions of the rights of man and traditional ideals of American liberty and democracy, in view of the task of government of other races politically inexperienced and undeveloped.[66]

Although there were many details to be ironed out in subsequent cases, the basic structure of the republican empire had been redefined to meet immediate felt needs. The United States would now have Athens's imperial structure of perpetually subordinate colonies. Equal power and full citizenship rights would only exist in those areas that Congress designated as States or officially "incorporated" into the United States as future States. Despite the Reconstruction Amendments, Congress could form its imperial policy upon an assumption of racial superiority. Rogers Smith summarized the new empire's racial structure:

> Congress decided that Filipinos, somewhat like Chinese laborers, were…too racially distinct, inferior, and troublesome to possess any form of U.S. citizenship or nationality. * * * They should be tutored as subjects for a time, then gradually expelled from formal affiliation with the U.S. via independence (which came, finally, in 1946). * * * The more compliant yet also racially inferior native residents of Guam seemed fit to be permanent colonial subjects… They did not obtain any measure of U.S. citizenship until 1950. Puerto Ricans…were thought suitable for citizenship, but only for something like the second-class citizenship of blacks and Native Americans, as well as women. Finally, there were enough nonaboriginal people in Hawaii and Alaska so that most of their residents could safely be treated as full citizens residing in a U.S. territory on its way to statehood, like the old Northwest.[67]

---

65 Ibid., at 282.

66 Turner, 'Social Forces in American History', Turner, op. cit., *supra* ch. 1, n.19, at 315.

67 Smith, op. cit., *supra* ch. 1, n.159, at 429-30.

The Fourteenth Amendment did not turn out to be a complete barrier to formal growth of the racist American Empire into foreign lands, but it did make it more difficult to fully assimilate those lands into the Republic. The American government solved this problem by only taking islands (and the Isthmus of Panama) that were necessary for trade and war. It would be relatively simple to pacify islanders, cut off from a reliable supply of weapons, but it would be profoundly difficult to maintain direct control over a large, well-populated country like Mexico or Brazil without eventually including them in the Union. It would be easier and cheaper to use military and economic force to keep these remaining areas under indirect control with the ruthless assistance of compliant local leadership. The only costs were the revolutionary commitment to equality throughout the empire and the Reconstruction Amendments' norm of racial justice.

Conclusion

One of the advantages of studying American constitutional history through the First World War is that America's rulers and citizens often spoke and wrote with great clarity and candor. The relatively permanent and semi-confidential letter, not the phone call or E-Mail, was the major mode of communication. Furthermore, the ideological rival of Communism did not yet threaten the American system. They were proud of their empire, wealth, democracy, and legal system, all of which helped protect them from such internal threats as unions and governmental regulations as well as external rivals such as England. Applying the nineteenth century's norm of nationalism, they had been enormously successful. But rival political forces often require modification of rhetoric. In the Twentieth Century, it became impolitic to refer to America as an "empire." It was too closely related to "imperialism," a damning code word of the Marxist Left.

This propaganda technique has had important internal and external effects. Like the Philadelphia Quakers who lamented violence against the Indians while greedily increasing their wealth thanks to the bloodthirsty efforts of men like Thomas Pynchon's fictional character Oily Leon (quoted at the beginning of this book), the average American has felt more comfortable when immersed in a political universe of sentimental euphemisms that blurred analysis and responsibility. To this day, America has been a Sentimental Empire. According to prevailing rhetoric and theory, every American is either virtuous or a victim. Nobody is responsible, or at least somebody else is.

Now that the Cold War is over, some Marxist analytical techniques and concepts should be revived, not for their rhetorical or predictive significance, but for their insights into existing practices. Until this Conclusion, I assiduously avoided using the word "imperialism," preferring to present a cluster or facts, observations, and statements to prove America's continual, widespread commitment to "empire." It is better to wrestle with those facts and propositions before entering into the semantic controversy over alleged differences between "imperialism" and America's dogged quest for "empire." It is far less important to squabble over normative political labels and categories than to determine, as best as one can, what actually happened and then make an overall moral assessment. Spending too much time on abstractions often leads to insufficient knowledge of facts and contexts.

Nevertheless, we need some word to describe empires that act immorally, instead of limiting our analysis of empires to the "analytical" definitions of size and growth. "Imperialism" seems an appropriate word. There are at least three historical factors to consider in determining whether a country has been "imperialist": the country's choice of ends (including its blend of motives), its selection of means (including development of institutions), and its effects on other peoples.

This book has revealed an American history of complex, frequently conflicting goals. A few Americans never wanted the country to expand. Some sought power, wealth, and glorious fame. Others wished to care only for themselves and their family, even if that desire required killing and displacing Native Americans. Some sought to purge the continent of rival nations and inferior, savage races; others believed they were liberating those they were going to rule. Just as saving souls for Christ justified European expansion in earlier centuries, spreading republican norms, Western civilization, the "rule of law" and, after a while, religious salvation to decadent and primitive civilizations provided Americans with moral justifications to supplement their quest for power and glory.

Nor were such altruistic beliefs implausible. There are powerful "natural law" and policy arguments in favor of republicanism. Most American male citizens had formally equal rights, a large improvement over feudalism. Later, all non-alien adults would become citizens, another great improvement. The electoral process helped keep rulers in line and provided the average citizen with some power. Of course, many people simply took pride in the country's ever-growing strength, preferring to win rather than lose. For a sophisticated analyst like Madison, the new empire also helped protect the wealthy, thereby stabilizing the republic. The poor could not threaten the rich, and the rich would be satisfied with what they had. Madison had brilliantly designed a republican system that would protect the rich, prevent majority tyranny, constrain the poor, and foster an empire.

Although many Americans dreaded war, the country's imperial ambitions required a standing army and an executive branch with sufficient "energy" to engage in combat or quickly make decisions like the Louisiana Purchase. Men like Jefferson preferred to expand through purchases on favorable terms, but it would be difficult to enter into and enforce such contracts without having military force lurking in the background. Many other leaders and settlers were willing, even eager to use brutal force – mass murder, invasion, and terror – against resisters, be they American Indians, Mexicans, or Spaniards. During the initial continental expansion, Americans usually preferred to extend citizenship equally. But when that republican norm caused complications, as it did in Louisiana after the Purchase, *Dred Scott*, and the *Insular Cases*, it was sacrificed by making the most ludicrous of legal distinctions. When the continental dream no longer was adequate, the country established colonies throughout Latin America and the Pacific. Thus America changed its conceptions of empire, republican, and citizenship in accordance with its most immediate needs.

Have the "other" Americans – the Native, and Latin Americans – benefited from this history, which at least immunized them from significant European intervention? They have certainly felt the wrath of a Machiavellian republic, which treats its citizens with some degree of respect but sees the rest of the world as a source of exploitation. In terms of actual policy, for well over a century the United States has been far more concerned to make the world safe for America and its corporations than for democracy. American leaders generally have favored "stable" dictatorships to turbulent democracies; Latin America has long contained a depressing mix of Athen's colonism in Panama and Puerto Rico and British mercantilism everywhere else. Admittedly, there has been much trade with Latin Americans. Nor were Latin Americans impressed into fighting on behalf of the new empire; America already had enough citizens to fight global wars successfully.[1] But America need not take formal responsibility for those countries, only intervening when necessary. In the meantime, Americans could wash their hands of local atrocities, just as some early Americans wrung their hands over injustices to Indians while supporting westward movement. Over the decades, millions have been sacrificed to this empire whether through direct violence, the slave trade, disease, or despair. Merely a decade ago, this country aided and abetted the slaughter of over one hundred thousand Indian peasants in Guatemala. Hundreds of millions suffer this very day, lucky if they can make clothes for our corporations (and our citizens) for a few cents a day.

---

[1] Machiavelli concluded that Republican Empires need to satisfy the citizenry's necessities to have enough troops willing to protect and expand the country, Machiavelli, *Discourses*, op. cit., *supra* ch. 1, n.134, at 70. One of the aftermaths of the end of the Cold War are that the ruling class no longer needs to take care of all of its citizens because there is no serious military rival. Furthermore, thanks to technology relatively few citizens may need to fight in most future wars. Finally, the country no longer needs to take care of its poor because the Soviet Union would use unjust internal treatment for propaganda purposes. For example, the State Department requested that the Supreme Court strike down school segregation in the South because the Russians were using that practice to persuade the new countries in Asia and Africa that the United States was racist.

The empire's domestic economy was also largely built by "others." Africans were taken across an ocean to become slaves. Most immigrants faced bias and oppressive working conditions. Now many of their descendants are dismissed as useless inconveniences. The country's domestic situation may deteriorate even more as the Global Market continues to determine so much of public policy with a strong bias against social services. Both NAFTA and GATT undermine the rights and hopes of citizens by forcing them to compete against incredibly cheap, exploited labor. Certainly the multinational corporations and markets will never value American citizenship as anything special. In addition, the ruling class appears to be convinced that technological dominance and the lack of any credible military threat eliminates the need for large armies. Empires have often protected a vast majority of their citizens so they would willingly and capably fight in war.

This book also has a more concrete legal implication. It calls into question the constitutional status of Puerto Rico, which is still not a State even though it has a large population on a significant land mass. As recently as 1920, the Supreme Court held that Puerto Ricans had no constitutional right to a jury.[2] Relying upon the numerous precedents – historical, legal, and political – set forth in this book, the Supreme Court should reaffirm *Dred Scott's* holding that Congress cannot create permanent colonies with less than full citizenship rights for their denizens. That doctrine flows from the Revolutionary principle that there should be equality throughout the empire. Some exceptions would probably need to be made for small island military bases, such as Guam or the Virgin Islands, but Puerto Rico is such a flagrant violation of ancient (and just) constitutional norms that the Court should no longer defer to Congress but should mandate its immediate Statehood.

Overall, we are caught in several Madisonian-Hobbesian dilemmas. We need a strong government to protect us not only from rival empires and civil conflicts, but also from the Global Market. At one time, corporations might have been an "intermediate institution" that protected us from governmental tyranny. Now, governments seem more like intermediate institutions that can prevent the Global Market from dictating our lives. After all, to the degree that the Global Market sees itself as the new Empire, it will treat all non-citizens, i.e., those who are not wealthy or major actors in the multinational corporate system, as potential candidates for exploitive profit-seeking. It is also worth noting that the Global Market is not "republican." These massive centers of power are not accountable to the people.

---

2 *Balzac v. People of Puerto Rico*, 258 U.S. 298 (1922).

The escalating debate over the roles of the Global Market and private power in the American constitutional system confirms this book's secondary proposition that Americans have perpetually contested the form and nature of their imperial republic. At the beginning of the Twentieth Century, the ruling class is divided among those who emphasize corporate trade and cultural propoganda, those who seek world-wide military dominance (presently with a heavy emphasis on space-based technology),[3] and those eager to override doctrines of state sovereignty to protect human rights (at least when the sovereign is no longer abiding by the will of the United States or NATO). There remains a dissenting tradition, barely audible in the mainstream media, that seeks a more humane, nonviolent approach based upon social and economic justice, human rights, and environmental enhancement.

This book will have accomplished one of its major purposes if it has convinced some of its readers that America has been an empire like so many before it. Perhaps America's empire has most of the time been better than most. But this is not the place to probe that argument.[4] Over the long sweep of history, America may well be seen as a generally progressive force. It could not have won three major wars during the Twentieth Century without having imperial strength. Defeating some forms of fascism, National Socialism, and the Soviet Union's imperial Communism counterbalances many evil deeds.

But, to return to the book's basic questions, has America been steadily fueled by imperial ambitions? Yes. Has it been and does it remain an imperial power? Yes. Has it been willing to use brutal means to achieve ends of power, glory, and wealth? Yes again. Has it acted the way most empires have, using its force and wealth to impose its will on others? Of course. For me, these answers are enough to conclude that America has been and continues to be "imperialist." Thus it does not completely accept Hardt and Negri's claim that "imperialism" has been replaced by "Empire."[5] Boundaries and nationalities still matter. The United States' overall imperial history has been rather ordinary for an empire, not exceptionally evil or virtuous. Indeed, one of its greatest contributions has been in the area of constitutional structures. The evolution from subordinate colonies of England to a political constitution that grants formal equality throughout almost all of its borders and provides basic citizenship rights to all adults is truly admirable.

---

[3] Peter Wilson emphasized this distinction to me.

[4] However, for starters, one should ask oneself if he or she would have rather been a political dissident in Latin America or in Eastern Europe during the 1980s.

[5] Hardt and Negri, *supra* Intro., n.2, at xiii-xv.

We must strip away a great deal of sentimental propaganda, emanating from both sides of our narrow political spectrum to determine who we really are. Only then we can thoughtfully decide how proud we are of our history and culture. Some of us will feel the need for changes, perhaps significant changes, in the basic constitutional structure and particular culture of our existing republican empire. Although my better emotions prefer Montesquieu's small republics that would avoid the evils of luxury and war, I don't perceive how such republics, even if clustered into federations, could provide a stable worldwide structure anytime in the near future. Some villains would eventually pursue vainglory. We need some sort of a Leviathan to protect us from internal violence, aggressive external threats, and that new semi-sovereign force known as the Global Market. Thus the immediate problem is to develop institutions and cultural norms that will somehow tame our existing empire that has often been far too Machiavellian in attitude and impact, forcing it to treat all its citizens and those living outside its boundaries with basic human decency.

Bibliography

Ackerman, Bruce, *We the People: Foundations* (Cambridge, 1991)

Ackerman, Bruce, *We the People: Transformations* (Cambridge, 1998)

Adair, Douglass, 'Fame and the Founding Fathers', Douglass Adair, *Fame and the Founding Fathers: Essays by Douglass Adair* (Trevor Colbourn, ed., Indianapolis, 1974)

Adams, Henry, *History of the United States During the Jefferson Administrations* (New York, 1986)

Adams, Henry, *History of the United States of America During the Administration of James Madison* (Earl N. Harbert wrote notes, New York, 1986)

Adams, Henry, *The Education of Henry Adams* (W.D. Brogan, intro., Boston, 1961)

Adams, John, *The Revolutionary Writings of John Adams* (Jan. 27, 1766) (C. Bradley Thompson, ed., Indianapolis, 2000)

Aleinikoff, Alexander, 'Puerto Rico and the Constitution: Conundrums and Prospects', 11 *Constitutional Commentary*, 15 (1994)

Amar, Akhil Reed, 'Some New World Lessons for the Old World', 58 *University Chicago Law Review*, 483 (1991)

Amar, Akhil Reed, 'Intratextualism', 112 *Harvard Law Review* 343 (1999)

American Political Writing During the Founding Era 1760-1805 (Charles S. Hyneman and Donald S. Lutz, eds., Indianapolis, 1983)

Ames, Fisher, *1 Works of Fisher Ames* (W.B.Allen, ed., Indianapolis, 1983)

Appleby, Joyce, *Liberalism and Republicanism in the Historical Imagination* (Cambridge, 1992)

Aristotle, Politics, *2 The Complete Works of Aristotle* (J. Barnes, ed., Princeton, 1984)

Baker, Leonard, *John Marshall: A Life in the Law* (New York, 1974)

Banning, Lance, *The Sacred Fire of Liberty: James Madison and the Founding of the Federal Republic* (Ithaca, 1995)

Beard, Charles A., *An Economic Interpretation of the Constitution* (New York, 1935)

Blackstone, William, *1 Commentaries on the Laws of England* (Chicago, 1979), 235 (italics in original)

Boorstin, Daniel J., *Americans: The Colonial Experience* (New York, 1958)

Brest, Levinson, Balkin, and Amar, *Processes of Constitutional Decisionmaking: Cases and Materials* (New York, 2000)

Brontë, Charlotte, *Jane Eyre* (New York, 1973)

Bryan, George, *The Imperialism of John Marshall: A Study in Expediency* (1924, Boston)

Calabresi, Steve G. and Rhodes, Kevin H., 'The Structural Constitution: Unitary Executive, Plural Judiciary', 105 *Harvard Law Review* 1155 (1992)

Calhoun, John C., *Union and Liberty: The Political Philosophy of John C. Calhoun* (Ross M. Lence, ed., Indianapolis, 1993)

Calloway, Colin G., *The American Revolution in Indian Country* (Cambridge, 1995)

Chomsky, Noam, *Year 501: The Conquest Continues* (Boston, 1993)
Circular to State Governments', *George Washington, Writings* (John Rhodehamel, ed., 1997)
Colonial Origins of the American Constitution: A Documentary History (Donald S. Lutz, ed., 1998)
Cornell, Saul, *The Other Founders: Anti-Federalism & the Dissenting Tradition in America* 1788-1828 (Chapel Hill, 1999)
Curtis, Michael Kent, 'The 1837 Killing of Elijah Lovejoy by an Anti-Abolition Mob: Free Speech, Mobs, Republican Government, and the Privileges of American Citizens', 44 *UCLA Law Review* 1109 (1997)
Davis, David B., *Slavery in the Age of Revolution, 1770-1823* (Ithaca, 1975)
Debate (1 The) on the Constitution 834 (Bernard Bailyn, ed., 1993)
DeVoto, Bernard, *The Course of Empire* (Boston, 1952)
Donald, David Herbert, *Lincoln* (New York, 1995)
Doyle, Michael W., *Empires* (Ithaca, 1986)
Draper, Theodore, *A Struggle for Power: The American Revolution* (New York, 1996)
Eckert, Allan W., *That Dark and Bloody River* (New York, 1995)
Elkins, Stanley and McKitrick, Eric, *The Age of Federalism* (New York, 1993)
Elliot, Jonathan, *1 Elliot's Debates* (Philadelphia, 1941)
Ellis, Joseph J., *American Sphinx: The Character OF Thomas Jefferson* (New York, 1997)
Ellis, Joseph J., *Founding Fathers: The Revolutionary Generation* (New York, 2001)
Farrand, Max, *3 The Records of the Federal convention of 1787* (New Haven, 1911)
Fehrenbacher, Donald E., *The Dred Scott Case, Its Significance in American Law and Politics* (New York, 1978)
Fehrenbacher, Donald E., *The Slaveholding Republic: An Account of the United States Government's Relation to Slavery* (completed and edited by Ward M. McAfee) (Oxford, 2001)
Feinman, Jay M., 'The Development of the Employment at Will Rule', 20 *American Journal of Legal History* 118 (1976)
Finkelman, Paul, *Slavery and the Founders: Race and Liberty in the Age of Jefferson* (Armonk, 1996)
Fischer, David Hackett, *Albion's Seed: Four British Folkways in America* (Oxford, 1989)
Foner, Eric, *Reconstruction: America's Unfinished Revolution 1863-1877* (New York, 1988)
'*Foreign in a Domestic Sense: Puerto Rico, American Expansion, and the Constitution*' (Christina Duffy Burnett and Burke Marshall, eds., Durham, 2002).
Franklin, Benjamin, 'The Albany Plan of Union', *Benjamin Franklin, Writings* (J.A. Leo Lemay, ed., 1987)
Freehling, William W., *The Road to Disunion* (New York, 1990)
Gibbon, Edward, *1 The History of the Decline and Fall of the Roman Empire* (David Womersley, ed., 1994)
Graymount, Barbara, *The Iroquois in the American Revolution* (Syracuse, N.Y., 1972)
Hardt, Henry and Negri, Antonio, *Empire* (Cambridge, 2000)
Harrington, James, *The Commonwealth of Oceana and a System of Politics* (J.G.A. Pocock, ed., Cambridge, 1992)
Henkin, Louis, 'The Constitution as Compact and as Conscience: Individual Rights Abroad and at Our Gates', 27 *William & Mary Law Review*, 11 (1985)
Hinderaker, Eric, *Elusive Empires: Constructing Colonialism in the Ohio Valley*, 1673-1800 (Cambridge, 1997)
Hobbes, Thomas, *Leviathan* (C.B. MacPherson, ed. New York, 1968)
Horsman, Reginald, *Race and Manifest Destiny: The Origins of American Racial Anglo-Saxonism* (Boston, 1981)
Horwtiz, Morton J., *The Transformation of American Law 1780-1860* (Cambridge, 1977)

Huizinga, Johan, *The Autumn of the Middle Ages* (Rodney J. Payton and Ulrich Mammitzsch, trans., Chicago, 1996)

Hume, David, 'Idea of a Perfect Commonwealth', *David Hume, Essays: Moral, Political, and Literary* (Eugene F. Miller, ed., Indianapolis, 1985)

Jennings, Francis, *The Creation of America: Through Revolution to Empire* (Cambridge, 2000)

John Marshall's Defense of McCulloch v. Maryland (Gerald Gunther ed., Stanford, 1969)

Journals of the Continental Congress, 1774-1789

Kant, Immanuel, 'Idea for a Universal History with a Cosmopolitan Purpose', *Kant, Political Writings* (Hans Reiss, ed., Cambridge, 1970)

Karnow, Stanley, *In Our Image: America's Empire in the Philippines* (New York, 1989)

Katz, Robert A., 'Note: The Jurisprudence of Legitimacy: Applying the Constitution to U.S. Territories', 59 *University of Chicago Law Review*, 779 (1992)

Kaufman, Burton I., 'Washington's Farewell Address: A Statement of Empire', *To the Farewell Address: Ideas of Early American Foreign Policy* (Felix Gilbert, ed., Princeton, 1961)

Kettner, James, *The Development of American Citizenship, 1680-1870* (Chapel Hill, 1978)

Klein, Christine, 'Treaties of Conquest: Property Rights, Indian Treaties, and the Treaty of Guadalupe', 26 *New Mexico Law Review*, 201 (1996)

Koebner, Richard, *Empire* (Cambridge 1961)

LaFeber, Walter, *The New Empire: An Interpretation of American Expansion 1860-1898* (Ithaca, 1963)

LaFeber, Walter, *The American Search for Opportunity, 1865-1913* (Cambridge, 1993)

Landever, Arthur R., The Indispensable Articles of Confederation – Stage in Constitutionalism, Passage for the Framers, and Clue to the Nature of the Constitution, 31 *Arizona Law Review* 79 (1989)

Landever, Carolyn M., 'Whose Home on the Range? Equal Footing, the "New" Federalism and State Jurisdiction on Public Lands', 47 *Florida Law Review* 557 (1995)

Lawson, Gary, 'Territorial Governments and the Limits of Formalism', 78 *California Law Review*, 853 (1990)

Levinson, Sanford, 'Why the Canon Should Be Expanded to Include the Insular Cases and the Saga of American Expansionism', 17 *Constitutional Commentary*, 241 (2000)

Lincoln, Abraham, *1 Lincoln: Speeches and Writings 1832-1858* (Don E. Fehrenbacher, ed., 1989)

Locke, John, *The Second Treatise of Government* 288 (Peter Laslett, ed.) Cambridge (1988)

Machiavelli, *Discourses on Livy* (Harvey C. Mansfield and Nathan Tarcov, trans. Niccolo, Chicago, 1996)

Madison, Bishop James, 'Manifestations of the Beneficence of Divine Providence Toward America', *Political Sermons of the American Founding Era: 1730-1805* (Ellis Sandoz, ed., 1990)

Madison, James, 17 *Papers Of Madison*

Madison, James, Hamilton, Alexander and Jay, John, *The Federalist* (Clinton Rossiter, ed., 1961)

Madison, James, *Writings* (Jack Rakove, ed., New York, 1999)

Madison, Thomas, *Notes of the Debates in the Federal Convention of 1787* (Adrienne Koch, intro., Athens, Ohio, 1984)

Magdoff, Harry, *The Age of Imperialism: The Economics of U.S. Foreign Policy* (New York, 1969)

Magrath, C. Peter, *Yazoo: The Case of Fletcher v. Peck* (New York, 1966)

Maier, John C., *American Scripture: Making the Declaration of Independence* (New York, 1997)

Main, Jackson Turner, *The Anti-Federalists: critics of the Constitution 1781-1788 130* (New York, 1961)
Malone, Dumas and Rauch, Basil, *Empire for Liberty: The Genesis and Growth of the United States* (New York, 1960)
Maltz, Earl M., 'Citizenship and the Constitution: A History and Critique of the Supreme Court's Alienage Jurisprudence', 28 *Arizona State Law Journal*, 1135 (1996)
Manville, Philip Brook, *The Origins of Citizenship in Ancient Athens* (Princeton, 1997)
Mark, Gregory A., 'The Court and the Corporation: Jurisprudence, Localism, and Federalism', 1997 *Supreme Court Review*
Marshall Chief Justice, Opinion and 8 How. 312 (1845)
McCoy, Drew R., *The Elusive Republic: Political Economy in Jeffersonian America* (Chapel Hill, 1980)
Miller, John C., *Origins of the American Revolution* (Stanford, 1943)
Montesquieu, *The Spirit of the Laws* (Anne M. Cohler, et al., trans. & ed., 1989)
Morison, Samuel Eliot and Steele, Henry Commager, *1 The Growth of the American Republic* 453 (New York, 1958)
Nelson, William E., 'The Eighteenth-Century Background of John Marshall's Constitutional Jurisprudence', 76 *Minnesota Law Review* 893 (1978)
Neuman, Gerald L., 'Territorial Discrimination, Equal Protection, and Self-Determination', 135 *University Pennsylvania Law Review*, 261 (1987)
Neuman, Gerald L., 'Whose Constitution?' 100 *Yale Law Journal* (1991)
Neuman, Gerald L., *Strangers to the Constitution: Immigrants, Borders, and Fundamental Law* (Princeton, 1996)
Neuman, Gerald L., *Whose Immigration Law?: Citizens, Borders, and Fundamental Law* (Princeton, 1996)
Newmyer, R. Kent, John Marshall, 'McCulloch v. Maryland, and the Southern States' Rights Tradition', 33 *John Marshall Law Review*, 875 (2000)
Nobles, Gregory H., *American Frontiers: Cultural Encounters and Continental Conquest* (New York, 1997)
Nonge, Jose Trias, *Puerto Rico: The Trials of the Oldest Colony in the World* (New Haven, 1997)
Noonan, Jr., John T., *The Antelope: The Ordeal of the Recaptured Africans in the Administrations of James Monroe and John Quincy Adams* (Berkeley, 1977)
Onuf, Peter S., *Statehood and Nation: A History of the Northwest Ordinance* (Bloomington, 1987)
Onuf, Peter S., *Jefferson's Empire: The Language of American Nationhood* (Charlottesville, 2000)
Pagden, Anthony, *Lords of all the World: Ideologies of Empire in Spain, Britain, and France, C. 1500-C.1800* (New Haven, 1995)
Paine, Thomas, 'Common Sense, Appendix', Paine, *Collected Writings* 50 (New York, 1995)
Parkman, Francis, *2 France and England in North America* (New York, 1983)
Parrington, Vernon Louis, *2 Main Currents in American Thought* (Norman, 1987)
Perkins, Bradford, *The Cambridge History of American Foreign Policy, Vol. 1, The Creation of a Republican Empire* (Cambridge, 1993)
Perkins, Dexter, *A History of the Monroe Doctrine* (Boston, 1941)
Peterson, Merrill D., *The Great Triumverate: Webster, Clay, and Calhoun* (Oxford, 1987)
Phillips, Kevin, *The Cousins' Wars: Religion, Politics, & the Triumph of Anglo-America* (New York, 1999)
Plutarch, *The Lives of the Noble Grecians and Romans* (John Dryden, trans., rev's by Arthur Hugh Clough, Modern Library ed.)

Pocock, J.G.A., *The Machiavellian Moment: Florentine Political Thought and the Atlantic Republican Tradition* (Princeton, 1975)
Potter, David M., *The Impending Crisis 1848-1861* (New York, 1976)
Presser, Stephen, 'Revising the Conservative Tradition: Towards A New American Legal History', 52 *New York University Law Review* 700 (1977)
Pynchon, Thomas, *Mason & Dixon* 343-44 (New York, 1997)
Rafael, Vicente L., 'White Love', in *Cultures of United States Imperialism* (Amy Kaplan and Donald E. Pease, eds., Durham, 1993)
Rahe, Paul A., *3 Republics Ancient and Modern, Inventions of Prudence: Constituting the American Regime* (Chapel Hill, 1992)
Rakove, Jack N., 'Fidelity Through History (Or To It)', 64 *Fordham Law Review* 1587, 1604 (1997)
Rakove, Jack N., *Original Meanings: Politics and Ideas in the Making of the Constitution* 55 (New York, 1996)
Ramos, Efren Rivera, 'The Legal Construction of American Colonialism: The Insular Cases (1901-1922)', 65 *Review Jurisprudence University Puerto Rico*, 225 (1996)
Ramsay, David, *1 The History of the American Revolution* (Lester H. Cohen, ed., 1990)
Remini, Robert V., *3 Andrew Jackson: The Course of American Democracy 1833-1845* (Baltimore, 1984)
Remini, Robert V., *1 Andrew Jackson: The Course of American Empire 1767-1821* (Baltimore, 1998)
Roman, Ediberto, 'The Alien-Citizen Paradox and Other Consequences of U.S. Colonialism', 26 *Florida State Law Review*, 1 (1998)
Rosenfeld, Richard N., *American Aurora* (New York, 1997)
Rousseau, Jean Jacques, 'The Second Discourse', *The Discourses and Other Early Political Writings* (Victor Gourevitch, ed., Cambridge, 1997)
Russell, Bertrand, *Power* (Kirk Willis, intro., 1995)
Simpson, A.W.B., 'The Horwitz Thesis and the History of Contracts', 46 *University of Chicago Law Review* 533 (1979).
Smith, Jean Edward, *John Marshall: Definer of a Nation* (New York, 1996)
Smith, Rogers M., *Civic Ideals: Conflicting Visions of Citizenship in U.S. History* (New Haven, 1997)
Stampp, Kenneth, *America in 1857: A Nation on the Brink* (New York, 1990)
Stannard, David E., *American Holocaust: The Conquest of the New World* (New York, 1992)
Stephanson, Anders, *Manifest Destiny: American Expansion and the Empire of Right* (New York, 1995)
Stephen, James Fitzjames, *Liberty, Equality, Fraternity* (Indianapolis, 1993)
Sumner, William Graham, *On Liberty, Society, and Politics: The Essential Essays of William Graham Sumner* (Robert C. Bannister, ed., 1992)
Sunstein, Cass R., 'The Myth of the Unitary Executive', 7 *Administrative Law Journal* 299 (1993)
Taylor, John, *Arator* 24-25 (Indianapolis, 1977)
Terrasa, Gabriel A., 'The United States, Puerto Rico, and the Territorial Incorporation Doctrine: Reaching a Century of Constitutional Authoritarianism', 31 *John Marshall Law Review*, 55 (1997)
The Mind of the Founder: Sources of the Political Thought of James Madison (Marvin Meyers, ed., Hanover, 1971)
Thomas Jefferson: Writings (Merrill D. Peterson, ed., 1984)
Thucydides, *The Peloponnesian War* (T. Hobbes, trans., Chicago, 1989)

Tise, Larry E., *Proslavery: A History of the Defense of Slavery in America*, 1701-1840 (Athens, 1987)

Tocqueville, Alexis De, *1 Democracy in America* (Phillips Bradley, ed., New York, 1945)

Tomlins, Christopher, 'The Legal Cartography of Colonization, the Legal Polyphony of Settlement: English Intrusions on the American Mainland in the Seventeenth Century', 26 *Law and Social Inquiry* 315 (2001)

Torruella, Juan R., *The Supreme Court and Puerto Rico: The Doctrine of Separate and Unequal* (San Juan, 1985)

Tribe, Laurence H., *American Constitutional Law* (New York, 1978)

Turner, Frederick Jackson, 'The Ohio Valley in American History', *Frederick Jackson Turner, The Frontier in American History* (New York, 1996)

Van Alstyne, Richard W., *The Rising American Empire* (New York, 1960)

Weeks, William E., *Building The Constitutional Empire* (Chicago, 1996)

White, G. Edward, *The Marshall Court and Cultural Change: 1815-1835* (New York, 1991)

Williams, William Appleman, 'The Frontier Thesis and American Foreign Policy', 24 *Pacific Historical Review*, 379-95 (1955)

Williams, William Appleman, *The Tragedy of American Diplomacy* (New York, 1972)

Wilson, James G., 'Justice Diffused: A Comparison of Edmund Burke's Conservatism with the Views of Five Conservative, Academic Judges', 40 *University Miami Law Review*, 913 (1986)

Wilson, James G., 'American Constitutional Conventions: The Judicially Unenforceable Rules that Combine With Judicial Doctrine and Public Opinion to Regulate Political Behavior', 40 *Buffalo Law Review*, 645 (1992)

Wilson, James G., The Role of Public Opinion in Constitutional Interpretation, 1993 *Brigham Young University Law Review*

Wilson, James G., 'Commentary: Noam Chomsky and Judicial Review', 44 *Cleveland State Law Review*, 439 (1996)

Wittgenstein, Ludwig, *Philosophical Investigations* (3rd ed., G.E.M. Anscombe, trans., Englewood Cliffs, N.J., 1958)

Wood, Gordon S., *The Creation of the American Republic* (Williamsburg, 1969)

Wood, Gordon S., *The Radicalism of the American Revolution* (New York, 1992)

Woodward, C. Vann, *Origins of the New South* 1877-1913 (1951)

Wright, Esmond, *Franklin of Philadelphia* (Cambridge, 1986)

Index

For Product Safety Concerns and Information please contact our EU representative GPSR@taylorandfrancis.com Taylor & Francis Verlag GmbH, Kaufingerstraße 24, 80331 München, Germany

Batch number: 10726009

Printed by Printforce, the Netherlands